After This...

After This...

An Inspirational Journey for All the Wrong Reasons

MARCUS ENGEL

Phillips Press

Phillips Press
St. Louis, MO 63122
314-822-9057
www.marcusengel.com

Second Edition

Printed in the United States of America

ISBN: 0-9720000-03

Dedication

For my parents…

The hell read in these pages is only surpassed by that of a parent
being forced to watch their child suffer.
Thank you for overcoming your pain
and giving me the freedom to fly with my own wings.

Acknowledgements

This book would not be possible without the assistance of three very special people. My gratitude toward each of you is immeasurable. Thank you, thank you and thank you!

Leah Atkinson –
You started my feet on this journey, read the map and pointed out the destination. Thanks for stocking my pack with the provisions I would need along the way.

Helen Fuller –
You joined me on the path and became my traveling companion. We covered the first leg of the journey together, stopping along the way only to take side trips that helped me become a better person.

Marvelyne Adams –
You guided me when I was lost, held my hand when the terrain was rough and ultimately taught me to travel on my own. I cannot imagine taking this, nor any future journey, without you.

Introduction

What you're about to read isn't pretty.

It is not some generic inspirational work accented by pictures of daisies and sunflowers. Nor is it littered with cutesy little phrases about reaching for the stars, achieving your dreams or any other crap like that. Please.

If you're looking for a book to bolster some already perfect picture of life, this isn't it. However, if you live a real life, if you know that human existence includes tragedies and set-backs, then maybe you'll choose to read on.

This story is, if nothing else, real. Reality includes images and pictures that might make you queasy, might make you cry and might make you see the world as senseless. However, read on. Read past the profanity to find the profound, go past the blood and guts to find insight and read past the bottomless pit of despair to find the light at the end of the tunnel. It's there. Trust me. I've lived it.

Still, this is your warning, up front, right here and now, that what you're about to read might be offensive. It might turn you off because you've never read something like this that you pulled from the inspirational section. Maybe it's out of the box, maybe it's innovative, maybe it shouldn't even be labeled as "inspirational." I don't care.

My only concern is, that this is my story, the way I want to tell it. Proceed with caution.

"Sometimes I ask to sneak a closer look,
skip to the final chapter of the book
and then maybe steer us clear from some of the pain it took
to get us where we are, this far…" [1]

~ *Indigo Girls*

I think that we waited for green &
Right then I saw the ond

other car caning. I cint swear I said Look oot bo,
I dint so why I waldnt have. We wee so
cold we wee in our own little worlds. Yos. when
visted at bed vext I drove to the arena front door, th
thats when the broter bhwe. Anything else?
Why did Tamn d I ccme here d kimd Vince to l
I s Tonnt hurl nore than I? Greed
Extra what flubes. Is my brain okay
Do ru think I lost any of my mind? Serious?

I don't want to be blind, i cant do anything
nod,

Chapter 1

"I can feel it coming in the air tonight..." [2]
~ Phil Collins

"See ya dude! I'm outta here!" I said, stepping into my friend's dorm suite.

Travis looked up from his bowl of Ramen noodles. Other than a blue St. Louis Cardinals baseball cap and half of my face, he could see nothing but the overflowing mound of dirty clothes I carried in my trusty laundry basket.

"Uh, you might want to re-arrange some of those clothes," Travis said, pointing at a pair of underwear spilling over the side. "Showing off your dirty drawers isn't going to get you a date any faster, man!"

I sat the basket down and pushed the tighty whities under a pair of jeans. Even this embarrassment couldn't put a damper on my excitement. We'd only known each other for a few weeks, but already Travis was one of my best buds at Southwest Missouri State University.

"I'm headed down to meet my ride in a few minutes. Tonight, I'm going to hit my high school's homecoming game, then tomorrow night I've got tickets to the Blues season opener! Dude, this weekend is going to rock!" I said, dancing around his kitchenette like a toddler with a full bladder.

"Sounds good, Marc!" Travis said, returning to his snack. "If you can, bring me something back from the game. Just a soda cup or one of those giveaways would be cool."

"No problemo! I'll see ya Sunday night when I get back!" I said, turned and stuck out the same hand that had just been touching dirty underwear. Travis looked at it, smiled and just shook his head. I shrugged, grabbed my laundry basket and took off down the hall.

When the elevator dinged, I stepped inside, smiled to myself and thought about the upcoming weekend. *Did life get any better than this?* Freshman life was great, but I was looking forward to seeing my old friends again- not to mention a few home cooked meals. This was going to be a weekend I'd never forget.

It was Friday, October 8th, and I couldn't get to my hometown fast enough.

When the elevator opened, I practically ran out the dorm's front door into the bright autumn afternoon. We had 200 miles of Missouri farmland to cover before we reached the city limits of High Hill, my hometown. Another mile would put us at my parents' front door, smack dab in the middle of the 100 acres of farmland on which I'd grown up.

As we loaded our gear into the trunk, the autumn sun beat down on my baseball cap. It was unseasonably warm, yet, even with bright sunshine and a light breeze, I felt cold.

You're just nervous about going home for the first time, I consoled myself. As excited as I was, something gnawed at the back of my mind. I shook it off and glanced back at the dorm as we pulled away. As the campus became smaller in the distance, I settled in for the long drive east on U.S. Highway 44.

Three hours later and just in time for dinner, we pulled into my parents' driveway. My mother was all too happy to treat us to an enormous amount of "real food." My recent diet of slop, more commonly known as cafeteria food, made the meatloaf and green beans my mother served seem like a five star dining experience. As

I sat stuffing myself, I wondered if my parents noticed any changes in me. Over the past six weeks, subtle little improvements caught my attention; smiling at strangers, offering help to friends and complimenting classmates whenever possible. I was feeling more mature, as if I had passed from one stage in life to another. I wasn't ready to give up staying out all night partying on the weekends or the college life I'd grown to love, but I felt like I was settling into a more focused routine. I had not celebrated my first taste of liberation by partying for six straight weeks, as some of my dorm mates had. With their grades sinking and arguments with parents rising, I was happy I'd chosen a more responsible route.

This new sense of self-discipline was capped off by a rigorous daily workout in the gym. What began as a social event with my next-door neighbor, Kit, had turned into a healthy addiction. My spare tire of a belly was shrinking and biceps were just barely shy of what you'd call, "buff."

"Do one more!" Kit encouraged as I had strained on the tenth repetition of my bench press set the night before heading out for Homecoming weekend.

"Okay, one more," I said through gritted teeth, my face flushed with exertion.

As I pushed out the eleventh rep, Kit looked down, grinned and said, "One more, man, you can do it!" With that kind of positive reinforcement I had to keep pushing myself.

Sitting up from the bench press, I tried to catch my breath. Kit clapped me on the shoulder before bending down to whisper, "A couple of girls walked by while you were benching. They both smiled at how much you were pushing up there, stud!" A grin was my only reply.

"What are you doing after we get done here?" he asked, laying down on the bench and moving his hands into position.

"Studying," I said, "Big test in Phys Ed tomorrow. Then I've gotta pack so I can get outta town."

"Need any help? I've got nothing to do tonight anyway," he offered. "Besides, Physical Education is my major, so I've been through all your classes before."

Surrounded by the generosity of friends like Kit, it was no wonder I was slowly transforming into a more acceptable version of myself.

Over dinner, Dad told stories of the daily happenings in our rural Missouri community. I listened without interruption. Normally I would have been slightly bored, but tonight Dad had some real news!

"Gene Schultz found a dead girl up by the junction," Dad blurted out in his matter-of-fact way; a style that was both blunt and endearing.

What was this? A girl murdered in the quiet little town of High Hill? Dead girls found in barren farm fields? I shivered at the thought, but I wanted to know more! Dad continued with the story as it had been passed on to him, the details of which were certain to be riddled with half truths, rumors and the downright inaccuracy of small town gossip.

The main facts were, however, indisputable. A nineteen-year-old waitress had been abducted from a restaurant in St. Louis and murdered. Her abductor had driven the 50 miles to High Hill and dumped her body in a field no more than 10 minutes from my front door. She had been beaten to death with a blunt object and the police were baffled by who had committed this heinous crime. The body had only been found the previous day, but the rumor mill was already churning. Undoubtedly, the football stadium would be buzzing tonight.

After dinner I said my hurried good-byes and beat a path to the game. Rounding the junction near where the girl's body had been found, ice shot through my veins. I craned my neck to see if there was any yellow police tape strewn near the highway, but saw nothing but a red setting sun over the rolling fields.

Five minutes later, I pulled into the high school's parking lot. The stadium lights and press box rose over the packed grandstand. Montgomery County R-2 had a better than average football stadium for a school its size, but it just seemed so much smaller than I remembered.

A horn blasted just as a beat-up gray Buick pulled up to my left. The two smiling faces that leaned forward and yelled their hellos belonged to Rodney and Jeff, two of my best friends. Both were freshmen at the University of Missouri-Columbia and I'd really missed them since we'd all left for college.

"Engel!" Jeff yelled as we piled out of the cars and shook hands for the first time in six weeks. "How ya doing, man?" he asked, smiling sincerely.

"Doing great, dude! How's Mizzou?" I asked, spotting Rodney's forest green sweatshirt bearing his fraternity's insignia.

Seeing my glance at the Greek letters on his chest, Rodney asked, "Do I look like a show off wearing this to a high school football game?"

"Yep! Pretty much!" I replied and gave him a playful punch; right in the Lambda Chi Alpha.

"Good," he said without shame, already starting to walk for the grandstands.

As we paid our admission at the gate and headed for the bleachers, the experience suddenly seemed surreal. So this is what it felt like to be a high school football fan in rural Missouri on a Friday night! I had lived on this football field every fall for four years. Everyday after school I sweated, ran, blocked, and practiced for the impending Friday night game. Now? Now I was a spectator. Looking over the field that had formerly been "mine," I was torn between nostalgia and excitement. I decided on excitement. After all, I was now back to show everyone that I was on my way to bigger and better things than the life I'd left behind. The college man had returned to his roots, his old friends and he definitely had an air of confidence about him. A year before, I thought there was no higher feeling than winning the Eastern Missouri Conference championship on the painted field just ahead. Now, I wasn't so sure. Simply put, I was on top of the world!

Glancing around, I spied an ex-girlfriend sitting with a group of friends. She avoided the looks I sent her way, but I knew she had seen me. Suddenly she seemed really... *young*! It seemed strange that I couldn't think of another way to describe how she looked until I realized I had become accustomed to girls my own age or older; girls who were more mature – and more interesting.

Rod saw me staring at my ex and smiled with a "Gotcha!" expression. He knew exactly what I was thinking. "Man, isn't it amazing that you can meet a dozen girls every day when, around here, you already knew everyone?" Rod asked. I grinned back, sharing in what felt like a secret that only we knew. We couldn't have been in greater form. This night was meant for us.

As we exited the stadium after the game, we prepared to move to the "field party." Field parties were just that, parties around a bonfire in the middle of a remote farm field. They were a weekend ritual, just like Friday night football games. As we chatted about the upcoming party, I couldn't help but mentally calculate how many times this exact same scene had played out in the previous four years. How many hours had we wasted sitting in parking lots waiting for parties to begin? How many times had we hung out on the hoods and fenders of cars watching traffic fly by? How often had I been overwhelmed with the feeling of being young and care-free? God, it was good to be home!

"See y'all there!" I waved as Rod and Jeff hopped into Rodney's car.

I slid into my beloved '72 Pontiac, cranked the engine and flipped the interior heat to maximum. While the engine warmed, I wrapped myself in a flannel shirt and waited for the heat to kick in. "God, why am I so freaking cold?" I said to the frigid darkness. Being chilly was, for me, weird. I was so warm-blooded that I rarely donned even a jacket before the first snow was on the ground.

Finally, tiny bits of warmth crept into the car. I steered the LeMans out of the parking lot and headed for the party. Even with the heater on high, I couldn't seem to hold in the warmth. Thirty minutes later, I turned off the blacktop, maneuvered the car over rough gravel roads and parked along a darkened drive, deserted except for the vehicles of partygoers. I hopped out into the night, the late evening temperatures washing away what little heat I'd been able to absorb. Listening to the crunch of gravel under my size thirteen boots, I walked the hundred yards on a shadowless path leading to the bonfire.

If I had any worries about being able to pick up with old friends where I had left off, they were quickly dispelled.

"Engel!" came a chorus of voices as I stepped into the light of the fire. Handshakes were exchanged with longtime pals and I moved closer to the flames. Leaning on the fenders of cars, we joked and caught up on the happenings of each other's lives. It was just like old times.

Standing there looking into the darkness over a cornfield, I felt that same happiness again, but also was aware that the moment might not last much longer. As I transitioned out of teenage years, I'd likely lose contact with most of these people. I was still connected to this place – it still felt like home, but how much would that change in the next three years? I could already feel myself mentally moving away from this small rural community. In a few years, would I still call this place home?

Just live in the moment, Engel! I said inwardly. *Worry about tomorrow when tomorrow comes.*

What would tomorrow bring? The reflective question was interrupted by the more immediate "tomorrow."

Tomorrow night would be spent at the Blues game with Tom and other friends I'd made at summer church camp. Tom and I were especially close and it had been months since I'd seen him. Although he lived more than an hour away, the distance hadn't slowed our friendship. Church leadership events, camps, retreats, dances and youth board meetings took place every month or two and we managed to work in visits to each others' homes in between – especially during hockey season.

Tomorrow would complete my three different circles of friends: college, high school and camp. I couldn't believe I would see all of them in just a two-day period of time!

Glancing around the party, I began to yawn.

"All right, dudes, I'm outta here," I said, rising from the truck's tailgate.

"What?! Engel! The night is young!" Rodney said, surprised.

"Sorry, dudes. Big day tomorrow and I'm beat," I said, shaking their hands. "I'll come up to see you guys at Mizzou sometime soon." That would prove to be a promise I couldn't keep.

Darkness enveloped me as I stepped away from the glow of the party. The laughter and raucous voices were soon swallowed in the chilly stillness. I had become accustomed to headlights crossing the ceiling of my dorm room all night, drunken students running down the hallways, the repetitive thud of bass in car stereos, but this? In six weeks had I forgotten what stillness and solitude were like?

Pausing for a moment, I draped my arms across the tan vinyl roof of the '72. I stared up at the heavens that glinted with the tiny white light of a million stars. My eyes traveled to the expanses of emptiness that lay to the west, then across the flat, dry cornfields to the south. For a moment, I was mesmerized by the vastness and natural wonder of the surroundings. Breathing in the clean, cold air, I stared in wonder at the skies for a few more moments before jumping in the car and shattering the dark stillness with the Pontiac's headlights.

Saturday was filled with the welcome routine of home and soaking up more gossip about the grisly murder. I had little new information, but knew I could always call my friend, Kista to get the low-down. After all, it was her father who had found the body of the murdered girl.

Shoving a sandwich in my mouth, I grabbed my backpack and headed for the door. The afternoon was getting late. There was still a long drive to Tom's house and I needed to hit the road.

I walked past my mom and didn't have "good-bye" out of my mouth before she fired off the usual round of questions: "Are you staying overnight? Where are you staying? Will you call if you're going to be late?"

She had followed me to the garage, but stood, hesitating in the doorway. "Be careful tonight," she called after me.

Without turning around, I called back my usual response, "Always!"

Be careful tonight. How many times had she said those words? Hundreds? Thousands? My response never varied. "Always!" The reply came without even thinking. What could have warned me that this time it wasn't my own behavior I needed to worry about?

An hour later, I pulled up to Tom's house. Walking through fallen leaves that littered the sidewalk, I felt that gnawing chill once again. Like the night before, I ignored it and rang the bell.

Tom answered the door with the tickets in hand.

"You're late. Dump your stuff and let's go," he said, unsmiling.

"Dude! Can I pee first?" I asked, ribbing him for being impatient.

Tom ignored me and walked out the door toward his Toyota. I shrugged and headed for the bathroom anyway.

Five minutes later, we picked up the other two friends that would be sharing the tickets, Vince and Kim. As they piled in the backseat, Tom revved the small car's engine. Almost before they had their doors closed, Tom pushed the gearshift into first. He wasted no time getting to the main streets and heading for The Arena. I was a hockey fan, but Tom was just plain passionate.

As the evening began to set in, I cursed myself for having left my jacket in the back seat of my car. Once inside the hockey arena, however, I warmed with the excitement of the game.

As we watched and cheered, the Blues skated to a win against Ottawa in the season opener. Details of the game and the final score were forever erased from my memory. However, for the sense of excitement generated by friends, life and hockey that Saturday night, I remain forever grateful.

After the final horn sounded, we navigated through the crowd and down the concrete hallways.

"You want to get some food?" Tom asked, shoving his hands into his pockets as we weaved through groups of happy fans.

"Definitely! You wanna hit White Castle?"

As we walked on, a strange sensation set in. It seemed like the further we went, the less distance we actually covered. My feet were moving, but it felt like I was trudging through thick mud. I shook off the feeling once again, figuring it was just fatigue from the night before. Still, the coldness lingered. I pushed open the heavy glass exit door and the outside air hit me like a blast from a frozen furnace.

Great, I thought, *I just want to be somewhere warm and go to sleep.* But I couldn't say that to my friends. How does an eighteen-year-old party animal come out and say, "Hey guys, I know it's only 11 o'clock, but I really just want to go to bed, okay?" They'd snicker and I'd never hear the end of it. So, I said nothing.

Feeling the way I did, an hour's drive back to High Hill was out of the question.

"Wait up a minute. I gotta make a call," I said, spying a pay phone. Tom nodded and I headed off to call my parents. Stuck in the transitional "gray zone" between childhood and adulthood, I wanted to be courteous and *inform* them of my where-abouts. Certainly there was no reason to cause them needless worry.

Digging through my pockets for a quarter, I reminded myself that this call was a sign of mutual respect, not an obligation from a child to a parent.

My father answered and, as was our custom, we made the call short. Since starting college, we hadn't spent more than 10 minutes on the phone. Idle chatter on long distance was expensive and I didn't want to endure a paternal lecture about frugality. Still, he sounded disappointed.

"What time do you think you'll be back tomorrow? In the morning or later?" he asked.

"Dunno, but I'm just too tired to drive tonight."

"Well, if you get home before 11 tomorrow morning, you can go to lunch with us," he said hopefully.

"Fine, but I really don't know when I'll get home tomorrow," I said, eyeing Tom and the others waiting in the cold.

Strangely, he seemed to want to talk; very unlike my Dad. But, I told him good-bye and hung up. Why didn't I stay on the phone just a little longer? Why didn't I let him explain their plans for tomorrow? Anything to keep me on the phone; just a few more minutes, a tiny bit longer. Mere seconds could have made all the difference in the world.

Returning the receiver to the cradle, it felt like an icy brick in my hand. I walked back to where Tom, Kim and Vince were standing under a streetlight. We began to walk around the ancient facility in search of the car. Jamming my hands into the pockets of my Levis, I pressed my arms tightly around me for extra warmth.

By the time we'd walked the half-mile to Tom's white Corolla, my body had begun to grow stiff.

I slid into the front seat, glad to be sheltered from the elements at last. Tom slammed the driver's door and said, "Let's get some heat in here."

Kim sat behind the driver's seat with Vince directly behind me. As soon as the doors were shut, Kim slid close to Vince. It was an attempt to get warm as much as show affection. I couldn't blame them. I secretly wished I had a girlfriend to cuddle up with.

As Tom slid the key into the ignition, the dashboard lights lit up. The "Fasten Belts" light flashed on and reflected a transparent glow against the driver's window. After a half minute, Tom pushed the climate control switch to "heat" and flipped on the interior fan. Just as it began to roar, a sharp 'pop' erupted.

"Shit! What was that?" Tom angrily muttered.

He flipped on the dome light and stared down at the floorboards. There, just inches from my toes, was a translucent green fluid dripping from the dashboard. The diagnosis was easy; a heater hose had blown.

After collective cursing, hunkering down for a freezing cold ride, and strategic placement of an empty cup to prevent the anti-freeze from splattering all over my Eastland boots, we finally left our parking space. Tired, no jacket, no heat and no girlfriend were bad enough, but now there was green crap soaking into my socks. I was ready for this night to be over... but it hadn't even begun.

As Tom inched the white Toyota through the gates of The Arena, I looked back one last time. The old barn-like building seemed so lonely sitting smack dab in the middle of acres of empty parking lots.

Staring straight ahead, I returned to my own little world. Tired, famished, and shivering, I tried to focus on the signs and lights along Hampton Avenue. Anything to stay awake. The only sounds came from Tom's customized car stereo and the slight crescendo of the transmission. The music helped break the silence, but the unspoken annoyance of everyone was all too apparent.

We slowed to a stop at a large cross street. Glancing up at the swinging traffic light, I spied a green and white sign that read, "Chippewa Avenue." Tom had already noticed that the light, still red, was about to turn green in our favor. As the light began to turn green, Tom's right hand grasped the gearshift. Suddenly, from out of nowhere, a blue sedan shot in front of us traveling east.

What the hell?! That guy just ran the light... and at that speed? All of us thought the same thing: *How stupid could anyone be?* There was only a car's length, maybe two car's lengths between our front bumper and the blue car's trajectory.

Tom, disgusted, swore under his breath. We'd all seen the car, but why even comment? Stupid drivers do stupid things every minute of every day on every street and road in America. Talking about it would do nothing but fog up the windshield.

Tom shifted into first gear, nosing the Toyota into the intersection. I instinctively looked to my right. Blinding halogen headlights exploded into my field of vision.

The lights grew closer with each microsecond. Time stood still.

Headlights! Too fast! White car! Dead insects on the grill. A white car… so close that the headlights split and traveled parallel on either side of my face.

What my mind registered were more like impressions than actual thoughts. *Going to get hit! Tell Tom! Who was screaming?! Was that me? Someone else? Tell Tom! Warn him! Watch out! Didn't anyone else see what I saw?*

There was neither time nor reason to think those lights would be the last things my eyes would ever see.

Chapter 2

"I don't ever want to feel like I did that day" [3]

~ Red Hot Chili Peppers

*W*hat happens right before someone dies? We've all heard the stories of someone's life flashing before their eyes, that sorta thing.
But is that true? Who knows? Certainly not me. From the split second I
saw the headlights until I heard the ripping of steel, I saw no images of
my childhood, no visions of my adolescence – nothing but those bright
beams of light.

Only a thin piece of Toyota metal separated me from the oncoming car. That's it. Traveling at nearly seventy miles per hour,
close to twice the legal speed limit. An almost indescribable force
bulldozed into our right side. Then, there was nothing.

The Toyota shot into the air and began overturning; spiraling
like an empty soda can blown by the October winds. Mercifully,
the car was launched high enough to actually shoot over the roofs
of the northbound traffic with a few feet of empty air to spare.

Descending as precipitously as it had been thrown, the Toyota flipped a final time before skidding to a stop. When the car had
ceased all movement, it lay at the southeastern corner, just a few
feet from some nearby buildings.

Upon impact, the gas tank was ripped apart. In a matter of
seconds, pungent fuel began spilling out into the street, soaking
everything within a dozen yards of the upturned car. A bad crash
soon became a highly volatile situation. A single cigarette tossed

by a passing motorist could have incinerated all four of us – not to mention half the block.

How long was it until I became aware of "me" again? It couldn't have been more than a few seconds, but time that is blocked from one's memory is a strange phenomenon. Those black holes are, believe it or not, greatly appreciated. Hell, I could have used a few more doses of shock.

Pain comes in all different forms; the thin, gasping feel of a cut, the fiery sensation of infection, the pounding force of a migraine. This; this can only be described as a bludgeoning. Even that doesn't do it justice.

The first thing to halt my trajectory from the car was the street. I flew teeth first into the pavement, my body crumpling into a melted pile. I awoke in the street – face down. My right arm raised above my head, twisted in an obscene waving motion. I clawed and scratched at the concrete, trying to get out of my own skin.

Moans were everywhere. Loud, sickening noises straight out of a horror flick. *Where were they coming from? Me?! That's me?!*

Both cheekbones shifted under the weight of my skull. As I tried to suck in the first bits of oxygen, a heavy, thick liquid bubbled inside my mouth: blood. I licked it from my lips, but it was everywhere. The thick, pudding-like gunk filled my mouth. Desperately in need of oxygen, I forced my tongue through the hole that had formerly been my mouth. My tongue felt like a torn muscle swollen to twice its normal size.

Have I bitten my tongue off? I wondered, trying to spit out everything between the air and my lungs. Sour blood clogged my nostrils.

Christ, I'm suffocating, I thought, trying to move my head and clear the blood from my palate. Lifting my head from the pavement was impossible, but I had to try. *Just a few millimeters, Engel, then you can breathe*, I coached myself.

With a huge amount of effort, I managed to lift my face a few inches. As soon as I did, I vomited and spat blood and teeth into the street. Instantly, my face crashed back down onto the concrete.

During the few seconds my head was aloft, another injury slapped me to attention. As I forced everything from my mouth, my left jaw involuntarily swung in a mechanical, rhythmic up and down motion.

Jesus Christ! My fucking jaw is broken! First things first, Engel… you've gotta breathe!

Forcing my tongue through the coagulated mess, I prayed for the cold night air to hit my taste buds. Finally, FINALLY! A miniscule passage had been opened! I gulped in air, hungry as a starving man for sustenance.

Breathe, dammit, Engel! No way in hell are you going to suffocate on your own blood! Breathe!

Inhuman wails and cries came between the sucking sounds of my quasi-breathing.

Dear God, am I going to die?! I can't die now! I'm not fucking ready to die! Hold on, Engel, hold on…Fuck! Don't die, man, hold on, hold on…deep breath, deep breath, my brain screamed. *I can't die, I can't die. Don't die, Engel… the pain, Christ Jesus the pain!*

Gotta live, don't die, don't die, don't die!

Whose body is lying in the street? How can that be me?

Obscenities continued to spew through the blood and teeth. Curses were interrupted by one jarring thought: death.

Engel, if you die, the last word to come out of your mouth will be the F-bomb! Do you really want that? Do you really want to die with profanity on your lips?

Swears and prayers soon joined hands.

God! Get me out of this! Oh God, don't let me die, hold on, please hold on. Please don't let me die!

Engel, you CANNOT die! Don't you fucking die! Breathe, Engel... NOW!!

The stone cold concrete was an oasis in this desert of pain. I wanted to fall into that coolness, be enveloped by it, to live in it. I thrashed and shuddered, my body involuntarily convulsing, trying to find any comfort.

What was this?! Hands on my back? Whose hands?

A female voice pleaded, "Marc, lay still. Please lay still."

Who the hell are you? I thought angrily. *Don't tell me to lie still when I'm choking on my own blood!*

"Marc, you have to lay still! The ambulance is on its way, but you have to stop moving!"

As the crash was taking place, a driver of a southbound car watched the events unfold, almost as if in slow motion.

After seeing the Toyota career to a halt, the young woman bolted from her car and ran to the injured teenagers. Luckily, this woman was a pediatric nurse. Had I known I was in good hands, I might have paid her a little more mind. I continued to writhe, ignoring her commands.

"Marc, LAY STILL!" she screamed. And, no matter how much I hurt, I knew that scream meant business!

I lay motionless, barely daring to breathe for fear of being yelled at again.

"The ambulances are here, Marc. They're parking now, they're going to get help for you," she said between nervous mutterings of, "Oh my God...oh my God."

I can't leave right now, I thought, feeling the cool pavement through hot, soaking blood. That concrete was my only comfort, a fragment of pleasant reality to which I could cling. If I was moved onto a stretcher and hoisted into an ambulance, I'd have to leave that feeling behind.

Vague recollections are all that remain of the ride to the hospital. A dreamlike impression of an oxygen mask over my face…a small sting as an I.V. needle was shoved into my arm, and loud voices. I would have been content to stay in that world forever because, strangely, I could feel, but there was no pain. Bits and pieces of reality crept in as I was rolled into the trauma unit. The 'whoosh' of the automatic doors, decidedly cooler air, and a warm blanket being thrown over my broken body.

Someone repeated my name as a pair of scissors sliced down the right leg of my jeans. Another sharp instrument cut up the side of my white Oxford shirt taking with it part of my undershirt.

Hey! Who the hell gave you permission to cut off my pants?! These were not some cheap ass jeans! Somebody is gonna pay for these!

I was exhausted, too weak to struggle and too drained to care. Lying stone still, I accepted the treatment as if my body was dead. As the clothes came off, I grew even colder. Shivering took too much energy. Lying there completely naked in front of the trauma team, there was no strength left for modesty.

Finally, I gave up trying to stay alert and slid into unconsciousness.

Maybe minutes, maybe hours, maybe days later I woke with a start, unsure of anything. *Am I alive? Conscious? Is it night? Day? Am I dead? If I am dead, why do I hurt so much? Death is supposed to be painless, right? No, there's no way I'm dead, is there?*

If I'm not dead, I want to be.

Something was very, very wrong. I found myself floating, no, falling. Floating and falling? *Huh?*

Dizziness and delirium invaded my skull. I took tiny, shallow breaths to survive. My tongue filled my mouth and felt like a football stuffed between the shards that had formerly been my teeth.

Am I stoned? Is this heaven? Am I laying on a cloud or something? This cannot be heaven; I am either alive or in hell... maybe both. God, how is this kind of pain even possible?

Waves crested and fell as if support was coming from a free flowing waterbed. *But, if this is a waterbed, who keeps making the waves?* The bed rocked harder and harder, almost as if someone were next to me, trying to throw me off. Up and down I floated, my head nodding like a buoy in a tsunami.

Stop it... NOW! I yelled at the unseen disturbance, but to no avail. The bed continued to try to buck me to the floor.

Inching my right hand across the sheet, I found a cold, metal cylinder standing upright. *What is this thing? A cage?*

I latched onto the bar and tried to stabilize myself, never once considering the tangible ocean was caused by an endless supply of morphine.

A foggy image began to materialize overhead. *Tom?* I thought aloud, or at least I thought it was aloud. *Is that you?* I inquired of a statuesque image of my friend floating nearby. He was just a few feet away, but made no movement toward me. *Dude, help me,* I pleaded, but he didn't acknowledge my screams. The Tom-thing just looked down with sadness in his eyes.

Don't just stare at me! Why won't you fucking help me? Shit, Tom, help me, please!

I frantically focused in on the vision, but then couldn't believe what I was seeing. Tom had no body... no arms, legs, neck, torso... just a face, not even a head! Fear seized my heart. I closed my eyes tight and tried to block out the image of the phantom face.

Somewhere in the night, I slipped into a true state of unconsciousness, only to be smacked back into the here and now.

What's that? I asked myself, concentrating on the noise I'd just heard. Listening hard, I heard it again. A gurgle, then a slosh. Sonar? It sounded exactly like the muffled, underwater sonar sounds on a National Geographic special. But, that couldn't be right, could it? The sound subsided. I held my breath for as long as I could, still trying to hear. As I took a breath, the noise came again. Now, though, it was more than a noise – it was a true, physical feeling. *Where? Huh?* Then, with a sickening realization, I knew. As my skull shifted the slightest amount, I could hear and feel the fluid inside my head rolling about.

Is my brain moving around in my skull?? I quickly dismissed the thought, too afraid to even consider it. Through the rushing liquid, I heard a voice.

"Marcus, can you hear me?" Voice. Quiet. Female. Past that, I could tell nothing.

I tried to nod ever so slightly, but it set off another tidal wave of pain. A small, soft hand gently slipped into mine. I lightly squeezed the fingers, hoping this would suffice for a nod.

"Do you know where you are?" she whispered.

Is this real? Or just some sort of hallucination like Tom's face?

"Squeeze my hand if you can hear me, Marcus," the quiet voice persisted. I did as I was told. As soon as she felt the slight pressure, the voice said, "Good."

"You're in Barnes Hospital… you were in a car accident."

Again I tried to nod that I understood, but the effort was just too great. I squeezed her hand, a bit more firmly this time.

"Go to sleep, just rest," she said quietly. Then, the most comforting words of all, "I'm here."

"Please, please don't leave me!" I mentally cried.

I drifted back to unconsciousness and relinquished all control to this kind voice and soft hand. Down, down, down, I sank to a place where no memories exist, still holding that hand as I took the first steps of a journey into hell.

Chapter 3

"I can't close my eyes and make it go away..." [4]

~ U2

The two boys laughed and slapped at the water, tossing a beach ball between them. As I watched, their play turned into a physics experiment. The taller boy bear hugged the ball and dove in headfirst. The ball's buoyancy overpowered him and soon it was rocketing back to the surface. Undeterred, he tried sitting on it, holding it underwater with his feet and legs. He kept it submerged for a few seconds, but then the ball found the point of least resistance and fired back to the surface.

Sitting in the hot sun and watching their play, my eight-year-old self was more interested in joining their fun than observing. But looking on was all I could do. I tried to throw my arms forward, but I couldn't move. Panicking, I turned to look at the boys, only to find that movement impossible, too. Struggling, I bent down and found that I could at least still control that vertical movement. What's more, as soon as my crown sank below the water's surface, I could move however I pleased. It was like being out of the water created some invisible straightjacket. But, after only a few seconds underwater, I'd rocket back to the surface; a place filled with fear and confusion and pain.

Hallucination or reality? Trying to tell the difference was exhausting. Only voices and human touch could ground me to reality.

Why can't I see? This question was real; that's for damned sure. I groped for an answer, any answer, any point of reference.

"Remember when you had surgery to fix that hernia you busted during football practice? You couldn't see at first then, either. This has to be a whole lot worse than some hernia surgery, dude!"

So many times my body had taken a sudden blow — football pile-ups, sledding accidents and a little mishap involving a merry-go-round, a concrete playground and the skull of a certain three-year-old. All these times I could recall not being able to see while my body adjusted. But *THIS*? Well, this had to be more serious than any of those times — a lot more serious.

You've just been knocked senseless, Engel. When the shock wears off, you'll be able to see again. Or so I hoped.

Without warning, a hand slipped into mine. Then, just as unexpectedly, another hand grasped my left.

The hand on the right was small and gentle, but the one to the left was just the opposite. The moment the weathered skin touched mine, my body fell limply in that direction and fluid sloshed inside my skull.

"Marc? It's Mom. We're here and we love you," came the hoarse, tear-soaked voice on my right. *Crying? What's wrong?* I'd heard Mom cry plenty of times, but this was different… unsettling. Tears were one thing, but her forced calmness was what really sat me on edge. She was fighting for control… and losing.

"Yeah, we love you, Marc," the voice of my father echoed from the left.

Wait a minute! My family doesn't say, "I love you" like this! Holy shit! I must be really hurt! Fear began to show its ugly face. My parents definitely are not the types who gush! Oh sure, when I was a kid I heard those words every night as Mom tucked me in and turned off my bedroom lights. But, as I got older and asserted my independence more, I repeated those three words back less and less. Soon, I really didn't remember hearing "I love you" at all any more. This is not to say our family wasn't close. In fact, I had no idea of just how strong of a family we were. Growing up, that bond was always present, but I never even noticed it... or maybe just never appreciated it. Of course, both parents were fans at my football games, attended every concert I performed and were fixtures at any play in which I acted. Those routine evening meals around the dinner table with all four of us present were also taken for granted. My sister, Cathy, and I were oblivious to just how difficult it must have been for Mom to get everyone gathered together. "I love you" wasn't always said, but it was always known.

When was the last time we'd actually used those words? Six months ago? Near the end of my senior year? Yeah, that had to be it. I was almost 18, a couple of months from graduation and all too ready to start college. Working nearly 20 hours per week at a Texaco service station gave me my own spending money and feelings of independence. Yet, I was still at home, still under my parents' roof, still in high school. I felt like a man with one foot stuck in the world of a child. The terms "growing pains" and "senioritis" were gross understatements.

That entire stage of growing up was captured in a senior English project. Mrs. Reynolds, our long-suffering teacher, assigned the class to read Charles Dickens', *A Tale of Two Cities*.[5] I had yet to become an avid reader and considered the assignment a huge waste of time. Being hopelessly stuck in my personal 'no man's land', I maturely decided I would not do the assignment. So I failed that section of the class... big freaking deal! I already had my acceptance letter to college. SMSU darned sure wasn't going to turn down my tuition money just because I'd slacked off on an assignment. Really, what was Mrs. Reynolds going to do? Flunk me and subject herself to another year of my brilliant presence in her English class? Not likely!

Impressed with my own logic, I didn't bother to read the first three chapters. Heck, I didn't even open the book. Truth was, I wasn't sure where I'd even stuffed it in my locker. Several classmates offered me the use of their *Cliff Notes*, but why? If you're going to screw off, do it right! Figuring I'd fake my way through the final, I'd probably pull off a "C" for the project. While it wasn't up to my usual grades, I could live with something less than normal if it meant all I had to do was slack off. However, I hadn't anticipated the land mine of every senior's existence, a pop quiz.

Knowing I was destined for a big, red "F", I proceeded to compound the problem with the unthinkable. For nearly a page, I lied, fantasized and fabricated a humorous story about ridiculous French characters with names like *Deja Vu*, *Escargots* and *Soufflé*. With characters named after the most basic French words, I poked fun at not only the French language, but the very work of Dickens which Mrs. Reynolds considered one of the greatest novels of the English language.

I summed up the manifesto of stupidity by saying "*A Tale of Two Cities* was a dumb book written by a dead guy named Darles Chickens"; a quip I borrowed from a Monty Python skit. The doomed essay ended with the words "Enough Said!" printed darkly at the bottom. I knew I had failed, so I thought I'd at least amuse myself in the process!

A few days later, my mother's unsmiling face met me at the front door. Her eyes filled with tears as she handed me an envelope bearing the school's return address. Inside was a letter from Mrs. Reynolds, which told, in great detail, of my latest brainstorm. A lump formed in my throat as I read the letter. Attached, in all its formerly humorous glory, was my essay from the quiz. Now, it didn't seem so funny.

Unable to hide my shame, I had to confess it all. Every last accumulated sin rose to the surface and spilled out – disregard for classes, weekend partying habits, and the strain of being old enough to do what I wanted, but not old enough to be on my own. My eyes swam with tears.

"I'm so sorry. I'm just tired of my life." I blurted lamely, sobbing on Mom's shoulder.

"I know, I know. You're almost done with school and that is a hard time for everyone. But, please, please take your classes more seriously." I promised I would. We hugged and I told her I loved her. It was the first time in years I remembered saying those three words.

So now? Both of my parents are here and saying they love me?! Mom? Well, that's one thing, but Dad? I'd never seen him cry, not even when he buried his own father. Yet, now here he was fighting back tears.

Breathing equipment left me unable to speak or make any sounds, leaving my hands as my only means of communication. I held up the only bit of American Sign Language I knew, the sign for "I love you." Making a tight fist, I raised my little and index fingers while pointing my thumb out at a 90-degree angle. It never occurred to me that they just might not "get it." Every time they were allowed into the ICU, I reaffirmed my love with my hand; a gesture they just didn't understand.

Days later, a friend, Pat, came for her first visit. Pat was a youth minister and had first introduced me to Tom several years before. With such a long history of friendship, and because Pat wasn't an untrustworthy teenager, she was the first visitor allowed in without the accompaniment of my parents. As Pat exited the ICU and said, "I love you, Marc," I signed back to her, "I love you, too." Surprised by the response, she hurried off to tell my parents.

"Marc is going to be okay, I just know he is. He even told me he loves me!"

My parents, baffled, couldn't get her explanation fast enough.

"He signed it to me," she said with a smile, holding up her hand as I had been doing for days.

"Is that what that is?" my father asked, already rushing out the door and headed for my side. Tears of joy followed at the first tangible sign that my mind was still in tact.

Glad to know my message was now getting through, this scenario brought along another worry. If Pat had been talking to my parents out of earshot, then other conversations were also probably being kept secret. Realizing this, a new question emerged: what had my parents been told and by whom? I didn't want to mix fact and fiction, but unable to speak, I wasn't going to be a whole lot of help sorting out the two. My heart sank when I thought of how my parents must have learned of the crash.

As my clothing was cut off, someone pulled the black leather Christian Dior wallet from my jeans. Among my cash, student I.D. and photos, they found my driver's license. The trauma team searched for identification knowing they had to deliver the unwelcome news to my parents.

Awakened by the call, Dad rolled over in bed and grabbed the phone.

"Sir, are you the father of Marcus Engel of High Hill, Missouri?" asked a tense female voice.

"Yes, I'm Phillip Engel," he said, immediately sitting up in bed.

"Mr. Engel, your son has been in a car accident. I'm an emergency room employee at Barnes Hospital in St. Louis. Marcus was rushed here by ambulance just a few minutes ago and the trauma team is working on him now."

"Is he hurt?" Dad asked, feeling as though he'd just been kicked between the eyes.

The calm, professional voice said, "He has some facial injuries and a broken leg. He's in surgery right now and will be for a few hours. Please come quickly, but carefully, to the hospital. There will be someone waiting to meet you."

Dad hung up the phone, stood quickly and relayed the news to my mom. In under five minutes, they were out the door and traveling the same route I'd taken just 12 hours earlier; not knowing what awaited at the journey's end.

A physician waited nervously for my parents to arrive. The moment they stepped through the emergency room doors, she ushered them into a private waiting area. She began explaining everything that had transpired in the hour since I'd arrived, but then came an even more shocking blow.

"With all the facial injuries Marcus sustained, his eyes were also hurt very badly. I must tell you there is a distinct possibility your son may now be blind." The physician sat quietly, waiting for her words to sink in.

"Marcus will probably be in surgery the rest of tonight and through most of the morning, too. I'll come back later with updates from the operating room. Mr. and Mrs. Engel, I want you to know we're going to do everything we can for him."

Everything we can for him… words that do not paint a picture of hope. The physician excused herself and closed the door behind her.

How do any parents sit alone in a private waiting room, unable to see or help their child? How could any parents do that knowing their child was barely clinging to life in a nearby operating room? Perhaps, it was as simple and as complex as the fact that they just didn't have a choice.

While the hours slowly clicked by, my parents began to formulate a plan to pass along the news. Powerless, this was the only thing they could do.

First, they had to let family and friends know. Starting with my sister, they would call everyone connected with me: Cathy, then grandparents, uncles, aunts and cousins. Mom and Dad divided up who would make the calls, hoping and praying word would travel quickly.

But, it was still the middle of the night. Everyone was home and asleep. Why get them out of bed when losing the night's sleep or driving into the city would accomplish nothing. People in the middle of a trauma can be amazingly sensible. Six a.m. was just a few hours away. Then the calls would begin.

To receive the call as my parents did, to numbly dress and race to the hospital is an experience no one would envy. But, to have to make the calls to loved ones is a task of even more courage. To have actually been forced to say the words, "The doctors think Marc is going to be blind" had to be equal to having one's heart ripped out of their chest.

After what seemed like an eternity, an orthopedic surgeon came in with news from the O.R.

"I'm Dr. Martin," he said, pulling up a seat by the worried couple. "I received a call around midnight to come and consult on Marcus."

Dr. Martin wasn't the only surgeon yanked from a night's sleep. It's not surprising that no resident in his right mind would want to cut his teeth on a trauma case this serious.

"Marcus' right hip was dislocated and he has a double compound break in his left leg. We have both legs in traction now, and that will be the initial treatment for the break. The hip is another story. Our goal was to manipulate it back into its socket. The procedure was successful, but I can tell you it wasn't the easiest manipulation I've ever done. Any procedure with the hip is delicate, but this one was more complicated because of your son's size. To make sure we minimized the potential for error, myself and another physician stood on the operating table to guide the ball back into the socket."

While his job was complete, Dr. Martin took the time to just sit and answer their barrage of questions. Finally, with all their queries answered, he left them with a bit of hope. His words were direct, simple and to the point and will always, always stay with me. "Marcus is hurt very badly. But, he's strong as a bull and he's going to be all right."

Strong as a bull... strong as a bull, yeah, I guess I wasn't exactly a shrimpy ectomorph, but strong as a bull? Was the exercise regiment I'd started at college enough to qualify me as "strong as a bull?"

My plan had been to get in shape and lose the fat that had accumulated since football season had ended nearly a year before. Plus, and more honestly, I wanted to impress some of the hot coeds I'd seen walking around campus! But, in one of those rare flashes of insight, it occurred to me much later that there might have been a more divine purpose for getting in shape.

Now, some 14 hours following the crash, they had finally been allowed to see their son. Could someone have prepared them for how I would look? Maybe someone as direct as the orthopedic surgeon said, "You probably won't be able to recognize your kid in there. He's just too beaten up." Even that could not convey the horrific vision that awaited them. There are no words to prepare a parent to look upon a child they cannot name as their own.

Naked except for a sheet that covered my mid-section, I lay in what was to be my home for the next several months. Both legs hung in traction above the bed. Each leg held a minimum of four stainless steel pins that protruded through the bones and out the skin of my calves. Suspended at the ankles by a metal apparatus hanging above the bed, my once muscle toned legs looked as though they belonged to an invalid. In less than a day, my body had melted from a tall, broad young man to that of a shriveled geriatric.

My torso presented an obscene version of their son. My face and head were swollen to nearly twice their normal size. Both eyes were sutured shut by a surgeon's stitches and tubes penetrated and covered my swollen chest. Both arms were black and blue with discolored skids and bruises covering the skin like a prisoner's tattoos. The hole in my throat held a plastic tube that pumped air into my lungs through an O2 tank. Another tube was protruding from my open mouth, pushed to the side by the chipped fragments of teeth that looked like they belonged to a jack o' lantern.

Who or what was this? Was this Marc? Was the Marc we loved still inside that body? What questions and worst fears were my parents unable to express, even to each other? How they managed to speak was as amazing as the fact I was still alive. Other than, "We love you," I have no recollection of what they said.

But I knew they were there. That was the most comforting thing of all. The simple presence of a parent during a child's trauma is as close to heavenly love as humans will ever know. They would remain with me, week after week as I fought battles no human should endure… and as they fought to make sense out of life.

Chapter 4

"But I can't respond to your sign language,
you're taking advantage, bringing me down.
Can't you make any sound?" [6]

~ Eric Clapton and Bob Dylan

The heavy toll of the church bell landed its first overpowering boom just as the telephone on the minister's desk began to ring. After a brief conversation, he hurried into the sanctuary, quickly scanned the crowd and located the youth director, Linda. He walked toward her seat, the look on his face broadcasting something was horribly wrong.

"Marc Engel was in a terrible car accident last night. He's been in surgery since about 1 a.m. For now, he's still hanging on…" he paused, purposely letting his words trail off to allow the information to sink in. Too stunned to pose any questions, Linda could only absorb what she was hearing. "Marc's eyes suffered some extensive damage. They won't know a full diagnosis until the doctors can operate, but there's a strong possibility he may now be blind. Right now, we just have to pray that he lives." Linda sat, numb. The minister continued, "I just wanted you to know before I announced it in church. I'm sure you'll want to tell Marc's close friends."

Without a word, Linda's head sank and she began to sob.

Instead of beginning the Sunday morning service in the typical fashion, the minister walked into the sanctuary and positioned himself at the pulpit. As he did, Linda gathered the youth together and quickly relayed the news, softening the blow before the minister shared the tale with the congregation. Within five minutes, the news had spread from one concerned minister to over 100 parishioners who would, as soon as church let out, spread the news to hundreds more. The network had begun.

An hour before the minister received the call, another phone rang in a bedroom in downtown Chicago. Elaine, my aunt, glanced at the clock before answering. Who would be calling before 7 o'clock on a Sunday morning? Her blood ran cold as she heard her brother's frightened voice.

"Marc has been in a bad accident," Dad said, his voice thin and hollow.

"How bad is it?" Elaine prodded, but she already knew the answer.

"It's bad…really bad," dad said quietly. Then, he could say nothing more.

"I'll be there tomorrow," Elaine said, hanging up the phone.

Without so much as a glance at her schedule, Elaine began to pack for a lengthy stay. And, the network continued.

The ICU waiting room soon became a virtual command post for sending and receiving information. My parents worked the phones to inform friends and family, interrupted by the occasional doctor bringing the latest word from the operating room.

In the midst of a crumbling world, they took control the only way they could; by telling everyone they knew. My parents, neither of who worked in the corporate world, ever perceived what they were doing as establishing a complex network of resources. The virtual machine they created would, over the next several months, pass along information about my condition, moods, surgeries, visitors, etc. It squelched inaccurate rumors, distortions of events and endless speculation with lightning speed.

During the first 48 painful hours, close friends and relatives quietly appeared at my bedside, most of them afraid it was the last time they would see me alive. When one of the voices would burst into tears and run from the room after getting a look at my ghastly appearance, I'd try to communicate to the others that I was still inside of this wrecked body – only to find I couldn't speak. Nothing but wheezing sounds came from my throat as tiny wisps of oxygen escaped around the tracheotomy tube.

Oh, Christ! Everyone is going to think I'm brain damaged! They'll think I'm a vegetable!

Inside, I panicked. *No, No! Please understand, please! I'm still in here! I'm still Marc!* But, I could do nothing to prove it.

Being unable to talk was such an inane problem relative to the medical nightmare I presented to the physicians. As they looked over my charts, some of them had to wonder if their plans were an exercise in futility. After all, the kid was hurt so badly that no one could really be sure whether he would live or die. Besides, with no official word on potential brain damage, was there really a point in reconstructing his face?

Meanwhile the hotline continued. One hundred and fifty miles away, the phone rang in the dorm room of three of my best friends, Jeff, David and Rodney. Their response shows more about their collective character than I could ever tell. The guys were spending a lazy Sunday evening watching football when my cousin called from the hospital. Conveying what few details were known, the looks that passed between them said as much as what was spoken.

Armed with nothing more than the name of the hospital and the words, "Engel is hurt," Rodney simply did what came to mind. He grabbed his coat and keys, looked to his friends and said, "Let's go." The bond of four young men and what they would do for each other in a critical time wasn't questioned; it was simply done.

Two hours later the trio walked into the waiting room and greeted my parents. "We just want Marc to know we're here when he wakes up. We'll wait as long as we have to until we can see him."

Had it only been a day or two ago that we were together and on top of the world at the Homecoming game? How was it possible that now one of our lives had been shattered?

Entering the ICU, 48 hours became a lifetime ago. As David, Jeff and Rodney gathered around my bed, four young men took an irreversible step into manhood.

It would have been impossible to look at the battered head resting on that pillow and think the friend they loved was still inside there. No one could blame them for wondering if my brain was intact. I knew what they were thinking… because I was thinking the same thing.

A year earlier four students from our high school had been hit by a train as they attempted to drive across the tracks. When the train stopped moving, two lay dead and two were changed forever; one by physical injuries and the other due to a traumatic brain injury. I loathed the thought anyone would think my brain had been damaged.

Dammit, guys! I am NOT brain dead!

Jeff gingerly held my left hand and began to stammer. Wondering if this may be the last conversation we'd ever have, he felt the need to confess a prank he and Rodney had played at the field party.

"Engel, you know what Rod and I told you about my ex-girlfriend the other night?" Jeff asked, hesitating and looking for any response. I gently squeezed his hand.

As Jeff and Rod had driven to the field party, they concocted a totally bogus story. By the time they arrived, they'd even rehearsed exactly what lines each would tell. If I bought into their tall tale, it would make me look like a total idiot, but their story was so ridiculous I knew it couldn't be true.

"Don't gimme that shit, dudes!" I had said, listening with annoyed amusement. "Y'all expect me to believe that? I don't know whether to kick you in the crotch, or congratulate you for trying!" I'd said, playfully taking a swing at both of them.

God, had that really only been two nights before? It hardly seemed possible that the world was now such a different place.

"Well, we were just joking about that stuff we told you. You know that, right?" he asked, his voice starting to crack with tears.

Now! Now, this was my chance! I could prove to them it was still me inside here, still the same guy who talked about girls, partied around bonfires, still the same guy with whom they shared the secrets of young life. I seized the opportunity. Sliding my hand from his, I made a fist. Then, as forcefully as possible, I raised my middle finger.

There! That ought to show you guys! And, they laughed! They actually laughed!

Now they could see that inside this unrecognizable face, I was still their buddy Marc. That only left the rest of the world to convince.

Until surgeries could begin in full, the only relief came from heavy doses of morphine. The drugs did a whole lot of nothing other than distort my thinking.

Concentration was impossible. Doctors would try to explain things with all their fancy Latin words and I'd get lost somewhere between, "Hi, Marcus" and "I'll be back later." Knowing the effects of morphine, they tried to speak in short, simple sentences. It was a bittersweet gratefulness, but at least I could understand when doctors would step into a layman's role.

"Pulverized" was the word one surgeon used to describe my face. It was harsh, accurate, and left nothing to the imagination; precisely what I needed to hear.

"Paralysis on the left side of your face, Marc," was another terse, clinical explanation. The shifting of my broken jaw was responsible for not only nerve damage, but had also severed my left ear canal.

Another even more painful injury had taken place as the concrete did a number on my face. Somewhere in the midst of the crash, my entire left ear was nearly ripped away. The doctor's exact words were "it looks like a piece of raw hamburger." I wanted descriptions, but I did not need to know my head resembled the floor of a slaughterhouse. The ear, re-attached during the first night's surgery, was a source of horrendous pain.

But that wasn't the worst. It was hard to convey the seriousness of my greatest discomfort when what hurt so badly was no place other than my ass! The skin had been coarsely sanded and scraped from my back, thighs and rear as I skidded along the pavement of Chippewa Avenue.

"Road rash" is a cutesy little term some jackass doctor created to lessen the pain of such a serious injury. Road rash is anything but funny.

As if the ear, jaw, road rash and broken facial bones weren't bad enough, the word "ventilator" kept coming up. Doctors and nurses continually discussed the trach, which itself felt like a hot bullet scalding my throat. *A ventilator? Isn't that life support? What is my condition, anyway? Stable? Critical? Or, was this so horrendous they had to create a new classification? Damn near dead? Really fucked up?*

No one bothered to inform me in which category I belonged, which, in retrospect was probably a good thing... I might have actually believed it.

I resigned myself to the necessity of the feeding tube inserted into my small intestine. With a broken jaw and shards left in my gums as teeth, I wasn't exactly going to be scarfing down a steak any time soon. I could handle the idea of the feeding tube filling my stomach with sustenance, but the inability to breathe on my own was terrifying. I lay there listening to the sickening sounds of my mechanical breathing, all the while praying the oxygen tank wouldn't run dry. If the hose got twisted and oxygen stopped flowing, a short alarm would sound. Immediately, a nurse would appear to correct the problem. But, what if the tube slipped out of my throat? What if the alarm malfunctioned? What if the oxygen concentration wasn't high enough?

I could still think – if you could call it that. Reality mixed with confusion mixed with hallucination swirled back and forth, never giving me a true point of reference.

Even if I could speak, what would people think if I started talking about visions of monsters and demons? Would they think I was nuts? I had to risk it… I couldn't handle not talking any more.

If speaking was out, the next best option was sign language. Problem was, I only knew a few signs… and those were profanities! The only remaining option was to try to write. *Write? With what, Engel?! You've got no paper, no pencils, nothing!* True, I answered in response to the naysayer within, but I can still trace with my finger. *I have to give it a shot!* Lifting my right arm, I smoothed the sheets in preparation. Then, I waited.

Finally, after what seemed like years, someone entered. I pointed with my index finger and began to move it along the bed sheet, hoping they'd understand. *All you have to do is figure out I'm writing, look at the letters and then do what I tell you.*

"Just checking the oxygen supply, Mr. Engel," a female voice said. I frantically motioned at the flattened sheet and started to draw.

I traced the word "who," trying to get the person to identify herself. Without looking at my writing, she simply twisted some knobs on a beeping device by the bed.

Dammit! I'm not dead! What are you doing? Mental irritation was getting in the way of my plan. Her task complete, she stopped just long enough to notice the wild movements of my hand.

She mumbled something, gave up and walked out. Frustrated, I imagined her returning to the break room and telling her co-workers that not only was the kid in the ICU beaten to hell, but now he was doing all this weird stuff with his hands.

But, it wasn't a total defeat. I had figured out that the person was a woman, probably a nurse, checking my oxygen supply. She had at least stopped and attempted to figure out what I was doing. *Sooner or later, someone has to get it, right?*

I tried every possible manner of writing: big, small, slowly, everything. Each time a nurse was able to guess first one letter and then two, I chalked it up to progress.

The fourth or fifth try was slightly more rewarding. The nurse was trying her hardest and even seemed to understand that smoothing the sheet was a symbolic indication I was going to start over; roughly equivalent to shaking the images off the screen of an Etch-A-Sketch. She couldn't decipher more than three letters no matter how hard we tried.

"Do you just want me to guess, Marcus?" she asked, hopeful.

I tried to nod my head yes, which set the weird fluid spilling around inside my skull. I slammed my hand down on the sheet trying to quiet the sloshing.

"Do you want some medicine for pain?"

I raised my index finger to answer in the affirmative.

"Okay," she said. "I'll ask the doctor and see if I can give you some morphine."

What?! I got through to her?! Hot damn!

"Do you want anything else?" she asked, probably hoping she hadn't started the guessing game again.

Before thinking, I held up one finger.

"Do you want your parents?" Her tone was pained, sounding as though this was a request she couldn't fill.

Yes, YES! I hadn't thought of it until she'd brought it up, but if Mom and Dad were here, then maybe they could fight off the hallucinations. I raised my index finger once again.

"Okay, I'll see if I can find them," she said before turning and walking out the door.

I waited another lifetime; totally forgetting she was coming back. When she finally reappeared, she began adjusting the plastic IV tubes that were taped to my forearms.

"This is pain medicine that should help you sleep," she explained, slightly tugging at the IV line as she injected the drug. At least, I think she injected something. I really couldn't tell. The relief was so meager that it was impossible to know if she'd shot me up or not.

She said nothing about my parents and I didn't have the energy to lift a finger to inquire. As she walked out, I slipped back into the dark world of hallucination, unreality and pain.

Chapter 5

"And I woke up in my hospital bed, I saw what it had done and I wished I was dead. Never knew there were worse things than dying..." [7]

~ The Pogues

"Marc? It's Elaine," came a quiet voice from my right. "Can you hear me?" the voice persisted. *Elaine? My Aunt Elaine? The nurse? What was she doing here?* She lived in Chicago, but I was sure this voice was really her; not a hallucination.

Dude! I must be seriously messed up if Elaine is here, I thought, apprehension washing over me.

"Don't try to talk," she said quickly. "You've got a tracheotomy in your throat and you can't speak right now." Well, back to square one. How can I communicate if I can't talk? I could keep doing the one finger / two finger thing, but that just makes the world a guessing game. Sheet writing? If the nurses hadn't gotten it, how could I expect Elaine to figure it out?

Suddenly, my mind flashed back to that same message I had to get across to my friends: *I am still me inside here!*

"Do you think you can write if I give you a pen and some paper?" she asked.

Yes, YES! Of course I can. Give it to me now!

Elaine's voice and words were even, giving no hint of how appalling my appearance was. No doubt she was viewing the crumpled body of the nephew she dearly loved while facing fears of her own. Was Marc even going to live? Would he ever be able to talk again? In a professional manner, which could only come from half a lifetime in the health care field, Elaine swallowed her emotions and pressed on.

I lifted my right index finger to answer in the affirmative.

"Okay" she said. "I'll go get some paper."

What?! She got it! I'm actually going to be able to tell her that I am okay! I experienced a fleeting moment of ecstatic joy.

A few minutes later, Elaine returned with what would be my means of communication for the next month. She handed me the pencil and pad, carefully laying them onto my mid-section. Grasping the pencil, doubt smacked me upside the head. *What if she can't read my handwriting? God! Just let her know you are not brain damaged, Engel! Or, at least not too much.*

The IV needles in the back of my right hand ached as I rolled the pencil between my fingers. God, even my fingertips ached. Bruised tissue near the nails caused stiffness as I struggled to bend my knuckles. The pain was just horrendous.

Morphine made concentration impossible. How would I be able to deliver a lucid, reassuring dissertation if I couldn't focus on a single thought?

"Okay, Marc, see if you can write your name."

Slowly, cautiously, I began to print. I could almost see her biting her lower lip in anticipation. Feeling her eyes on every movement, I tried to write legibly... something I wasn't very good at even without the "help" of narcotics!

After finishing my name, I laid the pencil to the side.

"Okay, very good!" Elaine said with approval. Pleased I could perform that simple task, she moved onto test number two. "Now, Marc, do you know where you are?" she asked, her voice quiet, but strong. The question was strangely intense. In fact, everything about her behavior seemed different, not at all the usual demeanor of my Aunt Elaine. Then again, I guess I wasn't acting like her usual nephew, either. I didn't know it, but she was making a quick clinical assessment of my cognitive functions: Did I recognize who she was? Did I understand her questions? Could I follow commands?

I answered, not even realizing I was being evaluated. I was preoccupied with letting people know I was still me, but I didn't realize others might have a way to test my brain functions. Short of me blurting out, "I'm not a vegetable!" I didn't know if the doctors and nurses would be able to figure it out.

The medical staff, my friends, even my family... everyone was treating me like I was an inconsequential child. I couldn't understand that they talked to me differently because I *was* different. Almost no one had ever come into contact with someone who couldn't see, talk, walk – or who was as injured as I was.

As I focused my concentration, Elaine nervously anticipated what she would say if I couldn't pass the second round. What if Marc really is changed forever, both mentally and physically? Her heart shattered as she thought back to summer days spent with her young nephew and how his future was still ahead of him. Now, his life had been reduced to an oxygen tank and a feeding tube.

Emotions are useless right now, she thought, what Marc needs more than anything is reassurance. She wiped away a solitary tear, swallowed hard and forced her focus back to the task at hand.

"Do you know where you are?" Elaine asked again, knowing from years in the medical profession just how much morphine trashed one's brain.

I scanned my memory banks for my location. Finally, I latched onto the last place I remembered and gave it a shot. "Barnes Hospital?" I wrote with an unsteady hand.

"Yes!" Elaine said clearly encouraged… and maybe a little surprised. I had understood her question and given a legible and correct response. Doubts about brain damage started to slip away. "Now, Marc, do you know why you're in the hospital?"

I forced my mind back, back to the headlights, to lying in the street, to the young woman who screamed for me to lie still. Unsure of the concrete details, I responded with a question. "Car accident?" I laid my pen to the side after trying to figure out how to spell "accident." Remembering how to spell, especially words with double letters, was nearly impossible due to the stranglehold of the drugs.

Elaine's heart leapt and she breathed a long sigh of relief. "Yes!" she said solidly, now almost convinced my cognitive functions were intact. What were obvious responses to me were critical, diagnostic pieces of information to her.

"How?" I wrote, praying she'd understand I wanted details of the crash.

"Do you remember going to the hockey game?"

"Y e s," I wrote slowly.

"You were with Tom, Kim and Vince. You guys were going to Tom's house after the hockey game. Another car hit your car on the way."

My mind begin to drift back to that night when a new thought slapped me into focus. Steadying my hand, I scrawled out the question that would forever change my life.

"Was anyone drunk?"

The force of Elaine's answer was startling.

"Yes! The people in the other car were very, very drunk." With every question and response, Elaine grew more and more assured that her nephew was still inside of this unrecognizable face.

"The other people were going home from a bar and hit you guys broadside."

Drunk driving? Now this was a whole new spin on the issue. I didn't have the strength to do anything more than dip my head in an almost imperceptible nod, accepting the information without much emotion. Emotions were just going to have to wait.

Confusion clogged my mind once again. *Wait! What had she just said? Drunk Driving? Did she think we were drunk? Did she think that Tom was the drunk driver? Tom wasn't drunk... was he?* I was positive no one in our group had even had a sip of alcohol. I needed to get that across and clear our names... fast!

"We weren't drunk," I wrote as legibly as possible.

Elaine seemed taken aback.

"I know. We all know, Marcus. You guys didn't do anything wrong." She said these words with such determination I had no choice but to believe her. Thankfully, there was no hint of accusation in anyone's mind about me or my friends.

Friends! Reality slapped me with an even harder blow. *Tom! Where is he? Where the hell are my friends?!* Terror grabbed my throat and began to squeeze. I was nearly frantic! I didn't even want to think about that possibility, but how could I keep from it?

A single word exploded like a grenade...dead! *They can't be dead! Can they? What if someone is dead?* Screaming inside, my heart raced. The fog lifted as adrenaline shot through my veins.

I thought back to the street, the screaming and the pain. I couldn't remember anything about my friends. But, I didn't *feel* like someone was dead.

What if someone really is dead? What if the funeral is already over? I had to know. But, my God, I don't even want to know. *Dead... Christ, dead! Nobody can be dead. We're just kids!*

Forcing deep breaths through the trach, I ordered myself to take control. I still held the pencil, but I had lost the desire to write… yet I had to. Finally, bracing myself for the answer, I wrote the question. "How are my friends?"

"Tom is here in Barnes, too. He has some broken bones in his neck and will be in a halo for a long time."

Okay, that's a good start. Tom is alive; he's hurt, but he's alive.

"Kim has some whiplash and she's wearing a collar, but she's not seriously hurt. Vince is a little beaten up, but he's okay. They were taken to a different hospital and released after a few hours." Elaine had neatly dodged an explanation of who went to a trauma center and who did not.

Good, no one is dead. As hard as I tried, I found I couldn't hold onto the explanation. "Tell me again," I wrote.

"Marc. No one died in the accident. Your friends are all alive," she said confidently. Then, as if pondering whether or not to continue, she took a breath and swallowed hard. Hating every word, she continued.

"Marc, you're hurt very badly, but you're alive, too."

Me? I had been so riveted on the fate of my friends, I hadn't thought about myself.

"What's wrong with me?" I quickly etched onto the paper.

"First of all, your eyes are hurt very badly. You had some horrible damage to both of your eyes and they are going to have to do lots of surgery on them." She paused, allowing me to digest the possibilities.

How badly could my eyes be hurt? Could I be blind? Wouldn't they already know if I was blind? Clarity took over again as I formed the inevitable question on paper.

"Am I blind?"

Elaine watched as I formed the horrid question. I'll never know how she kept her voice even while giving the response she hated even more than the question.

Did you see pictures of the car?
What do you know about the other driver.
The abrasion on my butt hurts.

Am I sleeping here?
which bed.
which bed. Show it w/ my hand.

"Marc, we just don't know yet. We hope not… but right now we just don't know."

How should I respond to the news that I would probably lose one of my most basic senses, my vision? Do I cry? Go into a rage? No, not right now. I needed more information before the drugs pulled me back into the waters of hallucination. I had to find out everything… and quick.

"What else is wrong with me?"

"You have many, many broken bones, Marc. Most of them are in your face. Your left leg is broken and it is hanging in traction right now. Your right hip was dislocated, but the doctors put it back together in the emergency room."

"Any internal injuries?"

Elaine's answer came as a breath of relief with the words, "No, thank God!" I slowly scrawled my one word response on the tablet, "Good."

"Marc, it's going to take a very long time for you to get better. You are hurt worse than anyone I have ever seen."

Really? Somehow, even after her clearly detailed answers, this was big news. Elaine had been a nurse for longer than I had been alive. *The worst injuries she'd ever seen? God, no wonder people are talking around me.*

"You are going to have to go through a lot of operations to get better, Marc. One of the first things they will have to fix is your face, but it will take many surgeries. It might even take a few years to get through all of them," she said before pausing to let me absorb this idea.

The pain I had been fighting for the last couple of days had already told me we weren't talking about easy repairs with a few stitches. I nodded slightly and Elaine continued. "When the doctors fix your face, they'll do bone grafts and maybe some skin

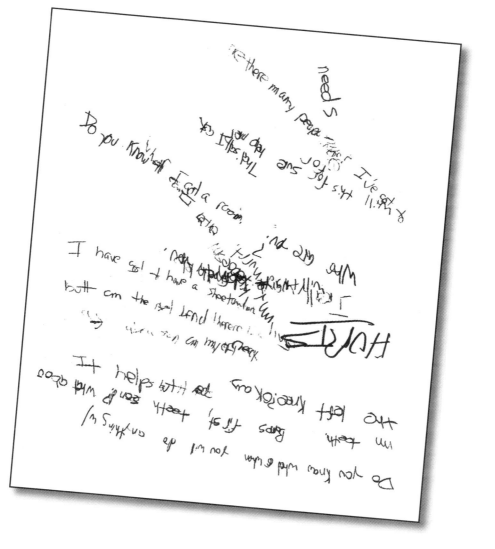

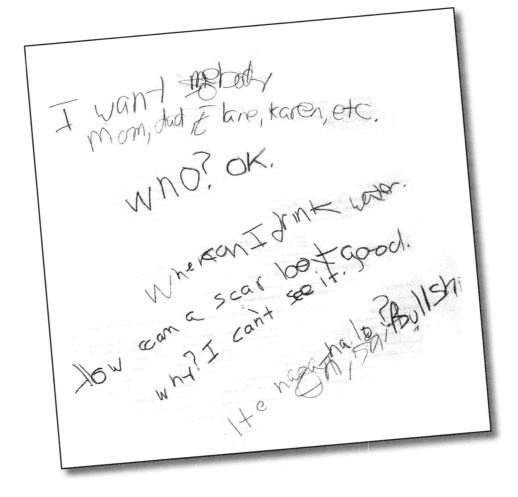

grafts, too. They won't do the surgery on your face until they know what condition your eyes are in. Then, they'll let you have time to heal between operations. It's going to be a long process and the doctors are going to have to do a lot of planning."

Before I faded into a stupor, my thoughts returned to my friends. I still had to know more.

"Tom can see, can't he?"

"Yes, his eyes were not hurt at all… only his neck." Elaine explained.

"Good," I wrote, thankful that only one of us would have to be blind. Having heard all the information I could handle for one time, I lay back, exhausted and spent. Hallucinations and unreality were waiting in the wings to take me as soon as Elaine stopped talking. I did not want to sleep, did not want Elaine to leave, and did not want to hear any more about my horrible situation.

Blind. How can I be blind?

God, I wanted to see again.

I just wanted to see.

Chapter 6

**"It's written on the chart at the foot end of the bed…
they say I'm blind, that I can't read it…
I've read it's every word and every word it says is death."** [8]
~ Richard Schindel & Dar Williams

"The surgeons who worked on your eyes are on their way." Elaine said softly, her fingers resting on my arm. She took a deep breath, swallowed hard and continued. "They need to talk to you…"

"Why? It didn't work anyway," I scrawled on the tablet.

In my heart I already knew what the doctors were going to say. I didn't need to hear the actual words to know the fate of my vision had been sealed before the surgery even began.

"Yeah, well, I know you're probably right…" Elaine whispered.

I lay there, drifting in and out of sleep, in and out of hallucinations, all the while waiting to hear the inevitable truth. I was blind.

An eternity later, a soft knock sounded at the door. Nervous conversations between family members immediately halted, voices hushed by the surgeons' arrival. I could almost feel the troubled looks that passed between my parents and the doctors. Footsteps moved toward my bedside, the room slipping into a death-like silence.

Elaine stepped away, letting her fingertips trail across my hands… almost as if she couldn't bring herself to break that human contact, as if her touch alone might protect me.

The doctor's assumed their posts.

"Marcus, I'm Dr. Del Priore and this is Dr. Luebeneski on your other side," he said, his voice kind, with no hint of arrogance or pride.

Dr. Luebeneski moved one step closer, but seemed to keep an invisible divide between us.

Clearly Dr. Del Priore had drawn the short straw and would deliver the sentence.

"Marcus, we did a surgery on your eyes yesterday. Do you remember going in for the operation?" he asked, stepping closer to read the reply.

"Yes" I wrote. I knew what was next.

"Marcus, your eyes were hurt very, very badly. We were hoping to save a small portion of your vision," he stated, his voice barely above a whisper.

Here it comes, I thought, *the words I don't want to hear*.

"Marcus, I'm really sorry. We did all we could, but your eyes were just too badly hurt. I'm sorry…" his voice faded out, but it felt like he was holding something back, almost like he couldn't bring himself to say the word "blind." But I had to hear it.

Dr. Del Priore skirted the horrible "B" word, possibly hoping that if he didn't say it out loud, the battered kid in front of him might not actually be blind. But, if he couldn't bring himself to say it, then I'd have to say it for him.

"Does this mean I am blind?" I wrote, bracing myself.

"Yes, it does…" he said quietly, his voice low and raspy.

"Any chance of a transplant?" I asked, grasping at the delicate straws of possibility, knowing all the while that if it was an option, it would have already been in the works.

"No," he said, sounding like a judge sentencing an innocent man to the gallows, "The damage is just too much. If it was only your cornea, we could do it. But, your whole eye would need to be transplanted. We just don't know how to do that yet. Maybe in 10 years we'll have a breakthrough, but right now, no. There's no chance."

I tried again, hoping I could come up with an idea they just hadn't considered.

"Are there any exercises I can do? Anything?" The paper began to tear under my desperate scrawl.

"No, Marcus, I'm sorry, but there's nothing that anyone can do." His voice had taken on the tone I needed to hear, final and sure.

Finality hit me square in the chest. The meager amount of air in my lungs was sucked out like a vacuum. Then, anger began to bubble up inside. *These guys are doctors and they can't save my sight? What the hell good are doctors if they can't help me?* Like a kettle set to boil, anger rose with each passing second. Fury raged toward the unfortunate messengers of bad news. It wasn't their fault, but I didn't care. *With all of the education and training doctors go through, you should be able to fix my sight! And you can't? A whole lot of fucking use you are!*

As the kettle neared the boiling point, I wanted to lash out at them, to punish them for their incompetence. I wanted to make them feel how I felt, to know what it was like to lay here in darkness. I wanted them to be blind, too.

Anger roared and grew, fast and violent as the kettle began to hiss. I knew deep down they'd done all they could, but obviously their efforts weren't quite enough. Rage took over as the first vapors of scalding steam poured out. Immediately, I had to tell them how pathetic they were.

I picked up my pencil and scrawled out their judgments as Dr. Del Priore read the words of condemnation and blame.

Lets give me a pain shot. –

No   Is there ever a chance for
So there is absolutely
no chance for improvement?
a transfusion or something?

Why didn't I just die –

Why though?
Why live like this?

I don't see it.

"How can you even call yourself a doctor?" he repeated, though I knew he didn't understand. I reloaded and attacked again. "How can you even look at yourself?" The words came quickly after the first insult. He read the assaults, but couldn't bring himself to answer. With the only weapon left in my arsenal, I scrawled, "I hate you!" Finally exploding in a burning, boiling fury.

I can only imagine how much Dr. Del Priore hated his powerlessness, too. Both doctors accepted my outburst with quiet grace and compassion, no doubt feeling helpless as infants. With nothing else to be done, they stepped away from the bedside, allowing my family to gather in close for comfort.

"I don't want to be blind," I wrote with one final effort, pain radiating from my body, my face, and my soul. A variety of gentle hands washed over my wrists and arms, simple human touch being the only help they could offer.

The excruciating pain from crying was so intense that I had to get control. More pain wasn't going to help anything now. I tried to stifle my cries, but I had no other way to grieve. Without the ability to create tears, make sounds with my sobs and fight the incredible pain radiating from my skull, I was defeated.

Silence reinforced the truth; *all hope was lost. This was no dream. This was my fate.* The adrenaline, which had only minutes before been boiling like lava, subsided leaving me emotionally and physically spent. I slowly and painfully tilted my head back onto the pillow concentrating on quieting my mind. I quickly slipped into unconsciousness.

At last, there was no pain. No sadness. And no wretched darkness.

Dad, I want to focus on you, Then I want only want you can in cat's crmmmy face

Marc was getting very frustrated.

ow the dr, is right in front of me?

Dr, would you show the damn lig

I can't see a thing.

When you were showing me the light in to the left was the patch completely

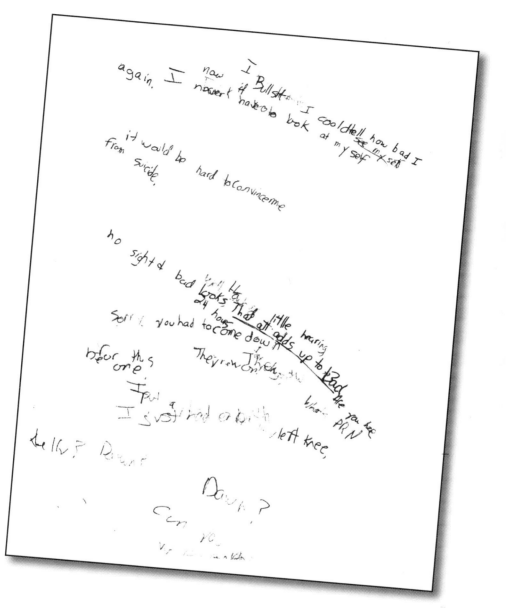

Chapter 7

**"It tangled up my mind, now people just get uglier
and I have no sense of time." [9]**

~ Bob Dylan

Elton John was in my head. Wailing in that tenor voice so familiar it could invade and take control of the morphine fog. His hands pounded the keyboard as the music roared to a crescendo. *And Jesus…He wants to go to Venus.* [10]

A mental finger hit instant rewind. Again, the words echoed, loud and lonely. *And Jesus…He wants to go to Venus.*

What? What does that mean? I asked, reaching for a tattered life preserver of reality that bobbed through the waves of unconsciousness. I grabbed the faded orange object and pulled it tight against my chest.

Do not let go, Engel. I bear hugged the life preserver. A wave crashed against my back, engulfing my body with frigid salt water. *Focus, Engel, focus… stay strong, hold on*, I repeated, kicking against the thick waters.

And Jesus…He wants to go to Venus.

Venus, I thought, trying to distract myself, *Venus is the planet nearest to earth. Is that it?* Over the water a pinpoint of light stood out among the shimmering stars of the universe. There, near what I thought was Venus, an illuminated figure came into focus. *A man?* From thousands of light years away, he slowly raised his hand and waved; a gesture made from obligation. He turned, his back slumped forward, and walked slowly into the nothingness of space.

Was this Jesus? Right before my eyes, the figure became nothing but a bright speck in the distance. Just before he disappeared, his image shone like a beacon through the darkness… then he was gone.

Suddenly the ocean became white capped and stormy. My fingers started to slip as something wrapped around my legs and began to pull me toward the abyss. I struggled toward the surface.

Wait! Which way is up? Instinct took over. I wasn't sure what I was being drawn to, but I knew I didn't want to be there.

I kicked and pulled at the invisible cord. With a heave, I contracted my legs into the fetal position and torpedoed toward the surface. The cord snapped and I floated back above the waves. Sweet oxygen filled my nose and lungs. I reached out, my right hand bumped a solid object sitting on the waves, my life preserver.

Cold air swept through my wet hair and caused a chill to rise over my pale, frozen skin. My stomach throbbed with hunger and my mouth was dry with thirst. *How can I be thirsty with water everywhere?? Food. When was the last time I'd eaten? Was it a week ago? Longer?* Vibrations from my stomach growled beneath my hands.

Engel, you idiot, I thought. *You're in the middle of a freaking ocean! It's not like you're going to happen past a McDonald's any time soon! And, even if you do, what can you eat with one hand? Don't even think of letting go of that life preserver!*

Giving up, I looked for land as another swell lifted me high into the air. In the distance, a familiar red sign glowed against the bleak horizon. I blinked to wash the seawater from my eyes.

Huh? How can that be? Before my eyes appeared the brightly illuminated sign of the supermarket that sat down the street from my dorm. I was starving and suddenly there was more precious food than I could ever eat!

As the glass doors whirred open, I drifted inside. It'd be easy to find something to eat, provided everything wasn't soaked.

Drifting past the check out lanes, I noticed something strange about the customers. Everyone seemed remote and zombie like, even the cashiers. Not even a smile or "Have a nice day," passed their silent lips.

I'm here for food, not conversation, I thought, turning down the next aisle. I glanced at the floor. The tiles were old and worn and looked like a mop hadn't touched them in years.

Wait! Where did the water go?

Not only was I now standing on a solid floor, even my clothes were dry. *Weird,* I thought, *but I can't worry about that now – I need food!*

The filthy aisle ended and I spotted the deli counter a few yards to my right. Turning toward it, I looked at the antiquated equipment of the meat department. The counter straight ahead was composed of old-fashioned white metal with a glass display case. A man stood behind the counter staring, annoyed at my very presence.

Looking into the case, I spotted a large shank of ham. It would not have been my usual choice, but it looked like heaven to my famished eyes.

WAIT! Just wait a damned minute! This whole picture is all wrong. The doctors just told me I am blind, so how can I see all this stuff, including a grimy butcher getting angrier by the second? What is going on here?

My rational mind suddenly reassured me I was not truly seeing, that I wasn't actually in this grocery store. Hallucinations were ready with a reply. "If you're really blind, then how come you aren't seeing darkness? No, my friend, this is true!"

My drugged self was impressively logical.

At least there was no argument about my hunger; however, the butcher was beginning to look more like a hostile Neanderthal. His straight, black hair had been replaced with a sloping forehead. His nose flattened and widened before my eyes. His jaw locked. Scowling, he let out a silent growl. I'd entered his world and I was clearly not welcome. Hatred blazed in his dark eyes. Although he looked as if he wanted to rip out my throat, he remained perfectly still.

What did I ever do to you? I silently questioned as I looked into that menacing gaze. The explosion mounting behind his stare was moving to the red zone. *Why does this guy hate me so much?*

Afraid, I turned to flee from the gaze of the brute, only to feel like I couldn't get away. The harder I pushed, the more resistance I found. Looking down, I saw the problem.

Christ! The ocean!

A tidal wave ripped over my head, and I grabbed the slippery life preserver once again. Cold and cramped, the world was turned into a fading memory.

Reality was now the hospital bed under my back, although even the sheets felt like I was on a skiff being thrown about in the ocean. Up and down I rocked. The slight movement of waves shifted my skull from side to side. I felt like a Raggedy Ann doll being carelessly slung around by a child.

Lying as still as possible I wanted to be absorbed deep into the bed.

Much better now, I can relax a little. As I stretched my tired, cramped legs, I smacked my parched lips together. I had to get something to drink, but how could I ask for a bottle of water? Although I was freezing, a glass of ice water would have been worth all the money in the world. A winter coat and a glass of water… my needs were simple.

I stretched my arms and tried to imagine the warmth of a heavy jacket and some cold water running down my throat. I pulled the jacket tight and viewed my new outerwear. The heavy material covered my arms, but I still longed for warm air to dry my soaking skin and hair. I had to get out of the elements to keep from catching pneumonia.

Looking around, I saw the welcoming glow of light coming from behind a heavy, oak door. Easing the door open, I slipped into the warmth of a beautiful room. *A cocktail lounge?* I dismissed the peculiarity of the situation and headed for the bar. I needed water and nothing else would do!

Taking a closer look around, I found myself in the lounge of a very classy ski resort. The dark, shellacked wood of the bar glimmered with the low lights that set the ambiance. A gigantic stone fireplace in the corner roared with a blaze that smelled of damp wood and snow.

I approached the bar, located the bartender and licked my lips in anticipation.

There were no sounds except for the occasional pop and spark of the fire.

Standing there with a towel slung over his arm, the bartender remained motionless. He looked into my eyes, but his concentration was elsewhere. He sadly shook his head and turned away to serve other customers. *Customers? How had I not noticed them before?* Yet, there they were... literally dozens of them, all wearing expensive skier's gear, sipping Zima and chatting in hushed tones. Even with the crowd, the volume was practically nil; almost as if everyone were attending a funeral.

I recognized no one in the group. Moreover, every face was surprisingly attractive. Each female could have stepped from the cover of Cosmopolitan and each guy looked like a GQ model. It was easy to see their perfect features because everyone, for some reason, had turned their gaze on me. I felt the hair on the back of my neck raise with the unwanted attention.

Why are these people all looking at me? They obviously knew something I didn't. Their eyes seemed to hold so much pity... *for me?* I glanced to the left, but before I could scan the crowd, an IV pole appeared. Then the ventilator. And there was some other piece of medical equipment I didn't recognize sitting atop the bar. *Huh?*

Once again, I was in the hospital bed. No wonder everyone was looking at the odd spectacle.

I would have run away, but of course, my legs were still trapped in traction. Helplessness turned to anger.

"Dammit, stop looking at me!" I screamed at their sympathetic faces. "Quit staring at me like I'm a corpse!"

Silence blanketed the lodge. Their expressions were clear enough, shock and sadness mixed with pity for someone they could not help.

A group of people this size should have been laughing and partying, especially since each one seemed to be quickly emptying their bottle.

Humiliated, I felt color start to rise in my face. *Why won't you just leave me alone? Stop feeling sorry for me!*

I was startled back into what could have been reality by a familiar voice.

"Hey, Engel...what's up, man?"

John? Is that you? I asked the darkness. But there could be no doubt. Since fourth grade John and I had been friends. There was no way he was a hallucination.

"We've got a whole bunch of guys here to see you, man." His voice never faltered, but I could tell he wasn't sure if his words were registering.

"Who?" I wrote, hoping John would guess I needed to know the names of those making the shuffling noises and nervous coughs.

He listed off the half dozen guys, then directed his attention back to me. "How ya doing, man?"

"All right," I wrote back. A bigger lie had never been told.

"Were you sleeping, man?"

His question was so simple, but within a half-second, my mind had gone blank. Why couldn't I think of an answer and write it?

"Because you're high as a fucking kite, Engel," a sinister voice snickered. "Yep, stoned to the limit!" The voice let loose with a demonic laugh... at me. Mocked by my own hallucinations, I got scared. Really scared. Any intrigue that hallucinogens may have held was now gone. The horror far outweighed the dancing colors and lights I'd read about in books from the 1960's counter-culture.

Concentrate, Engel, I ordered myself, *talk to these guys*. I'd have to watch what I said. The tiniest slip up about the hallucinations would make the dudes think I was nuts.

I sympathized with them. Hell, I hardly knew who I was right now!

"Hey Engel... they got you on any good drugs?" asked Chris, my old quarterback from high school football days. I was really relieved he was here. Chris was a freshman at the St. Louis College of Pharmacy. Surely he could understand how these drugs were trashing my mind.

"Yeah, I'm really tripping bad," I wrote, hoping enough of the letters hung together for him to figure out what I meant. A few nervous laughs sounded around the bed.

"You seeing some crazy stuff there, Engel?" John asked.

I wrote, "Yeah, really weird."

A rustling came from my right as Chris moved in close to see the tablet. I glanced up at his enormous frame. *Huh?* When I'd blocked for Chris on the offensive line, he was a thin, tall young guy. *Now?* Now he looked more like a grizzly bear! No, this was definitely not a "look-a-like" phenomenon. Chris WAS a grizzly bear! His sandy hair had turned to coarse, brown fur that extended down his neck, arms and back. His usual smiling face had now been formed into a stubby snout with white fangs protruding from black lips.

Right there in my hospital room, Chris had morphed into a large, brown grizzly bear. The bear casually draped Chris' high school letterman's jacket over his shoulder with a swipe of his huge, furry paw. The bear didn't seem bent on eating us or mauling anyone, but just stood looking over my bed. How had my friends not recognized that our buddy had been replaced by one of the most dangerous animals in North America? Was I the only one who could see this?

I grasped the pen and urgently wrote, "Chris is a fucking grizzly bear!"

I could almost hear their puzzled looks as they glanced back and forth at each other. What the hell is Engel talking about? A grizzly bear? Someone's attempt at a joke about Chris being a bear did nothing but anger me. I grasped Chris' hand again, knew he wasn't the least bit furry, but I couldn't escape the image of his brown coat of hair and massive, towering frame.

John tried to comfort me, realizing I wasn't joking. "No, man, Chris is just Chris… right?" he asked our very un-bear-like friend.

"Yeah, Marc… it's just me. I haven't changed into a bear and I don't plan on it, either!"

How could Chris be standing there, looking like a bear with an un-moving mouth, yet sounding just like he always had? I was sure I was crazy. I'd wanted to show my buds I was okay, but only ended up sounding like a lunatic.

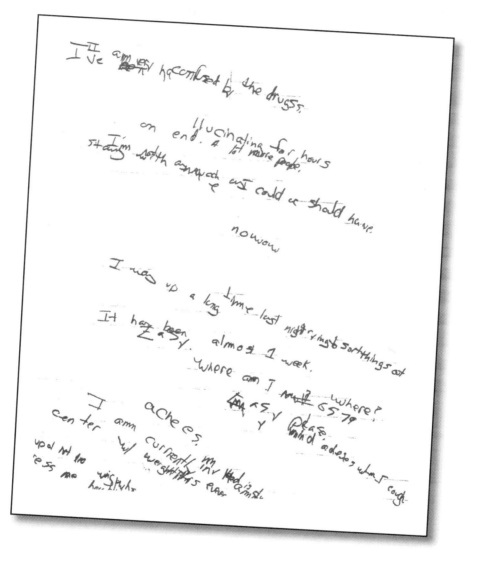

Then, I blanked out. I woke just a few seconds later. Exhausted and spent I waited. I no longer drifted off into a peaceful rest. Sleep came forcefully and violently; sort of like being knocked unconscious.

Blackness was now my life. But this was only night. Morning would again come in just a few hours. The eastern horizon would glow yellow and orange and then the sun would come up, just as always. But for me, darkness was everywhere. I prayed for even the slightest bit of light, a tiny flame to focus on.

Why can't I have light in my mind? I rifled through all the different kinds of light; candles, sun, halogen headlights, Christmas tree bulbs, streetlamps.

Just one streetlamp could create a pool of light hundreds of feet in diameter. That would hold the darkness at bay. If I stayed within that glow, nothing could touch me. No butchers, no bears, no buoys, nothing.

Why not run to the brightest light you can find, Engel? Just become part of the light.

I knew there had to be more light ahead, but how could I get to it without falling into the ocean of darkness? Of course! Another streetlight! After all, this was a parking lot, right? There has to be an entire path of brightness for pedestrians.

Walking to the edge of my illuminated circle, I stared down at the abyss of darkness. Suddenly the lights of an adjacent basketball court filled the night sky. I stepped from the pool of light directly into the friendly glow of the court. Dragging my fingers along the metal diamonds of the chain link fence, I looked at the basketball players scrambling under the hoop. I wanted to join the game, but something held me back. No. I couldn't be in there anymore. *I belonged outside the fence.*

The fence was now a fortress designed to keep me outside forever. I could walk in the light of the court, but I could never again enter.

I ran along outside the fence, frantically searching for a gate that didn't exist. Arriving back where I started, I scanned the horizon. *There!* I saw it! I couldn't believe what was ahead! Just over the tops of the trees was the Granddaddy of all lights: the object of my quest!

Just a few blocks down a cobblestone street stood the university's football complex. And overhead – light, glorious light! Row upon row of gigantic bulbs illuminated every square inch of the stadium.

As if on my way to heaven, I raced ahead. *If I can just get inside, I'll be nose to nose with thousands, no, hundreds of thousands of watts of electricity!*

I took the stairs that led to the complex two at a time. Reaching the top of the third flight, I flung open the hallway door and stared down the long corridor. I was now closer to those incredible bright lights. Just a little further until I could swallow and be swallowed by them.

As I ran, I spotted a short cut on the left. Breathing hard, I dashed up the stairwell.

Only a few more steps now.

As I reached the top of the stairs, the stadium lights exploded, drenching me in light! Lights everywhere! Lights bright enough to be seen from heaven!

The night sky was close, just out of reach but seemed so unreal. No, it didn't just seem unreal… it was unreal! The sky looked solid, almost as if it were made of clay and painted in a midnight blue. *Solid? The sky is solid?!* My mind raced back to the cold ocean water and my heart sunk with sudden realization. *Oh, God! It's the same as the ocean!*

I felt the burning in my lungs from the long run and tried to inhale as much sweet, pure air as possible. *Engel, breathe deep*, I coached myself again. *Breathe deep.*

I sucked in as much oxygen as I could take and raised my arms high. The air turned into a wall of ocean water and I was drowning again. I flung my arms in a wild attempt to keep my head above water. Something thudded against my right wrist. The life preserver.

Terrified at the loss of the visions, I clung to my preserver and desperately prayed to see those glorious lights again.

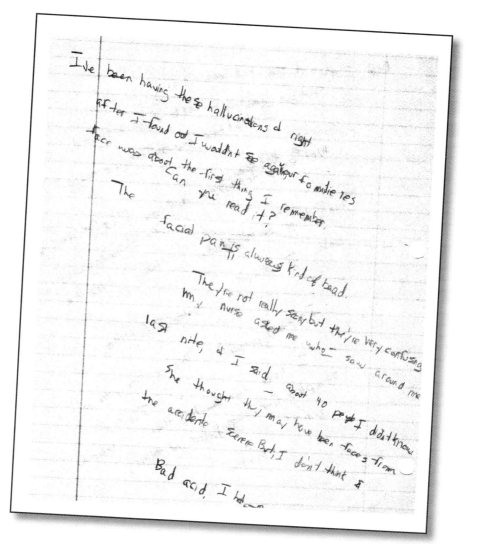

I've been having these hallucinations at night after I found out I wouldn't see again for a while. res face was about the first thing I remember. The

Can you read it?

facial pain is always kind of bad.

They're not really scary but they're very confusing. my nurse asked me who I saw around me last nite, & I said about 40 ppl. I didn't know. She thought they may have been faces from the accident scene. But, I don't think s

Bad acid, I

Chapter 8

"Then an angel appeared, she was just 17…" [11]

~ Gram Parsons and Chris Hillman

"Hi, guys, how's he doing?" Asked the young girl who approached my parents in the waiting room. Anticipating the arrival of even more physicians, her entrance came as a welcome surprise. Kista and her mother, Mary Ann! My parents smiled at the two familiar faces from our hometown.

So many friends visited that they couldn't keep up with all the introductions and explanations of how these strangers knew their son. They were amazed at how many friends were willing to travel, sometimes for more than three hours, just so I would know they'd been there. But no introductions were needed when it came to Kista and Mary Ann.

It had been more than half a year since my parents had last seen Kista. In the last several days, unthinkable losses had taken place in her life. While so many people were unsure what to say to mom and dad, now the shoe was on the other foot. Dad mumbled through a few "I'm sorry" and "It's just too bad" sorts of comments.

Two tragedies, two lives turned upside down, two horrible events that would shatter the world of any well-grounded adult. Now, within the walls of Barnes Hospital, were two young people living through disasters that took growing up from a gradual process to an immediate requirement.

Caught somewhere between a hallucination and a dream, I woke just enough to hear Dad ask, "Marc, Kista and her mother are here. Can they come in and see you?"

Morphine pounded through my system. With hallucinations and emotions running wild, I wanted nothing but to cry and wail and be held. *How the hell could I have visitors?!*

I shook my head with as much force as I could summon. *No visitors, not under any circumstances.* I'd probably end up moaning and sobbing or talking gibberish on my tablet. That was not the Marc I wanted to portray, especially to my friends. My insanity would be guarded from them, at least for now.

I darkly traced the letters N and O onto the tablet. No visitors right now… and, if I didn't start feeling sane again soon, maybe never.

I felt guilty for refusing them, but I had no choice. I had always tried to keep people happy, to go out of my way to be accommodating. Not this time. I just couldn't.

"Are you sure, Marc? They drove all the way down here to see you," Dad asked meekly, knowing that once my mind was made up, there wasn't a whole lot of hope of changing it. He continued to coax, but all the while seemed to be debating whether or not to tell me something. Dad paused for a moment. Then another. And another. I could almost see the debate whirring inside his mind.

"Kista's dad died earlier this week," Dad said quietly, probably wondering if sharing this was such a smart move.

What? Did he really say that, or was it just a hallucination? Reality marched front and center. *Gene can't be dead, can he? He wasn't even that old!* It had been just a few days before when the gossip circuit had stories of how Gene had found the body of the dead girl in the woods. Now Gene was also dead? *Huh?*

Set my drain
a little
Set up my bed alittle

Not now
I love you man
but I need
them now

Just be kalm So many
Visitors
I cant mom
I'm sorry

I mee... I'm not up
to it.

I'm not sure I'm doing
so good like a docter
Or nurse that everything
I mean right now vitals You

Only days ago, Kista's father had been hunting and discovered the murdered girl. No killing is pretty, but this was an innocent teenager who had been kidnapped and killed, her body left to rot.

However, no one stopped to think what the shock of finding the girl's body must have been like for Gene. What a bunch of vultures we were! All anyone did was compare our gory details to make sure we hadn't missed anything.

Dad continued, "Yeah, he had a massive heart attack and died earlier this week." If Dad was trying to distract me from the terrifying hallucinations blasting through my brain, he was doing a shitty job. I couldn't deal with any new disasters or the guilt that landed like another lead weight. I thought back to the last time I'd seen Kista and cringed with the memory. *God! I had been such a jerk! No. Wait a second… had I really been a jerk to Kista?* Reality poked its head through the curtain of confusion. I breathed a sigh of relief. *No, I hadn't. That was in the school play! It wasn't me being a jerk, just my character!*

A few months before graduation, Kista and I landed parts in the school play: a full-length murder mystery. My character, Charles Lansing, was a pompous, conniving millionaire… who also ended up with a bullet hole in his head. Reciting my chauvinistic dialogue, I spoke with the condescending tones and arrogance of the character's role. Dressed in a smoking jacket and with a walnut pipe protruding from my mouth, I was the image of an obnoxious tycoon. In my hand was a brandy glass full of apple juice posing as Courvoisier. Gazing into the amber liquid, I projected my bigoted lines comparing fine liquor to the opposite sex. There on stage in the gymnasium of Montgomery County R-II High School, all eyes were on me… and I got to play an arrogant bastard!

In elementary school, Kista and I had endured the crowded and raunchy round trip ride on ancient bus #17. Later, when we were in high school, I used to sit in her living room entranced while Kista and her mother spun tales of the ghostly visitations that occurred in their home. The story suggested the spirit was a young woman who met an unfortunate demise nearly 100 years before. Kista and her mother swore they had seen the phantom like apparition floating through different areas of their home.

"Whatever! Phantom schmantom! There's no such thing! You guys are just trying to screw with me!" I protested when the stories got especially frightening. I didn't want to think about a ghost haunting the place where I loved to hang out… because I believed every word!

Kista knew I was chickenshit, but allowed me to put on the contrived face of a skeptic.

"Here," she'd often said, walking with me down the hallway toward the bathroom, "I'll turn the light on so no spooks can get you!" The minute I stepped into the bathroom, she'd let out a bloodcurdling scream and pound on the door. Good thing I was already close to the john… otherwise I might have had to change my pants!

Kista had always been good company and never quite seemed two years younger. Although her witty personality was at the forefront, Kista was more level headed than most adults I knew. Her ability to be serious when the time called for it, and then quickly turn into the bubbly and energetic friend I loved, spoke volumes about her maturity.

When the cast began to stress during play practice, Kista always broke the tension with, "Hey guys! Want to hear some funny stories about Marc when he was in fourth grade?" Then, just out of playful spite, she'd tell everyone how I used to ride an imaginary motorcycle around the playground or how my underwear always hung out of my jeans. Each time she'd start spinning her tale, I'd try to melt into the backdrops of the stage.

Had it been a different member of the cast telling embarrassing stories of my youth, they would have never gotten away with it. But, Kista seemed to thrive on my playful infuriation. If I tried to counter-attack with an embarrassing memory of her as a second grader, she'd use that as ammunition to break out even more stories. I couldn't win… and I didn't care. Even being embarrassed by Kista became a joy.

"Parkus your Carcass Marcus," was one of her favorite sayings during the play. It had been resurrected from our bus riding past. Kista was frequently the first one to crack up, not so much at the story, but because she was well aware that she'd turned my face three shades of red. A vastly more mature upper classman, I would have to look the other way and hope she didn't see me laughing, too. I could never get angry with her. If there is one thing I learned from my father, it was that laughter is precious and should always be enjoyed, even if it is at one's own expense.

During the play, Kista and I had renewed our friendship, but I never imagined she'd be one of my first visitors. I hated to say "No" when Mary Ann and Kista had to be in such emotional pain, but I had no choice. Like a marathon runner who had just completed a 24K race only to be told he now had to turn around and run the course again at a full sprint, it just couldn't be done. There was simply no reserve of strength: Not physically, not emotionally, not mentally.

Kista and Mary Ann graciously understood and excused themselves, promising my parents they'd return soon.

A week later, my condition had improved, though I couldn't feel much difference. Again, my father told me Kista was there to visit, and again I didn't feel like having visitors. But, remembering the previous refusal, I swallowed the pain and agreed to see her. If nothing else, I hoped she'd distract me from my own problems for a while. When Kista walked in, she sounded surprisingly like her old self. She came straight up to my bed and said softly with a smile, "Parkus your carcass, Marcus." It was good to hear her voice again, but I wasn't sure how to act.

Remembering her father's death, I grabbed the pencil and wrote, "How are you?"

Kista gently placed a hand on my shoulder. I could almost see the pain in her eyes. "I'm okay, I guess," she said quietly, her smile fading. "It's really weird. I can't believe he's gone. When I come home from school, I just expect him to be sitting in the living room, watching TV. But he's not there… and he's not coming back."

God, I felt sorry for her. I couldn't imagine what it would be like to lose my dad. Kista continued telling the story that broke my heart.

"From the time Dad found the body until he died, he just wasn't the same. It was like he couldn't get that image out of his head. With the killer still on the loose, and the victim about my age, Dad got totally paranoid about my safety."

"That's understandable," I wrote, surprised at how well Kista could tell this story without breaking down.

"Yeah, it is. Finding a dead body would screw anyone up, but it became an obsession. Like, if I wasn't home within five minutes after my shift at work ended, he'd be calling the restaurant. I'd get home a few minutes late and he'd be in knots. I mean, he even timed me with a watch!"

I nodded and squeezed her hand.

"He wouldn't let me drive my own car. Dad said he was afraid I'd be cruising down the highway and someone would cut through the ragtop and get me. He took my keys away and made me drive his truck. Yeah, I got this great VW convertible and I couldn't even drive it. I guess I can now..." she said softly while fighting back the first tears.

As she continued, I was overwhelmed with sympathy for Gene. I couldn't truly understand what it felt like to be a father, but I figured I'd probably have been as overcome as he was.

"I'd wake up at three in the morning," Kista said softly, "and he'd be standing in my bedroom door, looking down at me. I'd ask him what was wrong and he'd say, "Just checking to be sure you're all right." Then he'd turn around, walk back to the living room and spend the rest of the night sitting up keeping watch. He'd only sleep a couple of hours per day and the rest of the time he'd be looking around to make sure no one was creeping up on the house. He was just so anxious. It's no wonder he had a heart attack."

Had I been able to, I would have wept for Kista. None of my friends had experienced the death of a parent.

Although I wanted to talk with Kista, I couldn't concentrate because of what I knew was coming. As soon as the orderlies arrived, I'd be making my maiden voyage from the hospital bed. How they planned to maneuver me was unknown, but I did know one thing: it wasn't going to be easy – nor pain free. I began to zone out. Fear formed a tight fist in the pit of my stomach. I needed every bit of support Kista could give, but how could I ask for help when she needed so much herself? I felt guilty that my own problems consumed me, but I couldn't help it.

As the minutes rolled by, my apprehension mounted. *Where are they taking me, anyway?* I nudged my memory bank for the destination. *Radiology? That's it!*

"Stay with me," I scribbled as a knock sounded at the door.

Kista, confused, agreed. "Sure, no problem," she said just as the orderlies entered the room. Three massive men gathered around my bed, one pushing a wheelchair.

What thanks for writing me.
I'm sorry.   Are you okay?
You need it more than me.
He has to wear a halo for 3 months.
So he won't move his head & neck.
Tell everyone from school to write me.
     I miss miss Gheens.
It was scarry. He lives in BFE.
   When was that?   It was the ghost
I believe you.   I believe in a lot of different
stuff since the accident. I totally believe our lives are
planned for us.   I could feel the finality
   a few days before & up to the accident
But I didn't know until afterwards.
What kind of car did you get?
What year? That's good.
   I usually don't have to do this.

She stepped out of the way and turned to my mother. "Where are we going?"

"Radiology," my mother answered. "This is going to take some time, Kista, but I think Marc really needs you right now."

"No problem! That's why I'm here!" Kista said, fully intending to keep her promise.

The conversation from the previous day with Dr. Jones floated somewhere in the recesses of my memory. Dr. Jones had expertise like no other in the field of facial reconstruction. In addition to being a plastic surgeon, this amazing physician had also served a residency in ear, nose and throat surgery. Although he was an expert in every sense of the word, the extent of my case presented a challenge, even for him. His election to the rank of my primary plastic surgeon came more by default than by his choosing.

His skilled fingers carefully ran over the top of my skull. "This is where I'll make the incision," he explained, closely looking at my scalp and the sides of my head. He stopped suddenly and said, "Tell me if I'm hurting you, okay, Marcus? I know this has to be a really tender area."

"Okay," I wrote, "what are you going to do to me?"

"First, I'm going to look at what sort of damage you have to your facial bones. Then, I'll start the reconstruction. I'll probably use your rib to fix your nose, maybe some fat from your belly or thigh, too." *Taking out a rib?* I mentally checked out. It was just too much information.

"Marcus," he explained with a slight southern drawl, "this is just the first step. You and I are going to be spending a lot of time together."

"Don't tell me anything else," I wrote and tried to block out his words. I just wanted him to do it and get it over with and not hear any more about it. Redirecting his explanation to my parents, he explained why the CAT scan and MRI were necessary.

"The surgical team will need to study the images before the reconstruction begins," he said, replacing my chart to its holder on the bed.

"I'm going to order an MRI for Marcus tomorrow. That should give us a couple of days to look over his pictures before we do the first surgery."

Not even my worst fears about the journey to radiology could have warned me I was worrying about the wrong things. The orderlies spent close to an hour lifting and positioning my broken body. I prayed the nightmare of pain would soon be over. After a count of three, the orderlies tugged the sheet high over the bed and I was, for all practical purposes, airborne in a make shift sling.

After gently lowering me into the wheelchair, we began the long, painful journey. Kista's hand rested on my shoulder as we navigated the labyrinth of the hospital corridors. Although the ride was uncomfortable, it could not compare to the horrors that awaited me.

The real nightmare came when, lying on my back stuck inside the cylinder of the MRI, this modern medical miracle malfunctioned. For two excruciating hours, I lay in silence and darkness, no one bothering to tell me what was going on or how close the workers were to having the damned thing fixed. Unable to keep my pencil and notepad while the scan was done, I couldn't even ask to be rescued, much less write obscene notes to the techs who kept me in this hell. What should have just been a short, uncomfortable procedure turned into two hours of agony.

When I was finally released from the restraints, Kista was waiting to comfort me. Frustrated tears spilled down my face. I was exhausted, afraid and lonely... and I still couldn't talk. I made a quick writing motion and Kista, my savior, placed my clipboard and tablet into my hands. "I want to go home," I wrote.

"I can't take you home, Marc, but I'm going with you back to your room and we're leaving right now," she said, giving my wrist a squeeze.

I'll never understand why Kista returned to the hospital after I had refused to see her, but I will always be grateful she came back. During the darkest days of hospitalization, I promised her again and again that I would someday, if it were in my power, return the gift she gave to me so freely.

An outsider would have seen two kids fighting incredible odds and promising each other that someday, everything would be all right.

Chapter 9

*"I came in from the wilderness, a creature void of form,
Come in, she said, I'll give you shelter from the storm."* [12]
~ Bob Dylan

Sweaty players gathered around the injured man. Shoulder pads and helmets bumped against one another in an effort to get an up close and personal view. The head coach was kneeling in a catcher's stance and slowly rotating the injured teammate's foot. The fallen man, a center, had his ankle severely twisted in a pile up on the frozen soil. It was the last game of the season and the chilly November wind stung exposed skin.

The coach stood and motioned to two second string linemen who carried the fallen soldier to the sidelines. The referee blew his whistle, positioned the ball and the game continued. A defensive lineman approached the makeshift infirmary and handed the benched player a cold bottle of Gatorade.

"Hey man, rub some dirt on it and get back in the game!" he said with a smile, attempting to lighten the mood with the usual football line.

Rub some dirt on it and get back in the game. Those words echoed through the ear holes of my helmet countless times during four seasons of football. I'd used them while overcoming jammed and dislocated fingers, blows that left me black and blue and the ultimate traumatic injury, a hernia.

But now this? What I was living wasn't one of those injuries. "Don't be weak… don't let your teammates down, get back in and play the game… whatever it costs!" I'd always known that was just football talk, but this was no game. This was my life. This was real pain, earth-shattering pain. I wanted to take that advice, but there was no way the hell I was living could be overcome with a pep talk. Besides, no one even had time to give me a pep talk.

Still, the football mantra sounded through my mind as the doctors and nurses prepped me for "the first big surgery."

"We're ready to go, Marcus. This will help to make the trip down to the operating room a little more comfortable," a nurse popped the plastic lid off of a syringe of painkiller and injected it into my IV. My parents' hands slipped into mine, they said a hurried "good-bye" and we took off down the hallway.

As I was pushed into the flurry of activity in the OR, I heard music. The opening chords of an Eric Clapton song sounded loud and clear above the beeping of monitors and hiss of equipment. *Well, at least the surgeon has good taste in music*, I thought as sleep climbed into my mind. Just before going under, I heard Dr. Jones' pick up a phone, dial a number and begin to speak.

"In about an hour, the mother of the young man I'm working on will be bringing a package for me. When it arrives, I need it brought down immediately," he said. His usual folksy conversational tone had been replaced with that of a commanding officer standing on the brink of battle.

What's in that package? I wondered. At his last examination, Dr. Jones had invited my parents into the waiting room for a private talk. He took a seat next to them and got straight to the point.

"It would be very helpful if you can provide a picture of Marcus, the bigger the better. I have a pretty good idea what he looked like before the crash, but I want to be as accurate as possible when we reconstruct his face."

Just after I headed into pre-op, my parents drove home to retrieve my senior picture from the shelf in the living room. To hold the picture of a child who, just a year before had been happy, healthy and carefree, is a feeling I cannot imagine.

As Dr. Jones hung up the phone, I felt someone place a breathing mask over my nose and mouth. Within a matter of seconds I began to drift off. Confused I heard someone call my name.

"Marcus," the nurse repeated in that tone designed to wake up groggy patients, "you're in the recovery room. Your surgery was a big one; it took more than 20 hours."

Twenty hours?, I thought through the anesthetic fog. It didn't feel like I'd been asleep for 20 hours. An hour or two of pre-op, a couple of hours in the recovery room and we're standing at a full day! No wonder everyone had been calling this "the first big surgery!"

"In a couple of hours, we're going to move you to the 7th floor ICU, the plastic surgery unit. For now, just get some rest." And rest I did.

Sometime later a nurse unlocked the wheels of my gurney and pushed me toward my new home. After what seemed like miles, the bed came to a halt. A familiar voice came from my right side. "Marc? It's Mom." Her voice was quiet and hoarse. She had obviously been crying. "We're going to step down the hall while they get you settled into your new room. We'll be back in a few minutes."

"Yeah, Brother, we'll see you later," my father said, sounding remarkably normal. I had no idea they were looking at their son's grotesquely swollen head with dozens of staples punched into his scalp.

My father's voice was reassuring, but even more comforting was his use of my childhood nickname, "Brother." As a kid, I always thought "Brother" was my Dad's unofficial title for me since I was the only sibling to my sister. Later, I realized the meaning was much deeper. The tradition of the Freemason went back generations in my father's family. In his opinion, initiation into the secret works of the Masonic Lodge went hand in hand with the last name, "Engel." "Brother" signified fraternal brotherhood and continuity, a safe heritage where many Engel men had gone before. It remained as a presence in my dad's life and the ranks of which he was sure I would someday share with him. It meant I would somehow make it through this. But for now, just being addressed by my nickname assured me that my dad was close by.

"We'll be back in a few minutes, Brother. They'll take care of you."

A nurse, busy arranging the tubes and IV lines, spoke with a calm patience. Her voice was strong and confident, but gentle at the same time.

"Hi, Marcus, my name is Barb and I'm a nurse. I'm going to be taking care of you up here for a while," she said, adjusting the oxygen tank attached to the trach. I liked her immediately. She wasn't using the patronizing tone others had taken when addressing my uncommunicative body, but speaking directly to me as if the fact I couldn't talk didn't matter in the least.

"Marcus… or, do you like to be called Marc?" she asked, pausing to watch my response. What?! Someone actually asked me for my preference? Someone asked me a question that was not related to where in my body the pain was the greatest? Someone wanted to know what they should call me?! How could I explain what it meant to once again be addressed as a member of the human race! I started to hold up one finger to indicate "yes" to the preference of "Marc," but quickly realized these new nurses would have to get used to my improvisational sign language.

"Do you want your clipboard?" Barb asked, seeing my gestures. Obviously, someone had briefed her about the kid who'd be under her care. I attempted to nod but the pain rushed to my face like an oncoming train.

"Okay, here ya go," Barb said, gently handing me the tablet. With this simple action, the world had once again opened up. I took the pencil and wrote "Either one, but my name is spelled with a *c*." I wasn't going to miss an opportunity to assert my identity. Within the first few days of hospitalization, I realized no matter what I preferred, the medical personnel were going to call me by the name on my charts. It just hadn't occurred to anyone that the kid attached to the chart had a preference about something as irrelevant as his name.

With her simple question and concern, Barb was quickly becoming my new best friend.

"Hey Marc… I tell ya, you've gotten hurt pretty badly," she said with a matter of fact tone.

"Do you know I am blind?" I wrote, unsure if they had arrived at that point in their chart reading.

"Yes, we know," Barb said, sounding as though she were conversing with any normal patient. Her bedside manner was one I hadn't yet experienced; no sugar coating, just confidence and competence. Why had this simple task been so hard to master for so many nurses before?

"You know, Marc, when I was a kid, I lost the sight in one of my eyes. I don't know exactly what you're going through because I still have sight in the other eye, but I do know what it's like to lose the vision in one eye," she said. Her tone made it clear that she felt pity for neither of us, once again, just stating the facts.

I desperately wanted to continue this conversation, but exhaustion was taking over. I already knew Barb was going to be one of my favorite people. I tried to form another question, but a morphine wave sent me toppling over into hallucination.

"Marc, you've had a really big day of surgery. Rest now. I'm going to give you something to help you sleep," she said as the other nurses exited the room. "We'll talk some more later."

During the next few days, I lay half in and half out of consciousness, my head swollen to unthinkable proportions. At least the bones in my face were no longer shifting with each turn of my head. The plates, screws and bone grafts inserted into my face by the skilled hands of Dr. Jones would, in the long run, be the glue that held my skull together.

For several days, I lay and contemplated how the new and not-so-improved Marc Engel might look. I wasn't sure I wanted to know.

As the mental fog slowly began to lift, curiosity was getting the best of me. Fearing my reaction if I discovered my appearance was less than acceptable, I waited until I was alone to satisfy my need to know. If I looked as grotesque as I felt, I didn't want anyone around to watch me wallow in self-pity. I raised my nervous hands toward my face, but quickly dropped them again, fearing what I might find. What if there was no improvement? What if Dr. Jones had done all he could, but I still didn't look human? What if I was even more disfigured than before? I had to know.

Gathering my courage, I tried again. Cautiously, I lifted an arm to feel the staples in my scalp and the two-inch wide line across my head where the hair had been shaved clean. My fingertips conveyed the deep incision over my crown, the tight, swollen skin of my cheekbones and the four-inch row of itchy stitches across my chin. I lowered my hands, accepted my fate and quietly began to weep. I was hideous.

Over the next few days, countless visitors arrived. I turned them all away. I was feeling terrible, but even more; I didn't want anyone to view the results of the reconstruction. As the days went

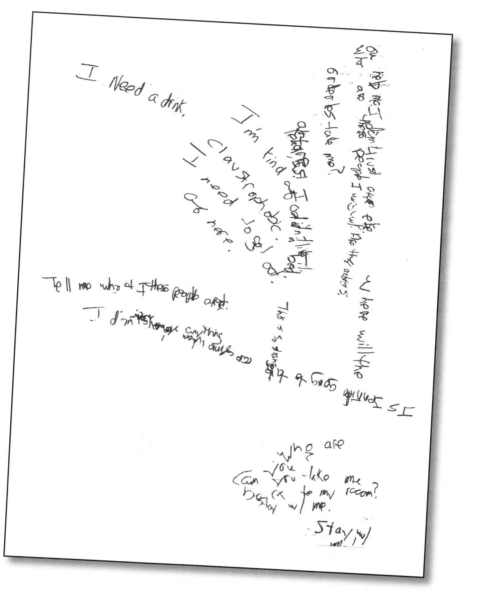

by, and the swelling decreased, I began to realize I couldn't lock my face away forever.

One afternoon my father walked in an announced, "A group of your friends from college are here Marc. Do you want them to come in?"

"Not really. But send them in."

When they came in, they made the usual small talk. Their unsaid words were even worse than criticism. I finally summoned the courage to ask, "So, how do I look?" I thought I was prepared for the answer. I was wrong.

"You ever see *The Goonies?* Dude, you look just like Sloth," one of them blurted out before anyone had a chance to muzzle him. All hope faded and the world fell apart.

The Goonies was a classic children's movie from the early '80's that my friends and I had all grown up watching. Of all the characters, Sloth was the most memorable. He lived in a cave dwelling underground, so hideously deformed and socially inept that he would never crawl out into public. Sloth's monstrous face and slurred speech did nothing but confirm that he should, in fact, keep himself hidden from the world. And now I was being compared to Sloth? I'd have killed my friend if I'd been able to grab him, but without that ability, I just waited until they left and cried some more.

Images of Sloth haunted my waking moments. I was doomed. Fortunately, my sentence only lasted until my sister's next visit. Cathy strolled in and exclaimed brightly, "Wow, you look great!" Her pleasant surprise was too genuine to believe she was sparing my feelings.

Overcome with thankfulness, the only thing I could do was write, "I love you!" All I needed to hear was that I might not have to keep this horrible face hidden underground. Cathy's pleasant surprise and compliment did more to bolster my self-esteem than anything since the beginning of this nightmare ordeal.

Not because I'm blind but it interrupts their

~~this~~ too. But then what? They won't
want to take me does I everything ways that so awkward

It's going to be even more awkward
for my friends. Yes.

No
kill me then. Yes. Well how about you
It all fell together them No. I know there is
I didn't say that the end now. I'm on the.
I was just happy

We up my options I won't be.
Page.
are either requird or you die

maybe 9 hours.

I know I'm not going to see again but that's not all so bad. The facial nerves are scary. I want to be able to smile

my hearing going is also scary

Those what is? Facial verves?

Yeah I gess so. Real good

Well, I know I'm going to live but what goes along w/ it is bad. Its hard for me to I only have

As Cathy relayed greetings from college friends, I started to miss everything… my dorm, the roommates whose irritating habits had only a few weeks before driven me insane, and just going to classes. I missed Kristin, one of the first girls I'd met at college who lived across the hall. I missed Travis, a friend I'd made in the dorm who lived just a couple of doors down. I missed Kit, my weightlifting buddy, and our workout routines with the sly glances we'd give each other when a good-looking co-ed walked by in exercise tights. Hell, I even missed the cafeteria's food; though not as much as looking at the tables full of girls who gathered in the dining hall.

Thoughts about the female gender started a new avalanche of questions and fears. How can you flirt without being sighted? Flirting has everything to do with eye contact. There'd be no more of those glances and smiles at co-eds as we passed each other on the sidewalks, no more spotting good looking girls across a smoky apartment living room and making eye contact that said, "I'd like to get to know you." All those things were gone… right?

Sighted life, as I knew it was gone, but I couldn't imagine my life without girls or without going back to school. It had taken several days for the reality to sink in: I was far too injured to go back to college this year. Returning the following year was also questionable. Even if I thought I could handle classes and homework, I still had many months of healing.

But, there was nothing else I wanted to do. I couldn't remember a time when college had not been part of my future. It was connected to finishing high school as the only logical next step. After all of those years of planning, why should I think of an alternative to college? The need of an education had not been lost with my sight. School would be very different now, but I suddenly remembered the blind student I passed every Tuesday and Thursday on the way to my French class. She navigated around crowds and obstacles, tapping all the while with her white cane. If she could handle campus, class work and college life, so could I!

All of those accumulated memories from the six week stint of college life came flooding back with a vengeance; happy memories of attending football games, going to parties, going to classes and loving my independence. I wasn't ready to give up on those things... not yet.

Slowly, I picked up the pencil and wrote, "I want to get back to school and see my friends Travis and Kristin."

My sister, standing nearby said, "They'll still be there when you get back." I wasn't so sure. Both of them, as well as Cathy and almost all the friends I'd made were juniors. If I weren't able to go back to school for two years, then half of them would have already graduated.

"Marc, trust me, no one goes through college in four years any more," Cathy insisted. "Not even me. I'm going to be there five years, too!"

I had no choice but to believe her. She was two years older and far more intelligent than me. Her experience as a college student was vast compared to mine. If she believed I could do it, then I believed I could, too. At that moment, the goal was set. I would return to SMSU when I was healed and ready to get on with my life. I didn't know how I would do it. I didn't even know when I'd get there, but I was going to do it. No matter what, I would get back to college as soon as humanly possible.

I penciled the news flash to everyone and anyone who walked into my room. Sometimes, I felt the expression of incredulity on their faces as they looked at me on the ventilator, still in traction and still unable to perform the simplest task for myself. The more my hold on reality was questioned, the more determined I became.

In the mean time, there was major healing to be done.

What felt like hundreds of nurses checked on me everyday, some good, some bad, some worse than bad. While I couldn't see, walk nor talk, I was still a person; not a body mass as some "caregivers" had treated me.

I wrote scathing notes firing one nurse after she shoved my body around and paid no attention to my hand gestures to slow down and stop. The less than compassionate nurses soon became known as, "The Evil Bitches." Luckily, the expertise and kindness of the other nurses was so great that any group objectification, no matter how enraged I felt, was impossible.

At the forefront was always Barb. In addition to her impeccable care, Barb helped fill my need for connection to the outside world. Her instinct told her that I was hurting inside just as much. Whether it was for this reason, or just because of the person she is, Barb's care was never impersonal. I treasured the times she was on call.

One desolate evening, hallucinations began to creep in. I needed someone to talk to and keep the visions at bay. Desperately needing help, I pushed Barb for some conversation when she came in to do the nightly tasks.

As she propped my left leg with pillows, I asked her where she lived, knowing I could lead into the guaranteed St. Louis conversation question about high school. The initiation of this question to native St. Louisans remains a mystery. Somehow the answer to this all-important query spoke volumes about your background, intelligence, socio-economic status, groups of friends and potential mutual acquaintances.

Barb quickly began telling me about her kids, her neighborhood, her son's high school football team, etc.

This conversation may not sound like work, but I was nearing exhaustion. Barb sensed my discomfort and exhaustion and gently lowered the back of the bed.

"Get some rest, Marc. We'll talk more later," she promised quietly while she closed the door behind her.

How could I ever thank her? She knew I needed those short conversations and a little extra time as much as I needed her skilled nursing. When I woke with a start the next morning, I immediately pressed my nurse call light and within moments, Barb strode into my room.

"Hey, buddy, did you get some sleep?" she asked with real concern. She knew all too well how horrible my sleep patterns were.

"I don't know," I wrote. "What time is it?"

"It's a little after four in the morning. You've been asleep for a pretty long time… for you, that is," she said, pleased her patient had gotten a bit of rest. I'd not slept for more than four consecutive hours in forever and the insomnia was almost as bad as the pain.

"Is there anything I can do for you, kiddo?" Barb asked. Her tone suggested she had nothing better to do than to fulfill my every wish for as long as I needed. That simple patience was so valuable when I was rushed by other nurses or ignored because they had too much to do.

"I'm okay. Can you stay for a little while?" I wrote. True, I didn't really need anything. No refreshment, no blankets, no shots for pain, nothing except the one thing I needed more than anything else: human contact.

"Sure, man, you just need some company?" she asked with a hint of sympathy in her voice. Barb quietly pulled a chair close to my bed and rested her hand on my arm, careful not to shift the tubes and surgical tape.

She sensed all the fears going through my brain and wanted to help. All I needed was her presence; just someone to stay and convince me I was not alone. A hospital bed in the middle of the night can be the loneliest place on earth.

"Yeah," I wrote, "I just need you right now."

"Then you've got me, Marc," she said softly. Those few moments of human contact, a hand to hold in the middle of the night and a compassionate minute spent just talking is a favor I'll never be able to repay.

Chapter 10

"The best thing you've ever done for me is to help me take my life less seriously; it's only life after all." [13]

~ Indigo Girls

"**M**arcus! Hey, how ya doing?" the voice thundered from just a few feet away. Surprised by the brazen entrance, I recoiled. I had been awakened out of a sound sleep by this booming voice stretching overhead. Groggy and trying to focus, I noticed the baritone came from higher than the usual voices. Whoever this new guy was, he was tall. I wasn't especially pleased to be awakened when my nights were so full of insomnia, but something was different… almost interesting! Whoever this person was, he not only had a powerful voice, but a powerful presence. I decided I was more intrigued than annoyed.

The voice boomed again, "My name is Dennis Fuller and I'm a speech pathologist. I'm going to do a little work with your trach here and see if we can get you talking."

As he introduced himself, he shook my right hand with a crushing grip. Whoever this guy was, he definitely wasn't going to baby me! I almost smiled!

Even with his enormous presence, I wasn't the slightest bit concerned this new doc would inflict any more pain. His friendliness was natural and not the forced bedside manner of so many other doctors. But, what was really intriguing was what he'd just said. *Talking again? After three weeks of silence, I was going to be able to talk?*

In blissful ignorance, I assumed my voice would return once I didn't need the ventilator. The physicians had wisely decided to withhold the negative possibilities until they'd determined an exact prognosis.

"There's no reason to cause Marcus needless worry if we look at his vocal cords and there's no problem," an ENT resident had explained to my parents. Well out of my earshot, the discussion was frank and factual. "I'll schedule an appointment for tomorrow in the ENT clinic."

Just a few days before this Dennis Fuller character roared in, I'd made the painful journey to the ENT clinic. Scrunched into a wheelchair with my broken left leg precariously pointing directly ahead, I shifted and twisted around looking for some relief for my butt. I was still getting used to the new face Dr. Jones had constructed… and I still hated it. The last thing I wanted was to expose my ghastly head to on-lookers. If Barnes Hospital were a circus, I was definitely the freakshow.

Wheeled through the hospital, I tucked my chin down to hide my disfigured face. As we passed people in the hallways, I wept at how much I stuck out. Three-inch round metal trays had been taped over each eye in order to prevent infection through the mucus membranes. The trays made me look like a gigantic spider. Even the most disinterested person had to stop and do a double take. Then, looking more closely, they'd see the uneven nostrils, the swollen cheekbones and the swath of hair that had been cleanly shaved across the top of my skull. It was easier to hide my face than feel their pity.

Once we arrived at the doctor's office, we by-passed the waiting room and were immediately ushered into an exam room.

I guess they don't want me to scare their other patients, I thought cynically. After only a few minutes, the ENT resident appeared, shook my hand, and introduced himself. I didn't care who he was, what his title was or anything about him. As far as I was concerned, he had but one commandment: Thou shalt not hurt Marc.

"Don't hurt me," I scrawled onto the tablet; a threat and a plea.

"I'm not planning to, Marcus," he said quietly. "I know you can't see what's going on, so I'm going to explain exactly what I'm going to do, then, I'll tell you what I'm doing every step along the way, okay?"

"Okay," I scrawled, "Just tell me before you touch me."

"No problem, Marcus. In my hand I have a lighted scope. First I'll use a numbing spray inside your nose so you won't feel anything. The scope will be inserted into your nasal cavity and will travel down the back of your throat. This will allow me to look at your vocal mechanism."

My mood quickly went from bad to worse. The painful wheelchair trip had been bad enough, but now I was going to get a nasal enema!

"Okay, I'm going to touch your left cheek now," he said, shaking a metal canister that sounded like spray paint. "You'll feel the nozzle of the bottle at your nostril. I'll give it three quick sprays. This will deaden the tissues and you shouldn't be uncomfortable when we do the procedure."

Easy for you to say, I thought bitterly. *You let someone shove a Mag Lite up your nose and we'll see if you feel it.* I was no dummy. The word "uncomfortable" when used in a medical environment translated to "painful."

"What is that stuff anyway?" I scribbled.

"This is a mixture of Tri-Cain, Bi-Cain and other topical numbing solutions. It is marketed under the name Hurricane and it's a really good product. You shouldn't feel anything except the spray may be a little cold when it first hits your nasal linings."

Tri-Cain? Bi-Cain? Novocain? Hmm, that sounds a little like cocaine. And, since he's sticking it up my nose, this stuff probably has some coke in it! Maybe I'm not going to feel a thing! Here I am in a doctor's office and they're using coke as medicine… what is this? The 1800's or something?

My mind hit the start switch on my mental stereo. My cranial jukebox was filled with songs inspired by drugs. The first that came to mind was a Grateful Dead tune, *Casey Jones*. [14] Unseen speakers introduced the song with the high-pitched licks of Jerry Garcia's guitar. *Driving that train, high on cocaine, Casey Jones you'd better watch your speed.*

All I wanted was to get that stuff up my nose, feel nothing and get this procedure behind me! Then, I wanted to get the hell out of dodge!

After the initial sting of coldness from the Hurricane, I cared very little about what the doc was doing in my nose. He was right! I couldn't feel anything! Hell, you can stay up there all day if you want, Doc! The spray not only worked, it improved my mood considerably. I was wheeled back to my bed in the ICU, back to safety, back to rest, back home again.

The results of the procedure were not provided as promptly as bad news. Good news would have been a welcomed surprise… if anyone had actually bothered to give it to me. As if reading my mind, Dennis said, "Marc, do you remember when the resident put the scope up your nose? We were checking your vocal mechanism. Everything is A-OK. Your voice is going to be fine!"

I sat there, too stunned to move. In the three weeks that had elapsed since the crash, this was about the only good news I'd received. I couldn't believe I was really going to get my voice back! I tried not to get overly excited. Yet, this Dennis Fuller guy and his booming voice seemed confident words would soon be springing from my mouth.

As Dr. Fuller explained what he was about to do, I sat in awe, thinking of the ability I would soon recover. I could yell at the nurses who had treated me like a body instead of a person. I'd soon be able to talk to my family! I'd be able to actually explain with real words, real intonation and real inflection what I was feeling!

"Okay, Dude," Dennis said, examining some device at the side of the bed. *Dude? Did this guy just call me dude? And he's a doctor?* I'd met a lot of doctors, but none, other than Dr. Jones, had really treated me like I was human, much less like I was a young guy. *Dude?*

"Dude" was what Dennis came to call me on a regular basis. I appreciated the nickname that let me have my own identity rather than the "Mr. Engel" new nurses and physicians always used. *For God's sake, I'm a teenager! Enough with the "Mister" crap!* Formality was obviously unnecessary when a physician called me, "dude." Better yet, Dennis embraced informality. Not once was I encouraged to call him "Dr. Fuller."

In fact, during our first meeting, the word "doctor" was never even used. I was left wondering if Dennis had that title or not. Not that his title really mattered; I trusted Dennis implicitly, prestigious position or not. His own title, as well as everyone else's, failed to impress him. What did make an impact on this guy was when he was able to help his patients speak once again. I was only too happy to oblige!

"Okay, Dude." Dennis repeated. "This isn't rocket science, I'm going to tell you what I'm doing here." I grabbed my pencil and paper as he explained that he'd be touching my neck at the trach opening for a few seconds. Enough physicians had poked my trach by this time to realize that "a few seconds" meant at least five straight minutes of excruciating pain.

Holding the collar around my neck, Dennis clicked a piece into place. "Okay, done!" he said with a magician's flare. *Huh? Done? That only took a few seconds! What do ya know? Maybe all doctors aren't lying bastards bent on inflicting more pain.*

"Okay, Dude, I placed a small plug in the plastic trach tube. This will force you to take in breath through your nose and mouth. When the plug is in, it'll prevent air from entering your lungs through your throat. If it gets hard to breathe, just pull the little string on the plug. Okay?"

I nodded and he continued. "Since you're breath won't be taking a shortcut through your throat, you'll be able to talk again, okay?"

I nodded again and scrawled "Okay" in response.

"No way, Dude. You're not getting off that easily!" He boomed, mocking anger. "I want you to say 'Okay.' So, take in a deep breath and say the word."

I waited a second or two, drew in a deep breath and uttered the first audible sounds in three weeks.

"Ho kay," I slurred, breathy and sickening and unnatural. It was hideous. I wanted to cry. If this was how my voice was going to sound, I might as well stay mute! It had none of the clear, baritone pitches which placed well singing "Plaisir D'Amour" just a few months before at the Missouri State vocal music contest.

Even if I had nerve damage on the entire left side of my face, a fractured jaw that was still wired into place, totally demolished teeth, and a trach, that still wasn't an excuse! If my vocal mechanism had indeed survived all of this with no injury, I wanted results… NOW!

"That was great, dude! Now, say it again!" Dennis boomed, beaming. *What? How can he be pleased with what he is hearing? None-*

theless, I repeated "Okay" with identical results. He was happy. I was horrified.

Ignoring my disappointment, Dennis said, "Okay, repeat after me. One, two, three, four. Okay, dude, now it's your turn!"

"Hwon, who, heree, whore," I slurred again. If I had known that my voice would one day return to its original state, I would have probably made a joke about the number four coming out as "whore." But we were working hard and witticisms were not flashing through my mind.

As we practiced, the words started to come a bit easier, but were still unintelligible. Snoring sounds erupted from my mouth. I was embarrassed to talk out loud. Now, I not only looked like Sloth from the *Goonies*, I sounded like him, too. *What if this doesn't get any better?* I thought miserably.

As if reading my mind once again, Dennis said confidently, "You probably don't sound like you remember. That's because you haven't used your voice lately. That will improve the more you talk, okay?"

I nodded feebly. Assuming we had finished the session, I promised Dennis that I would practice every day. But, Dennis wasn't finished with me yet. I heard a rustling coming from the end of the bed. *A newspaper?*

"You're a football fan, aren't you, Marcus?" Dennis asked, looking directly at me. I was still recovering from the surprise that we weren't finished and now I was bowled over again! The question was asked without even a glance in my parents' direction. Like Barb, He looked at me, posed his question and continued to look at me until he got his answer... just like I could see.

It sounds like such a small thing, but Dennis ignored my blindness and spoke directly to me, a fellow human being.

I nodded to Dennis and weakly said, "Yeah, I like football" though my words sounded as unintelligible as before. He folded the paper to the sports section and we launched into picking the winners for Sunday's games.

In 10 minutes, he'd taught me to talk, made me feel like the young guy that I was, treated me with respect by addressing me directly, shaken my hand like I was an able-bodied man and now we were going to talk football! With Dennis' entrance my world slowly began a positive shift.

"Okay, how about Cleveland versus Miami?"

"Cleveland!" I answered energetically. It required too much air and too much energy to explain that I loved the fans more than the team.

"Are you nuts?" Dennis asked, amused. "You'd pick the Browns over Marino and the Dolphins? Miami is favored by five and a half points! That's a sucker bet, dude!"

"Okay, Washington at Denver?" he feigned the sound of a drum roll as he waited for my pick.

"Enver!" I tried to say loudly, but the slurring still rang true. I was starting to care less, as it seemed like every word improved just the tiniest bit.

"Ready for another one? How about Indianapolis versus San Diego?" *Indy versus San Diego? Yah, right! Neither team would be making it to the Superbowl this season. Hell, neither team would probably even have a winning record!*

"Who cares?" I said, cynically. The words came out sounding like, "Ooo there's" But Dennis understood perfectly and laughed. He knew how to interpret the guttural sounds and never once made me feel like I was speaking with anything but perfectly enunciated English.

"Yeah, really…" Dennis said, echoing my sentiments. "Wait

a minute." he said, scanning further down the column, "Here's an even bigger 'who cares' game of the week! Who do you pick in New England versus Seattle?"

New England versus Seattle? A point spread was ridiculous against two teams that couldn't score a touchdown if their lives depended on it! I tried to laugh, but it came out a breathy, coughing sound. *Laughing? Was I actually laughing?*

In my state of total devastation, this guy had gotten me to laugh! I had to admit that laughing wasn't on my "to do" list that day, but here I was chuckling right along with Dennis. *Well*, I said to myself, *it is pretty funny*. Blind or not, it was still fun dissing on those sucky NFL teams.

Suddenly, I didn't want to put on a straight face again. Dennis had reached the end of the sports section and, even though I was exhausted, I wanted to keep going. I found it hard to breathe and grasped at the cord hanging from the trach plug. I took it out and rolled it between my fingers. It was very small, probably only a little bigger than the eraser on a #2 pencil. *This little piece of plastic gives me the ability to communicate?* It was odd, but my silence for the previous 20 days resulted from the lack of a plug barely the size of a fingertip.

"Take it out for a minute and then we'll do a little more." He continued, "By the way, Marcus, I was going to stop by yesterday, but you had a visitor and I didn't want to interrupt." Dennis said, drawing out every syllable of "visitor" like a junior high boy teasing a buddy about his crush on a girl. Dennis was obviously implying something, but I was drawing a blank.

What's he leading up to? I thought. My mind flashed to the previous day when Kista, my life preserver, had spent all afternoon telling me about the events of home. In a flash, I got his point! *No! He can't really think "that"? Can he? He couldn't!*

"Yeah, it was just you and a girl in here. She was a little brunette about 5'4" I think. So, who was she?" I could feel the "Nudge, nudge, wink, wink" look on his face.

No! No! Kista was one of my best friends. I'd never even thought about her in the way he was implying! Kista would have been as appalled as I by the insinuation. In fact, had she been there, she'd have probably socked him one! Kista was like a little sister, and here was this new guy suggesting we were romantically involved. There was no way he could have known the spiritual connection that had developed between us in the last few weeks. I really had to straighten this out… and FAST! I slipped the trach plug back in and nearly shouted.

"No! We're just friends!" It came out like "Ear gust sends." I wasn't sure he got it and this was no time to be misunderstood! Opting for the quickest and surest way to make certain he got it straight, I made a writing motion and said loudly, "Paper!" Dennis turned over a fresh sheet on the tablet and handed over the pencil. "We're just friends…we've been friends for a long time," I scrawled the words as quickly as I could. "She's not my girlfriend, she's just my friend," my words came fast and sloppy. I continued to protest until I had dismissed any possible notion of romantic involvement.

"Okay, okay, dude," he said, calming my speeding hand. "Now," he said, his voice taking on the tone of the Buddha ready to enlighten a mere mortal, "Why couldn't you have *spoken* all that?" I could almost see his Cheshire Cat grin. Shit… I'd been had!

I was embarrassed, but it was still funny. Anyone who could get me to laugh twice in one day was definitely cool; especially when one of the laughs was at my own naivety.

I doubt Dennis planned our first meeting this way, but no matter his intentions, it went well… not just well, but amazing!

Even during my darkest and most depressed times, I remembered that I could still laugh. Someone had teased me and it was still funny.

"By the way Marcus, I don't know if you are interested, but I'm going to tell you what I look like. I'm about your size, but you might be a bit bigger through the shoulders than I am. I wear a full beard and you might be wearing one pretty soon, too!" Dennis said, teasing me about the scruffy growth of stubble on my face. "Our hair is pretty much the same color, but dude, you've definitely got a lot more of it!"

I may have not recognized the importance of this exchange at the time, but it wouldn't take very long to realize I still had to laugh. It really wasn't complicated. If I couldn't learn to laugh at myself, then how could I laugh at anything or anyone else? After all there are so many things in this world that are worth laughing at, I better start with myself!

While Dennis provided the ability to speak and laugh once again, he also gave me the ability to do something less productive; scream and yell. Never did I scream more than in the days after Orthopedist's hammered an 18-inch nail through my broken left leg.

Once the pain began to subside, I slowly started to maneuver the leg, testing how far I could push myself. First, I'd just flex my foot as if I were pressing the accelerator of a car. Within a few days, I could lay my leg to the side and pull my left foot along my right calf, bending my knee in a way that seemed impossible only days before.

Anxious to show off these improvements, I waited for someone who would be truly impressed with the progress. Dennis came flying into the room one afternoon booming, "What's new, dude?"

Granted, my speech was getting better, but I really wanted to show off the leg.

"I can finally move my leg!" I said excitedly as Dennis approached. While he probably listened to my words more for their quality than their content, he still heard what I was saying. "Let's see it then, dude!"

I mocked seriousness, held out my palm and said, "Give me a dollar!"

Never missing a beat, Dennis replied, "Good luck finding somewhere to spend it, man. You're in a hospital, not a 7-11!"

Good point, I thought. I pulled my ankle back, almost to where my left heel lay alongside my right knee.

"Awesome, dude!" Dennis nearly shouted.

Dennis was hired to help fix my voice, not spend his time watching me flex my lower extremities. Yet another subtle lesson learned. The one and only reason Dennis celebrated the improvements was because I was excited about it. His demeanor mirrored mine and I'm sure he concluded, "Well, if Marc is excited about it, I'm excited about it, too!" This was just one of the scores of life lessons Dennis taught me without ever knowing he was in the role of educator.

Humor, voice, respect, and a life lesson I shall never forget; all from one person who probably never realized what a profound impact he was making.

Chapter 11

"You've got to learn to live with what you can't rise above..." [15]

~ Bruce Springsteen

The headlights of westbound interstate traffic snaked through the countryside and disappeared behind a darkened grove of trees. A half-mile of Missouri pastureland insulated us from the groan of tires on the highway. Microscopic glints of starlight reflected off the lake and littered the sky. Concentrating on the natural beauty, I'd momentarily forgotten where I was.

"So, what do you think?" a quiet voice asked.

I turned, smiled and sheepishly said, "Sorry, I got lost in my head there for a minute."

Amy smiled through the darkness and teased, "Oh, I see how it is! I sit here telling you all this deep, philosophical stuff and you don't even listen to me. Some friend you are!"

"Sorry," I mumbled, feeling like a complete heel.

Amy sat her drink between her bare feet on the seat of the picnic table, leaned over and rested her arms on top of her knees.

"I asked if you ever felt like there were just some things that were meant to be. Not like fate and falling in love and that romantic sort of stuff, but like things that we are just supposed to experience and, if we don't, our lives won't ever feel complete. Do you see what I mean?" she asked, wrapping her arms around her legs as her long, black hair fell over her shoulders. "I've just been thinking lately that, even at this point in my life, I can point to experiences and think, 'Wow! How different would my life now be if that hadn't happened?' Some are good, some aren't, but they all add up to make us who we are," she said, looking into my gaze.

A twinge of self-consciousness popped into my head. I quickly dismissed it. With Amy, I had no reason to put up a front. "Yeah, that makes sense. People learn things every day of their lives, even into old age, and those things all combine to create the person each of us is today, right? Like, what has happened in both of our lives that has led us to be sitting here right now?" I said, twisting at the label on my bottle.

As the hours grew long, I was nearly hypnotized by Amy's soft words. Whether I could turn to see her or view only the blackness that was now my world, those late night discussions had melded Amy's voice into my memory. She grasped my hand, careful not to disturb the tape and IV lines, and I was taken back in time to that peaceful night sitting by the lake. With those memories came comfort and longing.

"Here, I brought you something," she said, pressing a plastic cassette case into my hand. Standing and putting on her jacket, she said, "I hope you enjoy it... I think you will!"

"Thanks," I said, slipping into a doze.

"I'll see you soon," Amy said, leaning down and lightly kissing my forehead.

I clutched the cassette as I fell asleep, never imagining it would soon become the most definitive element of my recovery.

I woke an hour later, during what felt like the hundredth night of insomnia. The majority of sleep came from the sodium pentothal being washed into my veins during surgery. Sleep it may have been, but being knocked out by anesthesia could not replace the benefits of natural, restoring sleep. During the long nights when sleep would not return, I'd reach over to the table beside my bed and press play on the portable stereo. Soon the sounds of Amy's tape filled the room. Our mutual love of the music created in the 1960's and 70's had not only given us a common interest, but also perpetuated our friendship. We would invariably attempt to introduce the other to "new" music we'd discovered, although the artists were more often from our parents' generation.

After not seeing each other for several months, Amy and I could meet, hug and within seconds she'd exclaim, "I just heard this band the other day I know you would love!"

Each time I replayed her tape I envisioned Amy seated on the floor of her apartment, CDs strewn about the room as she created her masterpiece. The tape began benignly when the Georgia rockers, REM, took a slow and soft routine with their song, *Nightswimming*. [16] Piano and cellos began the poetic journey through the youthful experience of a late night swim in an isolated lake. The enchantment of the moment invited clothes to be dropped on the shore and a smooth dive into the still water. Michael Stipe's words and voice painted a picture so vivid that I could mentally see the reflection of a white, nearly full moon that peered through the bare treetops.

My introduction to the song, during such emotional times, secures REM's masterpiece as the definitive anthem of my recovery. It will forever be associated with lonely, insomnia riddled nights. I played it relentlessly, all the while wondering what it would be like to live the singer's tale of total, youthful lack of inhibition. Now, I would probably never know.

The next song took a step back in time. Neil Young's *Long May You Run* [17] will always seem the perfect song one friend would send another experiencing the difficulties of life. It spoke volumes about my friendship with Amy. *We've been through some things to-*

gether with trunks of memories still to come... we found things to do in stormy weather, long may you run. Long may you run, long may you run, although these changes have come.

The first time I heard the song, I wept. The line *although these changes have come...* expressed the notion of looking past the current adversity into the future. Maybe Amy and other friends no longer recognized me as I used to be, but the phrase *trunks of memories still to come* promised that I would never lose their love. Even when insecurity crept in, I never questioned Amy's loyalty.

Sending myself into a downward spiral of despair required very little imagination. I knew I had to get myself back into college, but how could I think of maneuvering around campus when navigating the perimeter of the physical therapy room with a walker left me exhausted? How could I consider participating in classroom discussions when I couldn't speak without sounding like the village drunkard? How could I contemplate rehabilitation school for blind adults when I couldn't even sit on a toilet by myself? God, how would I even exist outside of the hospital? Fear of the unknown can be the most debilitating force imaginable.

One dreadful, insomnia filled night, depression seemed ready to tip the scales of my self-control. Amy's tape had been playing, as usual, on low volume, when Bob Dylan interrupted the blackness of my mood. The name of the song escaped me, but the titles of Dylan's songs frequently didn't have much to do with the lyrics.

"When you're out in Juarez in the rain when it's Easter time, too..." Dylan sang on. No clues to the title yet. *"When your gravity fails and negativity don't pull ya through..."* [18]

Suddenly, I felt an unseen hand slap me through the music. *Wait, what did he say?*

"Negativity don't pull ya through..." I reached over and hit the rewind button; I had to hear those words again.

With the second playing, that same unseen hand grabbed me by the hair, shoved my ear against the speakers and said, "Listen to this! This is for you! What about this don't you get? This was meant for you to hear!"

I concentrated on the words. What if the lyrics were true? Who was I kidding? Of course they were true! Dylan's lines had even been noted in the tome of familiar quotations that resided on my shelf next to my unread copy of, *A Tale of Two Cities.*

A tiny shiver raised the hair on the back of my neck. With a shaking hand, I turned off the tape and sat in silence, my mind spinning.

Negativity? Hell, yeah! I had plenty of that! It was not some figment of my imagination. It was brutal reality. Well, Dylan had just provided me with a revelation. Focusing on challenges was not going to get me through the rest of my recovery; much less back to college any faster. I knew then that no matter what obstacles I faced, I would do my best to live Dylan's advice, look at the positive, the negative leads nowhere.

I began to think over the things that were good, solid and from which I drew strength; I was surprised at just how many positives there were. Family, friends, Barb, Dennis, Kista, my hope of returning to college… would these things be enough to override the mountain of negatives?

If I looked at the fact I was now blind, then I could immediately start to count up things I would never see… my wedding, my wife, my children, my grandchildren, myself, my home, natural beauty like trees, stars or mountains. I would also never be able to drive, live completely independently, or get around by myself.

Suddenly, I stopped my endless list of "nevers" in midstream. I quickly replaced them with good thoughts of Amy, her gift, tomorrow's visit from Kista, the fact that Barb was my nurse on duty and how, little by little, people were beginning to understand my speech better. I smiled a little, realizing that, almost as if by magic, I could change a bad mood to a good mood. I could and would take control of those negative thoughts instead of letting them control me. If I constantly looked at the good in my life, then maybe, just maybe, I could even have a good life. *OK, Engel, You've got to use every opportunity to prove to everyone your life still has good in it!*

The next day, my attitude had greatly improved, but it couldn't prevent me from grouching. When I caught myself complaining, I tried to stop cold. With more than a twinge of conscience, I realized how my family had born the brunt of all my mood swings.

If I bitched at a nurse, she'd just finish her job and leave, usually mumbling something like, "I don't have to put up with this." It's not too hard to walk out on a blind and mostly mute patient. When no nurses were around, my family was forced to listen to my endless complaints.

Now trying to live Dylan's advice, I knew I couldn't continue to take out all of my aggression on the people who loved me the most. It was hard enough for them to see me in this condition, much less for them to have to be on the receiving end of me shifting the blame.

Kista was the first person outside my family to test this new view of life. One night, while attempting a good mood, Kista popped into the room saying, "I've got something you've got to hear! I just got this new CD and I've been laughing over it for the last week!"

This was one of the things I loved about Kista; she came to visit, not to force me to re-live the mundane daily hospital events. So many visitors asked about the surgeries, the doctors, what other operations would be coming up soon, and so on. While I didn't mind answering, I loved Kista for showing me what was happening in the outside world.

Mom excused herself, saying she would go get a cup of coffee.

Kista was a good person to leave on duty while Mom took a break from her posted position at my bedside. Trusting my care to someone else was one of the smaller adjustments my parents had to make.

"I'd better close the door. Your doctors and nurses may not want to hear this," was mom's parting comment as she grabbed the handle and pulled the door behind her.

"This is a CD by Adam Sandler and it is the funniest thing I've ever heard," Kista exclaimed excitedly. "You'd better grab that big jug you pee in or you just might wet the bed!" Only Kista could get away with a statement this humbling, but I was used to it considering all the "Parkus your carcass Marcus" comments.

Kista pressed the play button and the room filled with the heavy feedback and squealing of a microphone. Before even one minute had elapsed, I was in hysterics. I'd never heard anything so vulgar, twisted, profane and hilarious, all rolled up into one!! If laughter is the best medicine, I almost overdosed.

When the CD finished playing and Kista was putting on her coat to leave, I knew I had to squeeze in one last obnoxious comment.

"Hey... think you could hand me my piss jug? I've really gotta go!"

She bopped me on the arm with the empty jug and dropped it in my lap. "I hope everything comes out all right!" she called over her shoulder as she walked out.

As the weeks wore on and my speech improved it was easier to convince visitors I was on the road to recovery. I could write

"I'm okay" on a tablet until my hand fell off, but when people heard me joking with them as I had a million times before, they began to believe it.

With each visitor I improvised different ways to reassure them I was getting better. A visit from Travis, my college buddy who lived down the hall, inspired a moment of genius.

During the daily hour of physical therapy, a nurse stepped in and said, "Your friend Travis is in the waiting room with your parents… and he brought dessert."

Travis was simply an amazing friend. Knowing my parents had been living off of hospital cafeteria slop, he treated them with something he knew they'd appreciate: home cooked food. Although he had never met my parents, he found them in the waiting room, introduced himself and left them speechless when he presented them with a homemade pecan pie. Not only was I impressed with the fact Travis had driven the three hours from college to visit, but now he'd also given my parents a great showing of the kinds of friends I had at school. Mom and Dad stood behind my decision to return to college, but knowing I'd be around people like Travis helped ease their mind.

Realizing they were all sitting in the waiting area enjoying their treat, I convinced my physical therapist that my obligatory stroll down the hall with the walker could be extended just a few more feet to the waiting room. My real motivation was a plan that would send them back to school with news that I was definitely on the road to recovery!

Stepping into the hall, I asked the therapist, "Can you walk at my side instead of behind me?" No doubt she thought this was an attempt to look strong, healthy and independent… and in a way, she was right! As she complied, a devilish grin crossed my face. "Sucker," I mumbled, almost laughing at her naivety.

Every few steps sparked rapid-fire questions, "Do you feel all right? Are you dizzy? Let me know if you start to feel woozy, okay?" She was getting annoying. I'd entered the hospital at 255 pounds, and even though my weight had dropped to less than 205 I was considerably larger than my therapist. She did not relish the thought of catching that much dead weight as it collapsed to the floor.

After reaching the waiting area and inviting my visitors to the room, I turned back down the hallway. When I heard Travis and his girlfriend directly behind me, I knew the time had come!

Stopping abruptly, I reached to the back of my robe and pulled on the lowest tie. Wearing the typical hospital attire with the typical lack of anything underneath, I pulled open the gown and gave them an eyeful of my, not-so-attractive bare ass.

I could not have been happier when I heard them howling with laughter! If actions spoke louder than words, they had to be convinced that blindness was not enough to keep me down! I was remanded to my room after the mooning incident with a not nearly stern enough lecture.

"There should be no screwing around when you're walking, Marcus! Your leg is still healing and if you had fallen down, the pain would have been horrendous and..."

"Blah, blah, blah," I chimed in, Laughing and quite pleased with myself. I sat in an armchair and waited for my friends to arrive.

Still laughing, they entered, shaking my hand and clapping me on the back. For the next hour, they caught me up on all the happenings back at the dorm, what my friends were up to and stories about how the guy who had taken my place wasn't as cool as me. For some reason, this gave me a perverse satisfaction.

"Well, man, we'd better be getting on back to school," Travis said, shaking my hand.

"Dude, thanks so much for coming," I said, truly meaning it, "I really appreciate what you've done for my family."

Just as they stepped into the hall, Barb rounded the corner into my room and said, "Hey Marc! Mail call! Want me to read these to you? There's a whole big stack here, like always!"

"Sure!" I said, still on an emotional high.

She launched into reading the multitude of cards and letters, one of which was from the mother of a close friend, John. The same John who had the "privilege" of being present during the infamous grizzly bear, morphine produced hallucination.

During our younger high school days, John's mother, Joan, fed me, checked up on me and in general, treated me like one of the family. I was at her home so often that I started to call her Mom, even responding in unison with John when he said, "Yes, Mom."

Joan didn't mind at all. At that point in most teenagers' lives, they don't even want to admit they have parents. Yet, here was Joan who had a young man volunteering to be her son.

Her note was the most sincere, direct and honest communication I had received. Barb cleared her throat and began to read.

"Marc, I've been sitting here thinking of something uplifting to say that may brighten your day. I just can't come up with anything. I can't think of a single thing good about this situation. I can't stop thinking about the horrible mess you're now in and how rough this must be on you and your family. I wish there was something I could say to make the situation better, but there's not. Every time I think of you, I just think how senseless this all is. You're a strong young man and you don't deserve any of this…Love, Joan/Mom.

These were feelings that my family and closest friends would not, or could not, give voice to. But finally hearing them spoken brought such a sense of relief!

It wasn't unusual for a new visitor to get their first good look at me and choke out "I'll be right back" before running for the door. Sometime later, after they had time to regain their composure, they'd return upbeat and happy, ready to give me a pep talk. While I appreciated their intention, the cheerleader routine was complete crap – they knew it and I knew it.

How could they expect me to believe everything was going to be all right when they couldn't even treat me like the same old Marc?

The "No Nonsense" approach is so much better – not optimistic, not pessimistic, but realistic. The reality was that, no matter how inspirational a visitor's words, their true feelings were of sympathy. I was happy Joan had "shot me straight" and skipped the pep talk.

It seemed so odd that, knowing how severely my life had been changed, everyone still felt the need to "protect" me from the obvious. Dr. Fuller's respect of addressing me directly and Joan's simple honesty showed me people would, in time, come to treat me as they had before.

Plus, Joan's words treated me with a maturity I wasn't accustomed to. True, it was difficult to be teetering between childhood and manhood for anyone, but throw in the fact I was now as helpless as an infant, but inside felt like a man and you've got a catharsis so complicated it would take a dozen shrinks to figure out. When the sheltering attitudes started up from visitors, I wasn't sure whether it was because I was young, disabled, injured or what.

Joan by-passed her maternal desire to treat me like a kid, gave me her feelings, no holds barred, and had successfully brightened my day. No one could imagine that her direct honesty, which sounded discouraging on paper, would be a boost to my ego throughout not only the rehab process, but also the complicated journey of growing into adulthood. A passage now compounded in its difficulty by factors that seemed insurmountable. Maybe it was. But with friends like Joan who refused to coddle a grown man, no matter his disability, that rocky road was one I could surely travel. And at the end of that hazard-strewn highway, I would reach my goal. All that was left to be determined was when I would arrive and what I would encounter along the way.

Chapter 12

"All the anger and the eloquence are bleeding into fear..." [19]

~ Counting Crows

"Thunk!" came the muffled sound just inches from my face. I stopped, startled by the soft noise. Bewildered, I asked, "Was that me?" Rick, my only male nurse glanced up and saw the triangular bar swinging from its chain just inches from my face. When I heard him chuckle, I figured the situation couldn't be too dire.

"Yep, Wild Man, it sure was! Stick your hand out and see what you hit," he said, amused. Cautiously extending my fingers, I found a cold, metal handle-still swinging to and fro. I grasped the heavy duty alloy bar and steadied it.

Man this thing could really do some damage! I pressed my fingers to my forehead, checking for blood. Finding none, and unable to even feel the impact due to neuropathy, I made light of what could have been a painful injury.

"Thank God for nerve damage! It's a good thing I can't feel that or I'd be screaming to wake the dead!" Just a week before, I'd have thrown a tantrum of childlike proportions. Now, my amusement showed Rick that his patient was progressing – and fast.

"Yeah, and if you were deaf, you wouldn't have even heard that *thunk* at all!"

The offending equipment was a handle and chain that hung from a metal framework over the bed. Nicknamed "The Jungle

Gym," it really did look like something that should have been on a playground. In hopes of preventing bedsores, doctors ordered my body be turned every few hours. I could help by using the handle.

Through the turning ritual, Rick and I talked, joked, laughed and did everything we could to make the hour-long task easier. Sometimes, if our competition of wit was heated, I could almost forget I was blind… almost.

Slowly but surely, I was getting better. It would be a long, long time until someone would give a diagnosis of "recovered," but compared to the nightmare I'd been just a month earlier, the differences were like night and day.

Even as physical improvements were made, the war with insomnia continued to give battle. On yet another sleepless night, I asked for some company. Rick was on duty at the intensive care end of the floor; a place I'd escaped from several weeks earlier.

He was happy I was getting better, but deep down I think he missed caring for me. He must have strolled down to my end of 7400 just as the nurse call light flashed on above my door. As I lay there, Rick entered with his usual greeting, "How ya doing, Wild Man?"

"Wild Man" was Rick's nickname for me, much as Dennis referred to me as, "Dude." I couldn't help but wonder if their other patients also received nicknames. Selfishly, I hoped not.

"I'm just going to lay here all damned night again and get pissed," I complained bitterly.

"You want me to come by after I get stuff settled down in the unit? It's a pretty slow night down there. I can drop by and hang out for a little while, if you'd like." It was like music to my ears!

"Thanks, man," I said, with true sincerity, "Chances are, I'll be awake when you come back."

For the next hour I tried to fall asleep. Relaxation exercises, self-hypnosis, counting sheep, nothing worked. I gave up and sat thinking. It had been a few weeks since I'd arrived on the 7400 floor after "the first big surgery." At the time, I didn't think any other nurse would be able to care for me as well as Barb. I was pleasantly surprised to be proven wrong!

Rick not only had a great personality, but impeccable nursing skills. He was probably assigned to my case because he was strong enough to handle two very big things: my size and my attitude.

I met Rick in the middle of the night shortly after arriving in the ICU. Groggy and annoyed that this guy was not my new favorite nurse, I decided to find out if he was competent. I wasn't up for being his guinea pig so God help him if he was a novice!

I reached for my notepad and wrote, "How long have you been a doctor?"

"Marcus, I'm not a doctor. I'm a nurse in the ICU and I've been here for four years. But, I'm not a doctor," he said, explaining more than I had asked. The extra information saved me the time and trouble of interviewing him. I liked Rick. He could live.

Plus, there was just something more manly about fighting the battle of the bedsores on my ass with someone of my same gender.

As if on schedule, an hour later, Rick walked into my room for the second time that night. "Still not asleep, Wild Man?" he asked, with a touch of empathy in his voice.

"Nope!" I responded with more than a hint of exasperation. Think you could punch me really hard and knock me out?" I asked, only half joking.

"I think Dr. Jones would have me by the balls if I ruined his work on your face!" Rick said, chuckling and pulling up a chair.

For the next hour, Rick and I talked about growing up. We shared similar stories of our teenage years of parties, girls, more parties, and more girls. We talked of the nursing profession, gossiped about some of my other nurses and Rick concurred that I definitely had my fair share of "The Evil Bitches."

"Have you always been a nurse?" I asked.

"I've had several different careers, some where I made a heck of a lot more money than you can in nursing," he said, leaning back in his chair, "But they just didn't fulfill something inside of me. I wanted to be able to help people and nursing gives me that ability."

"Well," I said quietly, "I, for one, am glad you're doing what you do, man."

Although Rick was close to 20 years my senior, he treated me as he would any other adult. During these conversations my blindness slowly became irrelevant. Rick and I were just two friends, swapping tales as if one of us wasn't disabled or injured at all. Those things that had governed my life over the past month were now simply non-issues.

After an hour, Rick bade me good-bye and shook my hand. Those 60 minutes of conversation were more precious than any tangible gift I could receive.

Late one night during yet another endless battle with insomnia, I was seething with frustration. Finally, with no relief in sight, I hit the nurse call light. Barb cheerfully strode into the room, unprepared for a barrage of complaints.

"Why won't they give me something that'll let me sleep?"

"Well," Barb said sympathetically, "you're on so many drugs already. They probably don't want to put you on any more. Besides, if you're complaining this much, chances are that you won't be in the hospital much longer anyway."

What? Did I hear that correctly? Up until that point, no one had even mentioned being discharged. My release always seemed light years away.

"Are you serious?" I asked, skeptical that there may not be an end to this home away from home.

"Of course I am. You don't want to stay here forever, do you?"

Home! By this time, I had spent as much time in the hospital as I had at college. I'd considered SMSU my home, but it just didn't seem sane to call this hospital room, "home."

My mind had shifted into its favorite gear, *Worry Overdrive*. I couldn't imagine what it would be like when I first stepped inside the familiar house I would never see again. I wasn't especially concerned about finding my way around. After all, I'd stumbled around in pitch darkness every time I came in late and my parents were asleep, but how I was going to feel definitely had me worried. What would it be like to walk into my room and never again see the posters plastered on the walls, never again read the books on my shelf, and never again be able to look through the photo albums of people I loved? Would I be able to handle that? I wasn't so sure. But, I really didn't have a choice. Barb was right; I couldn't stay here forever.

"I'll have to cross that bridge when I come to it," I said. *At least when I get home I'll finally be able to get some sleep!* Sweet, nourishing rest in my own bed. I'd have some peace and quiet without doctors and nurses always competing for time, attention, and vital signs. As I mulled over the thoughts of home, the idea of a familiar household was starting to become more appealing.

However, the next thing on the schedule was one more big, damned surgery. I was still facing a 13 hour-long operation where my left facial nerve would be bridged, my left ear canal repaired, and some more reconstruction done to my nose. I was sick and tired of surgeries and all the pain and nervousness that went along with them.

While my acceptance of the surgery wasn't graceful, I tried to keep the drama to a minimum. I just wanted to get this last operation behind me and then have everyone leave me the hell alone.

Half a day later, I exited the post-op recovery room in a foul mood and just wanting to sleep. The surgery had been much more extensive than I'd expected, but with one pleasant surprise. Instead of an incision and staples running over my entire head, this time the bloody mess only crept up to my crown. *Thank God for small miracles,* I thought cynically as my fingers explored the hideous incision. This must have been an easy surgery for Dr. Jones compared to the rest, but it had still taken over 15 hours.

Three days later, a resident came in to check how well I was healing. He finished his examination and turned to my parents. "Has anyone talked to you about when you might be getting out of here?" he asked, matter-of-factly.

I hadn't shared the late night conversation with Barb because I really had nothing concrete to tell. This surgery had been such a major ordeal that all other thoughts had been temporarily erased. The question caught my parents off guard. Shocked, my father could barely blurt out his single word response, "No!"

"Well, Dr. Jones and Marcus' other doctors have been talking. We think he'll probably be able to be released on Thursday," the young resident said, having no idea the joy he'd just brought to room #7489.

Thursday? That was only three or four days away! "Well, what do you know, Brother?" my father said excitedly. "You're going to be home for Thanksgiving!" His enthusiasm was contagious, but I tried not to let my hopes rise too high. I was all too accustomed to one more unexpected complication.

Things immediately shifted into high gear. No one had lived in our home for the last 46 days and the house was apparently feeling abandoned. The water in the pipes had become stagnate and, when any faucet was turned on, the smell of sulfur invaded the room. Uncle Steve, Elaine's husband, was dispatched on the mission of supplying bottled water until tap water could be restored.

For weeks, Uncle Steve had looked on helplessly. Doctors and nurses took care of my medical needs, and what they couldn't take care of, Elaine did. I turned to my parents every time I needed anything else. Sometimes I could feel Steve's helplessness. Now, at last, he had been given a mission he could accomplish. He performed his task with absolute zeal, buying up gallons of every conceivable kind of bottled water: Evian, Natural Spring, Clearly Canadian, the variety was amazing. Our home soon resembled the bottled water aisle at a supermarket! We had more bottled water sitting in the house than we could drink in a year.

Thanksgiving Eve was a celebratory event all its own. I had a flood of visitors who were home from college and who wanted to visit one last time before my release. Thankfully, the visitors exhausted me and I slept well as soon as the last one left. The morning of my discharge, I woke, grabbed the talking watch at my bedside and pressed the button. The electronic female voice announced the time as 5:30 a.m. I couldn't believe it! For the first time in nearly a month, I'd slept through the entire night! If ever there was a good omen, this had to be one! I pressed the nurse call button and Barb appeared for the last time.

"You ready to get outta here, buddy?" she asked brightly.

"Sort of," I said with unexpectedly mixed emotions. "I'm going to miss you guys," I added quietly. I really was. Barb, Rick, and several other nurses and therapists had been my caregivers and friends. It was going to be strange and lonely to wake up in the night and not be able to talk to them.

"Yeah, we're going to miss you, too, kiddo. You've made quite a mark on this floor!" Barb's tone was upbeat, but there was something in her voice that showed she was also having trouble letting go. She gave my arm a gentle squeeze and softly said, "You know, when I first got you as a patient, I had no idea you'd end up affecting all of us so much. You've been here so long now that it's going to be strange not having you around. Still, I'm glad you're going home. You've improved so much. I'm sure that will continue and you'll accomplish all your goals!"

I wished I had half as much confidence in myself as Barb did. My optimism was teetering as the hour of discharge approached. For the first time, I wasn't sure I really wanted to leave. Yet, there was no point in postponing the inevitable. Barb took my vitals one last time, recorded the numbers and helped me dress for my departure.

Later that morning my family arrived, surprised to find me awake, dressed and waiting in a wheelchair. The logistics had been planned in advance and now all they needed was to plug me into the equation. I'd ride with Uncle Steve and Aunt Elaine back home while Mom and Dad transported the hospital equipment, flowers, gifts and cards. Steve and Elaine's car was the largest and it would offer ample room to maneuver out of the wheelchair. While the discharge papers were signed, I fidgeted, drumming my fingers nervously.

I silently listened to the hustle and bustle of the people around me, hoping and praying no one would notice my sullen mood. No one but Barb knew I had misgivings about leaving the hospital. My parents had enough to worry about without their son getting unnecessarily emotional.

I buttoned my flannel shirt as high as I could without it disturbing the trach. The metal trays, which covered my eyes through most of the last several weeks, had been replaced with a cheap pair of black sunglasses. The shades made me feel a little more acceptable to the outside world, but they didn't fit well across my swollen nose. The staples up the side of my head were, thankfully, not blatantly visible due to my hair being long enough to brush over them. The only other signs of trauma were the bandages on the backs of my hands from where Barb had removed the IV lines. Hopefully, I could get through the lobby with some anonymity.

I sat silently in the wheelchair. This was a joyous day for my family and I would do nothing to ruin their celebration.

Several of the nurses came by to wish me well before I re-entered a world now totally unknown. Just as I was being rolled toward the elevators, Barb grabbed my hand and bent down to hug me. As I lifted my arms to hug this woman who had become one of the greatest assets in my recovery, I felt tears well up in my dead eyes. Not out of sadness or loss, but out of gratitude and love for the person who gave so much of herself.

"I love ya', buddy," she said holding me close.

"Love ya', too. Thanks for everything. Thanks for taking care of me." I said, choking on emotion.

I let go of my favorite nurse as my father positioned himself behind the wheelchair, unlocked the wheels and we pressed on. Nervous and timid, I was pushed through the unfamiliar lobby of Barnes Hospital. It seemed strange that, after weeks locked inside I'd never even visited the lobby.

A fountain on the left splashed water and muffled our conversations. Approaching the bank of automatic doors, I could feel blasts of cold air as they opened and closed. *Fresh air!* I hadn't been able to touch or breathe it for the last 46 days and it tasted wonderful! With my first lungful of oxygen, I forgot the mountains of worries I'd been feeling… at least for a while.

So what if St. Louis was experiencing one of the coldest days on record? I was glad to once again breathe fresh air like a normal person, frigid temperatures or not! Steve arrived in the Lincoln just as I was begging for a wheelchair ride around the circle drive.

"All right, here we go!" my father said as the automatic doors opened. The feeling of cold, fresh air washed over me like diving into a lake on a blistering August afternoon.

I wrapped myself tight in my flannel shirt as we pushed over the small ridges in the sidewalk. I was outside once again, in the real world and I was going home!

"Okay, Brother," Dad said, pushing the wheelchair up to the car door. "Stick out your right hand and find the inside of the car. I reached out and my hand rested on the buttons for the power windows. I would be riding shotgun, the front passenger seat, once again. The last time I'd sat in an automobile, my life had almost ended. I fought through the desire to run back inside and hide.

Holding tight to the door handle, I slowly, carefully, sank into the front seat. I think I surprised everyone except myself when I reached out and slammed the door behind me.

While everyone stood outside getting last minute instructions from the nurse, I sat in solitude and ran my hands over the cold, leather interior. As fear began creeping up my spine I pulled myself in check. "Okay, Engel, just do this thing. Fear and flashbacks be damned, you've got to learn to ride in a car again," I muttered.

After thanking the nurse, Elaine and Steve piled in the Lincoln and we eased out of the circle drive. I gripped the door handle with white knuckles, more out of the anticipation of fear than actual fear itself.

As we pulled onto Highway 40, Elaine cautiously asked the very question I'd been asking myself, "Are you afraid to ride in a car now?"

"I don't know," I responded honestly. "I guess we'll see how it goes. So far so good."

We rode in silence for a few moments until Steve said, "Just in case you want to know, we're passing The Arena."

The last time I'd breathed fresh air had been at the hockey game at The Arena. The last hours I'd spent as a sighted person had been at The Arena. Now, out of the left window, Steve looked at the very building where I'd spent one of the greatest nights of my life... right before it turned into one of the worst.

Out of habit, I turned my head the direction Steve was looking and felt a shot of emptiness. I'd never again see The Arena, never watch a hockey game there, never drive past the old barn-like structure while looking at the sign that announced the upcoming games and events. Yet, even knowing I'd never again gaze upon that building, I could see it perfectly with my mind's eye.

I didn't answer Steve, too lost in my own thoughts. Wondering where my life was now headed, I began to get sleepy. I was mentally and physically exhausted. Unable to hold off the sleep that had eluded me for so long, it took only seconds to drift off.

When we arrived at home an hour later, the house was warm and full of life. As soon as I was wheeled in, I transferred from the wheelchair to the plush Lane recliner sitting in the living room, now known as "Marc's chair." It felt like heaven.

Soon, family members began showing up with mountains of food for Thanksgiving. An impromptu dinner erupted from the kitchen, but unless the turkey and stuffing was to be put through a food processor, I'd be enjoying none of it.

As relatives piled in the house, the wind with its 20 degree below zero chill whipped through the front door and sliced at my feet. It felt absolutely wonderful! Still exhausted from the day's events, I opted for napping instead of enjoying Thanksgiving dinner with the family.

When everyone had left, my sister, Cathy, approached me with a gift, of sorts. "Hold out your hand," she directed without giving any other clues. I did as I was told and into it she placed my black, leather wallet. Not since the crash had I even thought of it.

"Where'd you find this?" I asked as she sat down next to me.

"Mom and Dad went to the E.R. a few days after the wreck to see if they could collect your personal belongings. They were able to get your wallet and your shoes, but everything else was destroyed by blood and gasoline."

Cautiously, I lifted the wallet to my nose, searching for the slightest odor of fuel, but found nothing except the scent of worn leather.

"Is there anything in there you need?" Cathy asked. *Need? No, not really.* I didn't need money and had nowhere to spend it anyway. I didn't need my student I.D. now and probably wouldn't for at least a couple of years. With a sting I thought of the inside fold of leather where I kept my driver's license. *Nope,* I thought sadly, *I won't be needing that, either.*

As she searched through the wallet, Cathy discovered something I'd forgotten, a letter from Tom. My mind drifted back to the afternoon of October 9th before the hockey game. When I arrived at Tom's house, there was a folded piece of paper lying on his bureau. "Know how I said I'd write to you at college? Well, there's your letter!" he said, pointing at the folded paper which had just caught my eye. "I ran out of stamps, so don't complain that it didn't come through the mail!" he quipped. Figuring there was no reason to read it when he was standing right in front of me, I stuffed the letter into my wallet. "Cool! I'll just read it sometime when I get homesick," I had said, stuffing the wallet into my back pocket.

Cathy asked quietly, "Do you want me to read it?"

I wasn't sure. So much had changed since Tom's pen had scratched those words.

"It might be the last letter anyone ever sends me," I said, wondering how I would handle the invasion of privacy that was necessary for me to receive mail. *You've got nothing to lose, Engel,* I thought as Cathy patiently waited for a response. Finally, I nodded and took a deep breath, preparing myself to be transported back to a carefree time in the life of a teenager.

As she began to read, a flood of memories came rushing back. For the next five minutes, I heard tales of Tom's life and the adventures of his senior year, his thoughts on the chance of the Blues making the NHL playoffs and a few off-color memories of some of the pranks we'd pulled earlier that summer.

Now, that letter represented so much more than just the teenage happenings in Tom's life. Cathy finished reading and said nothing, but handed the letter back. I couldn't say anything. Tom's words were absorbed and processed, but what was even more intriguing was my lack of feelings over the letter. Maybe I was just punch-drunk with all the changes that had gone on since that day, maybe I was just too tired to care, or maybe it had gotten to the point where I realized that nothing could change the past and I had to move on. Whatever the reason, I just couldn't cry over my lost innocence. I carefully refolded the letter and placed it back in my wallet.

"That's all in the past," I said quietly, "And it doesn't change anything."

With a sad smile, she said, "You're right… so what are you going to do now?"

"The only thing I can do," I said calmly, "keep pushing on."

Chapter 13

**"Fed through the tube that sticks in me,
just like a wartime novelty..."** [20]

~ Metallica

"Hey, I've gotta piss!" I called to my parents who were seated at the kitchen table watching the nightly news, much as they'd done before this nightmare ordeal began.

Mom disappeared down the hall saying, "Okay, I'll set the commode up in the living room."

"Like hell! I'm not using that overgrown potty chair!" I spat out. She started to reply, to say it was not a problem, but I cut her off.

"No, no and no! Just help me get to the bathroom and I'll be fine," I said and grabbed the walker. *Commode... yeah, right.* No cutesy little French word could change the fact that the toilet I'd used for the last month resembled a toddler's high chair with a bucket. Bedpans and commodes had been the order of business in the hospital, but no longer. Anyway, I'd be so embarrassed at submitting to nature's call in the living room that I doubted I'd even be able to squeeze a drop!

Thanksgiving dinner had consisted of several glasses of red fruit juice. I'd fought off the pressure on my bladder as long as possible, knowing the journey to the bathroom was going to be difficult.

"You're doing fine, Brother," Dad said, following me as I maneuver down the hall. His voice had all the encouragement of a parent watching their child in a sporting match-up, but this was no game. After rounding the corner into the bathroom, I paused to wipe the sweat from my forehead.

Once I arrived at the foot of the can, I backed up until I felt the cold porcelain against my calves. "You can leave now… and shut the door," I said to my paternal cheerleader.

At last! I was alone! Complete solitude and self-sufficiency.

Nearly two months had passed since I'd sat alone in a bathroom. Now that I was solo again, I felt independence like I hadn't known in a long, long time! If I only could flip through the magazines sitting on the back of the toilet, life would again be complete. Since that wasn't going to happen, it just reinforced the desire to learn Braille… and quick! After all, what male does not long for those moments of complete manhood, sitting on the can and reading whatever is handy? Never had there been a more powerful motivator to make myself literate again.

Days turned to weeks and new daily tasks became routine. Despite Christmas approaching, the feeling around the house seemed strangely out of focus. I couldn't concentrate on celebrations knowing I was facing a major surgery before the 25th of December.

Dr. Jones would again be performing his artwork, though this time it would be in a more sensitive area; my mouth. He would be taking a piece of skin from my waistline and transplanting it over an area of exposed bone along the roof of my mouth. He had already transplanted bone, nerves and fat to different parts of my face, but grafting skin into my mouth was going to be especially tedious.

"Skin grafts don't always work on the first try, Marcus," Dr. Jones explained on the pre-surgery visit. "Surgery inside the mouth is very delicate work. If we can't establish blood flow, we'll have to try again."

Upon Dr. Jones' delivery of the horrible news, he became the archenemy, the target of all my frustrations. The torturer.

Two days later, I was released from the hospital with a strict diet of clear liquids and more clear liquids. Once the graft ceased bleeding and a few more days passed, my appetite returned with a vengeance. My stomach soon began to grumble. Not thinking about eating was futile. Nutrients injected by the pump shot the mixture directly into my small intestine, bypassing my stomach altogether. The 3000 calorie per day diet helped maintain weight, but was now the only means of food intake. My body was receiving plenty, but my stomach believed my throat had been cut!

I dreamed of rare cheeseburgers with mayo and pickles, egg rolls and Crab Rangoon. I was tortured by thoughts of steaks, omelets, pizza, bagels, cereals... anything that wasn't a clear liquid.

The days dragged on and my spirits sank lower with every loud noise that came from my belly. With every pang of hunger, I hated Dr. Jones more. The only relief came when I contemplated new ways to berate him. As my next appointment approached, I even rehearsed the profanities Dr. Jones would be receiving. Somewhere deep down, I knew Dr. Jones wasn't to blame, but depression, starvation and pain overshadowed rationality.

Finally the day of reckoning arrived. It had been nearly two weeks since the surgery and I was ravenous. For the entire hour of the car ride, my thoughts jumped from pleasures of food to inflicting damage to Dr. Jones, back and forth, neither leading to anything but a downward spiral of emotions.

I was wheeled through the hospital, to the plastic surgery office and directly into an examination room. The target of my hostility entered after just a few minutes and greeted my family with his usual cheery, "Hello, Engels!" His greeting was returned with a scowl and a grunt.

"How are you doing, Marcus?" he asked sincerely, shuffling through an instrument cabinet, no doubt looking for something sharp and metal to jab into my mouth.

"Shitty!" I blasted back, venom dripping from my voice.

"That's an honest answer," he said sympathetically, adjusting his stool and moving it closer in order to begin his examination. Before he could even say, "Open wide!" I broke out the big guns and started firing.

"I want to eat, dammit!" I nearly shouted, though no volume would ever be loud enough to convey my frustration.

Dr. Jones stopped, let out a sad sigh and sat motionless. I could almost feel the quick look he directed to my parents, a sympathetic glance that seemed to say, "I wish there was something else I could do to help..."

My outburst had landed a direct hit. As I felt the hurt I inflicted, I immediately wished I could take the words back. I'd tried all along to ignore Dr. Jones compassion. Disregarding his empathy made it easier to justify my hatred.

"I know you do, Marcus, and I want you to eat, too," he said, placing a hand on my knee. "The skin graft is still healing. I wish I could give you permission to eat, but I can't just yet. We've simply got to get this mouth problem resolved, or you'll never be able to go back to solid foods. I don't want that any more than you do, okay, Marcus?"

Tears welled up and I immediately felt shameful for my childish behavior. Anger at Dr. Jones was unfair, but the whole situation just sucked. I was only asking to eat, not for my sight back or for the cancellation of more inevitable surgeries. I was just so frustrated, but more than anything, I was ashamed.

I sat silently for the rest of the appointment. As Dr. Jones finally returned the dreaded metal devices to their storage place, I asked quietly, "Okay, so when do I get to eat?" My voice had taken on an apologetic tone.

He sighed again and reluctantly said, "I'm sorry, Marcus, but it's going to be at least another two weeks. I think by the end of January it should be healed enough for food to pass over it, but right now, the risk of infection is just too great." Dr. Jones laid a hand on my slumping shoulder and continued, "I can't imagine what it's like not to be able to have food, but please believe me when I say I'm not trying to hurt you…"

I couldn't take it… the tears fell like rain. *Damn it!* That was nearly a month of living with an empty stomach. I just wanted to go home and cry. Dr. Jones had every right to walk out of the exam room and dismiss me for my deplorable behavior. Instead, he patiently waited for the crying to stop.

"I got you a little something for Christmas," he said, reaching into the pocket of his lab coat and pulling out a small gift. *A Christmas present? Since when do doctors give Christmas gifts, especially when their patients are as ungrateful as I have been?*

I tore open the small package and found a cassette tape, still in the cellophane wrapper.

"My kids picked this out, "Dr. Jones said warmly, waiting for my reaction. "I hope you don't already have this one. You had quite a collection when you were on 7400!"

Heat rose to my face. I held the cassette in my father's direction, hoping he could read the band and album title.

"It's R.E.M. and it says *Automatic for People*," my father said, mispronouncing both the band and the title.

"Thanks, Dr. Jones," I said through my remaining tears. He had every right to take pleasure in the double serving of humble pie I was about to devour.

In addition to a slew of tunes that were ingrained with

my senior year, the tape also included the song, *Nightswimming* which had already been such a memorable element of my hospitalization.

After bidding Dr. Jones good-bye, we headed for the car. While waiting for an elevator, my father laughed and said, "I think Dr. Jones just got about ten times better in your opinion, huh?!" My surgeon had slipped me a bribe, pure and simple. That short appointment and a $10 cassette taught me the value of putting myself into someone else's shoes. It also reminded me to keep my mouth shut whenever the opportunity presented itself! Still chuckling as we entered the elevator, my father said, "Yeah, I think it's probably about time you took your big old size 14 foot outta your mouth!" And, he was right.

Dr. Jones' "couple of weeks" stretched into a month and a half. For six full weeks, my stomach remained empty while I continued to dream about food. Finally the day arrived when permission to eat was granted... and eat I did! I started with a light, succulent snack of a half dozen White Castle burgers, two orders of cheese fries, a milkshake and a gigantic piece of cheesecake. I ate like there was no tomorrow, finished and spent the rest of the afternoon on the toilet with a case of diarrhea. Life again seemed tolerable.

Just a few days before Dr. Jones gave permission for the feasting to begin, I'd been reacquainted with the orthopedic surgeon, Dr. Perry, who had inserted the rod and pins through my left leg. After bending and twisting my leg, he gave me some great news. "Well, Marcus, the bones have mended nicely. When it feels ready, you can begin bearing weight. You're not ready to run a marathon, but you can try walking whenever you feel up to it."

A week later, I sat alone in the living room thinking about how easy it had been to maneuver the walker down the hall that afternoon. Quietly so as not to attract attention, I carefully eased myself out of the chair. Standing and balancing with my good leg, I stepped away from the confines of the walker for the first time in four months.

My family had not seen me standing upright since the October afternoon before the crash. When I turned the corner into the kitchen, a silence fell over the room. Slowly and carefully, almost as if their excitement would knock me off balance, they quietly complimented my progress. Once again, the world improved another notch.

The months of homebound recovery dragged on. Once per week, the cycle of monotony was broken by the bubbly personality of Judy Burch, my rehab teacher. She would arrive with her Seeing Eye dog, Splash, and lead me through lessons of Braille and adaptive daily living skills. Judy was the first blind person I'd met and I immediately knew she was going to break down every stereotype my young mind had created.

"Can you meet on Thursday instead of Wednesday next week, Marcus?" she asked after one of our sessions. "I'm in a bowling tournament Thursday night and I want to save my energy so we can beat up on the other team!" *Bowling? And she's blind?* I thought with amazement, *who would have imagined that?*

Our weekly sessions laid a foundation, yet we knew it wasn't enough.

"You're just going to rock when the doctors finally give you permission to go to the rehab school, Marcus! I mean, I give you an assignment due in a week, and the next day you're calling me at the office asking, 'Okay, it's done. What do I do now?'"

"I just want to get back to college," I said innocently, "So anything I can do to move that along, I do it. What will I be doing when I finally get to the rehab school?"

"Well, at any rehab school, you'll do the same things we've been doing, but it'll be all day, every day. You'll learn everything from adaptive computers to Orientation and Mobility and so, so much more!"

Attached to a feeding tube for 10 hours per day, that possibility seemed remote. Once I had healed enough to stay out of the hospital for more than a week at a time, rehab school became much more of a reality.

Acting upon Judy's advice, I began researching rehab school options with a thoroughness I hadn't even used when selecting a university. I needed to be challenged if I planned to lay the groundwork and develop the confidence needed to continue the road of independence.

Research and interviews helped to narrow the field to one standout program; the Colorado Center for the Blind. I was starting to get excited! If all went as planned, I'd arrive at the school in late October. College should be on the horizon in less than a year! My plans now had a definite shape and time frame!

With the rehab school decision made, I began to give serious consideration to another option. Judy had introduced me to the possibility of acquiring a Seeing Eye dog. When this idea came up, I peppered her with endless questions: "How does the dog know where to go? When you travel, how do you know where to take the dog to the bathroom? If the dog gets sick, how do you get around? When you go out, does the dog always go with you?"

"Gosh, Marcus," she laughed, "You ask more questions than a little kid!" We'd taken a break from my Braille lesson and discussions had once again turned to the Seeing Eye and the wonderful dogs they train. "You know, I'm not the only person to ask. I think you should talk with a few Seeing Eye grads other than me. In fact,

I'm married to one and I know if you call my husband, Rick, he'll be happy to talk to you!" I quickly used my limited Braille skills to punch out their phone number.

I called Rick later that week and got a lot more than just some additional information on Seeing Eye dogs. After answering all of my questions, our conversation turned to sports, music, world events and whatever else we could think to talk about. Soon, I felt comfortable enough to question Rick about his blindness.

"Marcus, you're going to learn a lot in Denver, but you're also going to learn a lot on your own. When I lost my sight, I didn't have the option of a rehab school. I learned practically everything by trial and error and, really, I haven't fallen off a cliff or been hit by a truck more than a couple of times!" Rick teased. His comfort level with his disability was not only amusing, but made me wonder, "Will I ever be okay enough with everything to joke about it?"

"You know, Marcus, I got in a little trouble with my dog last year. One day, I decided to play a little trick on my boss. I went into a novelty shop and bought some fake dog poop and a can of stink spray. I mean it was bad! This stuff smelled worse than a porta-potty in July! When I got back to the office, I laid the fake poop in the hallway and squirted the spray all over it. Man, it stunk so much I thought I was going to die! I ran back to my office and waited for the fun to begin! Half an hour later, I heard drills and hammers in the hallway, so I went out to see what was going on. There were maintenance men everywhere checking heating vents, looking at the electrical outlets, everything. I asked one what they were doing and he said something smelled like there was an electrical fire. I went back and checked the smell of the spray again and yep, you guessed it! That stuff smelled more like melting plastic than poop! Man, I'm lucky I didn't get fired for that little prank!"

Rick and Judy showed that the lives of the blind are really no different than the lives of the sighted. Their average daily routines proved that if others could function in a world without sight, so could I!

In addition to the input from Rick and Judy, I'd received a packet of information from the Seeing Eye, Inc. in Morristown, NJ. Along with the usual forms were several tapes entailing the experiences of other graduates and their dogs. It all sounded too good to be true! After much contemplation, I took the first step, filled out the extensive application forms and stated specifically what my time frame was. I also described what sort of life a Seeing Eye dog would live alongside me.

The unwavering goal to be back in college for the summer semester was only about nine months away. If I spent five or six months in Denver, then trained for a month with a Seeing Eye dog, that would leave at least a month to prepare for returning to college! The plan was finally coming together; and what a great plan it was! No one, and I meant no one, would deter me from my goal!

After spending the winter, spring and better part of the summer sitting at home recovering, I really needed a change of pace. I was bored out of my mind! My days rarely consisted of more than reading, radio, napping, TV and dreaming of being back in college. Day in and day out, this routine almost never changed. It did, however, offer a great chance to create a more aesthetically pleasing version of myself.

With nothing better to do, every sunny afternoon from May through September, I pulled a lounge chair onto the back deck and basked in the sun's rays. By Memorial Day, my skin looked as if I was of an ethnic descent rather than the 99.9% Germanic blood that ran through my body!

I didn't realize quite how dark I'd gotten until I ran into Dennis Fuller while walking to a doctor's appointment at Barnes. It had been close to a year since he'd made me pick that week's NFL games.

"Well, I'd say 'Hello!' but I think I need to say 'Aloha!' to this guy," he said, playfully poking me in the ribs. "What the Hawaiian Tropic have you been doing to yourself, dude?"

"Trying to overdose on vitamin D!" I said, poking him back.

As much as I hated to admit it, I enjoyed going back to the hospital, if nothing more than for a change of pace. Being 18 years old and homebound can get old really, really fast.

Late one afternoon, the phone rang. Roused from a nap spent in the lounge chair outdoors, I sleepily answered, "Hello?" The bright voice at the other end belonged to Kista.

"Hey Marc! Whatcha doin'?" She asked.

"The same thing I do every day... I sit, I read, I eat, I go to the bathroom... you know, the life of your average nursing home patient," I responded cynically.

"Want to go for a ride?" Kista asked.

"Is the Pope Catholic?" I tried to hide my excitement; not wanting her to believe my life was now so uneventful that a short joy ride was the highlight of the week.

"Okay, I'll be there in 15 minutes," she said as I rushed inside to change clothes.

Just as I was combing my hair, Kista beeped the horn and pulled the VW convertible into the gravel driveway. I stepped out to greet her and immediately felt the warm sunshine and soft breeze against my face.

"Hey man! Get over here and help me get my top down!" Kista called as she piled out of the car.

Having the gutter mind of an average teenage guy, I realized her mistake and jokingly called back, "With pleasure!"

Kista let out an exasperated sigh and said, "The convertible top, you pervert! Not my top!" Using my white cane and what limited Orientation and Mobility skills I'd acquired thus far, I made my way down the sidewalk to the VW. Reaching out, I grabbed the edge of the ragtop and helped Kista lower it behind the back seat.

"Let's go!" she said, jumping back in the car.

I squeezed in the convertible next to her, grabbed the gearshift, turned to Kista and feigned seriousness.

"Can I drive?"

"You were a crappy driver when you could see, what makes you think you'd be any better now?" she asked playfully slapping my hand off the gearshift.

A few minutes later, we were flying down the interstate with the wind whipping over the windshield. The sun beat down on my bare arms and face and I felt more alive than I had in a long, long time.

Chapter 14

"Not a word was spoke between us,
there was little risk involved / everything up to
that point had been left unresolved…" [21]

~ Bob Dylan

The alarm clock rang with the sound I had been dreading all night. I fumbled for the switch, wishing I could go back to sleep and not have to go through this day. The whole damned thing would be nothing more than a waste of time. Crawling out of bed, my knees felt weak. Today, I'd face the man who had changed my life forever.

Two weeks earlier, I'd sat in the prosecutor's office as she explained the possible sentences the court could hand down.

"Drunk drivers really don't get heavy sentences in this state. I know that isn't what you want to hear, but our best bet is to make an agreement with the defense."

"So, how long are we talking then?" I asked for the second time. She'd already dodged the question, instead opting for an explanation about the legal process. I was determined to nail down a time frame, even if we had to play this ridiculous question and answer game all day.

"Unfortunately, I think the best we can hope for is the plea bargain where he'll do 120 days," she said, bracing herself. *120 days?*

"That's bullshit and you know it," I shot back, not giving a damn if my language offended her. How could anyone overlook the mountain of medical bills and doctor's reports, the blind teen-ager sitting across the desk, or the defendant's driving record showing blatant disregard for the law and really believe that four months in the pen was a fair punishment?

"I know you're not happy with this sentence, but let me ex-plain the options. If we do this 120-day call back, the offender is guaranteed to serve the full sentence. Afterward, he'll have five years of probation. If he screws up, bam! He goes back to jail. Those five years are a sword hanging over his head."

As I absorbed the possibilities, the phone on her desk rang. "Excuse me for a moment," she said, picking up the receiver. Sit-ting in the tiny office, I had no choice but to eavesdrop on her end of the morbid conversation. Attorney/client confidentiality seemed laughable in this sewer.

After sifting through some papers, she found one and spoke into the receiver. "Ma'am, the agreement looks like the offender will get 230 years for the first offense, and 125 years for the sec-ond offense." I did some quick mental math and thought, *"That's nearly 400 years! That has to be a murder case... what else could trans-late to that long of a sentence?"*

By the time she hung up the phone, I had a little more under-standing of her position. Every day, she was assigned to represent innocent people who had been harmed by the dregs of society; killers, rapists, child molesters. Now, sitting across the desk from her, was a 19-year-old kid who had been hurt in "an accident."

The crime against me wasn't premeditated nor intentional, right? The drunk driver was beyond negligent, but he never *in-tended* to hurt me. Did that put him in a different category? The law seemed to think so, no matter what I thought. Besides, the sentence that was handed down didn't really matter anyway. What did it change: a whole lot of nothing!

"Okay. Here is the other option. Let's say the judge gives him the maximum penalty. You, Kim and Tom each have one assault charge against the offender. In a perfect world, that'd be a grand total of 21 years. But, I've worked in this office for a long time and I have yet to see a judge hand down consecutive sentences to a drunk driver. Almost always, the sentences run concurrently."

I bit my tongue and suffered through the rest of her feeble explanation.

"If you look at how criminals serve their time, most don't even do half their sentence. If the judge runs the sentences concurrently, then the offender is looking at seven years. My best guess in that scenario is he'd be out in about three years, and then he'd have no probation requirements, nothing."

While her hands weren't completely tied, it was obvious there wasn't an option that could come close to justice. I left her office feeling sick.

Driving to the courthouse on the day of sentencing, I cued my Walkman to some intense and angry music to match my mood. I was sure I'd leave the courtroom pissed off at the state for shafting me, one of the citizens it swore to "protect and serve."

After we arrived at the courthouse, I took my father's arm as sighted guide. We made our way through the metal detectors and up the marble steps to the designated meeting room.

My stomach churned as I greeted Tom, Kim and Vince. The last time the four of us had been together was nearly a year ago when we were laying in the street, bloody and screaming. As if this wasn't excruciating enough, we were about to be "reunited" with the reason we were here in the first place. Being with Tom again was especially hard. More than a month had passed since we'd last spoken. An awkward tension hung between us; something I hadn't anticipated.

Several weeks earlier, the prosecutor had called each of us when the plea bargain had been reached. As soon as Tom heard the news, angry and fuming, he phoned me. "Are you going to be home?"

"Yeah," I answered, "Why?"

"I'm coming over. I'll be there in an hour." He hung up before I could protest. When Tom was determined to do something, there was no point in trying to dissuade him. Being stubborn myself, it is a wonder we ever became friends at all.

An hour later, I greeted him at the front door and felt an almost imperceptible twitch in his handshake.

"You want to take a ride?" Tom asked, already turning and walking into the bright summer afternoon. It was more a command than a request.

As we passed through the rolling hills of Missouri farmland, Tom flipped off the radio.

"So, what do you think about all this?"

"All I know is that it sucks, dude," I answered. "What's worse is there's nothing you or I can do about it."

"I know," Tom whispered, and then swallowed.

We'd both been avoiding this conversation for nearly a year. Now, it was time.

"Pull off up here, man. Let's just talk this out," I said, knowing this wasn't going to be easy. Tom turned onto a deserted gravel drive. If a farmer happened along and saw two teenagers parked in a German sedan, he'd probably assume they had something to do with the local marijuana trade. He'd return home, phone the sheriff's department and we'd soon have a large man in a brown uniform tapping on the window with his nightstick. But, we had nothing to worry about. It was the time of year when crops were too tall to cultivate and farmers had little to do but watch the skies and pray for rain.

A deafening silence engulfed the car as we pulled to a stop. For a moment, we sat unspeaking; each hoping the other would take the first step. Time stood still. Heat from the engine and the call of a bird flying over the bone dry cornfields were the only things that broke the silence.

I sighed. If this was going to happen – I was going to have to go first. Swallowing hard, I opened the Pandora's box.

"Tom, I don't give a damn about all this, okay? I don't care what happens to him. I don't care if he dies. I don't care if he goes to prison and becomes someone's jailhouse bitch," I said, hoping my obscene comment would chip away at the tension. Tom smirked, but we were a long way from laughing.

More than once, I'd tried to put myself in Tom's shoes… and more than once I'd cursed the feelings of guilt. What would it be like if I'd been the one driving?

Pushing the conversation further, I stepped onto some shaky ground. "And I don't care what anyone, including you, says about all this, okay? We didn't do anything wrong. YOU didn't do anything wrong. It was the other guy who screwed up. Nothing, NOTHING was your fault, okay?" I struggled to keep my emotions in check. If I had a meltdown, it wouldn't dispel any of my buddy's guilt.

Then, it was Tom's turn to talk. I waited. He didn't speak, but his nervous breath came in quick, shallow gasps. Staring straight ahead, his eyes fixed on some unseen event. Finally, he whispered, "No, it was my fault. I don't know how I could have stopped it, but it was my fault. I was driving, I was responsible and it was my fault."

I exhaled a frustrated sigh and blasted back, "That's bullshit and you know it! He was the one who was drunk, he was the one who ran the light, he was the one who was speeding, and he was the one who was racing. He was even in the wrong freaking lane! That was all him! Where in that equation did you do anything wrong?" I wasn't going to wait for Tom to answer. Hell, I didn't even want him to. I was on a roll. If he was going to verbally beat himself, then he was going to hear every last bit of what I had to say. "Dude, what happened was no one's fault except his, not yours, his, got it?"

My previous attempts at trying to put myself in Tom's skin had been painful enough. The reality of what he'd been living with was even worse.

Finally, Tom gritted his teeth and whispered, "It was all just so fast. I feel like I could have done something, but I don't know what. I just wish it never happened…" his voice trailed off as he fought back tears. "I'm sorry, man," he said again, "I just wish it had never happened. I'm so sorry."

Saying nothing, I let him cry. He needed it.

"What do you remember?" I asked after he regained some composure.

"Everything… well, almost everything," he said, his voice raspy and low. We were talking facts now, not emotions, and Tom's mood eased a bit. "I remember driving down Hampton and seeing the first car go flying through the intersection. You were saying something about stopping to buy CD's at the music store on the corner. The last thing I remember you saying is, 'It looks like it's open… want to stop?'"

"Yeah," I broke in quietly, "I remember saying that."

"After that, I don't remember anything until we were laying in the street." Taking a deep breath and pausing for what seemed like an hour, Tom waited for the right words to come. "The woman who ran to you asked what your name was. I told her, but she couldn't understand me because Kim was screaming. She kept calling you 'Mike' and I was shouting that your name was 'Marc'," he said, his voice trembling. "I was so pissed that she kept calling you by the wrong name. For some reason, I really remember that."

"How close together were we when we were in the street?" I asked, but I knew I didn't really want to hear his answer. The horror of the dark blood, mangled car, and broken bodies thrown onto the pavement had to be burned into the memory of anyone unfortunate enough to have witnessed that sickening scene.

"About four feet," Tom said, now strangely calm and turning to look directly at me. The sudden change in his temperament set me on edge.

Dammit... I never knew that Tom lay so close to me, his broken neck making it impossible for him to turn away from the ghastly image of my nearly dead body. That scene was traumatic enough for the paramedics, let alone a 17-year-old kid.

He turned away and quietly said, "I saw your eye, man."

Dammit, I thought angrily, *Dammit, dammit, dammit!* I felt like I'd just taken a direct kick to the crotch. Ever since learning of the injuries to my eyes, I hoped and prayed no one but the paramedics and the surgeons had seen them. Maybe even eyewitnesses, but definitely not by my friend. From just over a yard away, through a fog of spattered blood, twisted metal and gasoline vapors, Tom looked straight at my battered head and saw the injury that caused the blindness in my right eye; structural damage so severe that the eye had been enucleated.

We sat in the stifling heat, but there was nothing more to say.

Since that summer day, Tom and I hadn't spoken. We had bared our souls and now, neither of us knew quite how to bridge that gap. While we waited to make the trek through the courthouse, I fumbled for something, anything, to say to Tom. He'd opted not to speak during the sentencing, and I could understand why. No one really wanted to prolong this matter even one additional minute. Even so, I needed that moment to at least have my victim impact statement read, to have some words ring in the memories of the drunk driver.

The prosecutor finally escorted us down the marble hallways to the courtroom. I sat in the first bench, biting my lip and fidgeting with my white cane. After the charges had been read and all parties identified, the prosecutor invited me to join her at the front of the courtroom.

Stepping to my bench, she whispered, "Here, Marcus, you can take my arm." I loathed the thought of having to touch this woman, but I really didn't have a choice. As I stood alongside her, she introduced me to the judge, a woman of about 50 with a personality that was all business.

As I handed the victim impact statement to the prosecutor to deliver to the judge, I heard muffled sobs slightly off to my left. The judge took the document and said strongly, "I will now read Mr. Engel's victim impact statement."

I shifted from one foot to the next, listening to words that didn't even sound like my own. *Hurry up and get this over with.*

As the judge continued, the quiet crying became louder. I leaned toward the prosecutor and whispered, "Where is he?" She put her arm around my shoulders and said quietly, "At the table in front of you. He's the one who is crying."

Although it made sense the offender would be at his own sentencing, until the prosecutor told me he was nearby, I wasn't sure I was sharing the same air with the man who took my sight. My heart skipped a beat as I thought how close I was to this individual who had put me through so much hell. For some reason, I was scared. I knew he wasn't capable of hurting me now, but I couldn't help being a little afraid.

His sobs became stronger as the judge continued to read. *Crying? He's crying? Why? He's not the one who is blind!* Slowly, realization crept in. *This man may be a miserable excuse of a person but he is still a human being.* As his sobs grew more pronounced, I was forced to notice his humanity. Even the most heartless of criminals would have been moved by the damage that his reckless stupidity had caused. True, this guy was low enough to try to get a reduced sentence. Worse, he was a parent and his kids were both under age five. What kind of a father goes out driving drunk and drag racing? Yet, even as despicable as he was, I couldn't help but think of his kids asking their mother where daddy was going to be for the next four months. In spite of everything he'd put me through, he was still a human being and still a parent... even if he was a pathetic example of both.

I thought back to the conversation in Tom's car that hot August day. Tom's guilt was overwhelming, even though he couldn't control what had happened. But this guy? He shared the blame with no one. Yet, I couldn't even begin to grasp how horrible it must feel to be inside his skin.

As the judge continued to read my statement, I noticed a sniffle and a sad sigh coming from my right. *The prosecutor?* This hardened woman, who on a daily basis witnessed the horrors of society, was crying. I had accused her of not caring, but, as I listened to her quietly swallow her tears, I wondered if I might have been wrong after all.

After the judge finished reading, she asked, "Mr. Engel, do you have anything else you'd like to say?"

"Your honor, I'd just like the defendant to look at me and see what he's done..." I said quietly, slipping off my Oakley sunglasses. My naked face revealed the structural bone damage, the angry, red scars across my chin and the atrophy that had already begun in my eyes.

As I turned to face the defense table, the offender's crying became less controlled. Even I was convinced his distress was sincere. I waited for a few seconds, hoping to burn the image of my disfigured face into his mind for eternity. *Think about it the next time you get drunk; think about it every minute of every day.*

After a few moments, the judge asked, "Anything else, Mr. Engel?"

I quietly answered, "No, your honor," and stood waiting for the sentence to be read. That was premature.

The judge turned to the defense and asked, "Does your client have anything he'd like to say to Mr. Engel?" The offender took the cue and stood.

This man who had altered my life forever, who'd hurt me in more ways than anyone could imagine, the man who would be responsible for every step my life now took, simply said in a soft voice, "I'm sorry… I never meant to hurt anyone. I'm sorry…" I have no reason to believe his tears were anything other than genuine. I shrugged, knowing that all the apologies in the world wouldn't change anything.

Finally, the judge said, "It is my understanding that the two parties have reached an agreement for sentencing. Is this correct?"

The prosecutor and defense attorney answered in unison, "Yes, your honor."

"Then I will read the agreements for sentencing." She cleared her throat and began, "The offender will serve 120 days in the custody of the state with five years probation to follow his release. The conditions of probation are attached to this document and will include 1,086 hours of community service, a time equaling that which Mr. Engel originally spent in the hospital."

When the judge finished, she slammed down the gavel. Two deputies from the sheriff's department escorted the offender from the courtroom while we exited out the heavy wooden doors. It was over.

Chapter 15

"I ain't asking for a miracle, Lord just a
little bit of luck will do" [22]

~ *Steve Earl*

"**M**y part is done. I'll see you when you're home for Christmas," the dentist said casually, having no idea that those words meant freedom.

Dr. Gay snapped off his surgical gloves and extended his hand. I gave an awkward smile, the new bridgework making my mouth feel unnatural and full.

Through the last months of sensitive fittings and tedious shaping of the prosthetics, Dr. Gay had proved himself a master of his craft, a virtual artist with his attention to detail. Now, his masterpiece was complete, I could eat solid food again and, best of all, the path was cleared for me to leave for Denver!

That evening my mother treated us to an entire home cooked meal with all the trimmings. Over dinner we discussed the plan for departure to Denver.

"When we go out there, Brother, we can't stay long, okay? We'll probably just drop you off one day and come home the next." Dad said.

"I know," I said, not the least bit offended, "I don't need you to hold my hand or anything." As we talked, departure was scheduled for exactly two weeks away. I would arrive in Denver on October 31st and return home for Christmas break in mid-December, ready for another round of surgeries.

I began packing, preparing to live on my own again. But first… I needed a vacation!

"Can we go to Springfield next weekend?" I asked. "I really want to see Cathy and everyone before I run off to Denver for six months."

"Sure! You deserve a break," my mom said, "and we haven't seen your sister in a while, anyway."

When the weekend finally arrived, I felt like a little kid headed for Disneyland. When we finally reached my sister's apartment, she and several friends were waiting.

"How ya doing, Marc?" a familiar voice said while grabbing my hand. *Travis?* Cathy and Travis didn't even know each other, but she'd tracked him down to let him know I'd be coming to town.

"I'm taking you out on the town tonight, man! Just don't go showing your butt to anyone like you did the last time we hung out, okay? I don't have enough cash to bail you out of jail!" Still laughing, we hopped in Travis' car and headed downtown for some nightlife.

Until the early morning hours, Travis and I showed up wherever the action was; parties, clubs and bars. Everywhere we went I had my hand on Travis' shoulder for sighted guide. I hoped it didn't make him uncomfortable, but if it did, we'd go home right then.

Finally, worry got the best of me. I stopped Travis after we exited a club and asked, "Are you okay with me using your shoulder for sighted guide?"

"Sure, why wouldn't I be?"

"I don't know… it just might look sort of weird with two guys walking around and one touching the other…" Travis knew exactly what I meant.

"Let them think what they want! Who cares? It's pretty obvious you're not using my shoulder because you want to, so screw what anyone else thinks. Let's just go out and have a good time!" There was no way Travis could have known how his confidence made me feel more normal than I had in forever.

When the weekend finally drew to a close, I hugged my sister and friends goodbye. Springfield and SMSU had become a virtual Mecca. When I returned, I would be an equal, no longer just a visitor.

A few days later, I packed my suitcases, loaded them into the car and set out west on I-70. 800 miles later we arrived at the massive complex that housed the apartments occupied by students of the Colorado Center.

Kim and Dan, two blind alumni of the program, met us at my apartment to help me move in. The small dwelling didn't seem any better or worse than some college apartments I'd seen at SMSU. As I started the unpacking process, Kim briefed me on the living arrangements and my new roommate.

"Your roommate's name is Robert, he's 22 and you probably won't meet him for a couple of days. He'll tell you he's at his grandmother's house, but he's really staying with his girlfriend!" After Kim and Dan left, I explored the living room. Next to a gigantic home entertainment system was a black acoustic guitar. A couch and love seat surrounded a small coffee table and faced the stereo.

Searching around on the coffee table, I stuck my fingers straight into an ashtray full of cigarette butts. *Well that's just lovely.* A corner end table held a tower of Robert's CDs.

"Hey Dad...tell me what he's got in his collection."

"Pantera, Black Sabbath, Ozzy Osbourn, Tool," my father read monotonously. My assessment of my new roommate became more and more grim.

Great, I thought, *an Ozzy Osbourn fan. I wonder if he also bites the heads off of live bats!*

"Pink Floyd, Led Zeppelin, Big Head Todd," my father read on in a voice that clearly conveyed all of these groups sounded the same to him.

Did he say Pink Floyd? Maybe there was reason to hope. Between those three groups and the acoustic guitar, Robert and I might find common ground, after all!

After a quick run to the grocery store, my parents drove away. I was left in a new place. Alone. I nervously wandered around the apartment, feeling every wall, window, counter and doorframe. If I was going to live here, I'd better get to know my own space. All the while, fear gnawed at my belly.

After I'd explored every last inch of the apartment, I dropped to my knees and began to pray. "God, help me get through this," I said silently, trying not to focus on the threadbare carpet under my knees, "I'm really scared right now and I need all the help I can get." A car drove past on Evans Avenue, its stereo pounding so hard that it shook the apartment's un-insulated windows. "You know how badly I want to be back in college and I'm going to need your help to get there…" My mind began to wander as I heard heavy footsteps cross the ceiling overhead, then the sounds of a man and woman having a vicious argument.

Distracted, I whispered, "Amen," and stood up, still listening to the couple on the fourth floor.

"Man, what is this place made of? Cardboard?" I thought, rapping my finger on the cheap sheet rock. Discouraged, I sank onto the couch, wondering what on earth I was doing in Denver. Ever since we turned the key to the front door, my will had been crumbling, little by little.

How am I supposed to go through with this? I'm 19, for God's sake, I thought wearily, *I've never lived in a city that even HAD a public bus system, much less one I'd actually have to use! I'm blind, I'm 800 miles from home, I have a Satanist for a roommate, I'm in a shitty apartment and I'm supposed to learn how to be blind.* My self-pity becoming more and more exaggerated with each item I marked off the mental list entitled, "Marc's Crappy Life."

Depressed, I retreated to my bedroom and readied myself to weather the first night in this place. I fell asleep while cars rolled by my window, and tears rolled down my cheeks.

The next day my parents showed up at the apartment, unaware I'd almost dialed their hotel half a dozen times during the night demanding we pack up and go home. I swallowed the fear, grabbed my backpack and followed them to the car.

As we pulled into the center's parking lot, I opened the door before Dad could even shift into park. They probably deduced my anticipation as excitement about getting started on this second leg of the journey. They were wrong. The truth was I knew that the longer I put off walking into the school, the less likely I'd be to actually do it.

We stepped through the building's front doors and were greeted by a secretary who buzzed the director, Diane, in her office, just like this was a corporation with a busy CEO. After a cursory tour of the facility and a brief description of the program, we were invited into Diane's office. Once we were seated around her desk, her focus centered on me, disregarding my parent's entirely.

"Marcus, we're ready to get you started. You're going to learn so much while you're here and I hope you're excited. When you leave this place, you probably won't even recognize the person you were when you first walked through the doors," she said with assurance.

We conversed for the next ten minutes, but not once was a comment made to my parents. I found it odd to ignore the other people sitting at her desk. Suddenly I realized she was disregarding them on purpose. The cold shoulder was intended to show them they would not be a part of my education.

As rude as it was, I understood her logic. The longer the caretakers remained, the longer it postponed the beginning of the rehabilitation process. It was more than slightly insensitive, but since I needed the education of the center, I kept my mouth shut. I bade my parent's good-bye and we agreed to meet later.

"I want to introduce you to Trina," Diane said as soon as my parents were out the door.

"She's the head Orientation and Mobility instructor and she always gives students a new cane on their first day."

Diane buzzed the front desk and a few minutes later, Trina appeared, shook my hand and introduced herself. "Here ya go!" she said brightly, handing me my new means of travel, a solid white cane. I'd been using a telescoping cane for the last year, but this seemed much more sturdy. "Let me show you around the building, let you get a feel of your new surroundings and I'll introduce you to everyone along the way."

As we stepped into the hallway, she pointed out the coat closet, the kitchen, each classroom and the room that contained the soda machines. "You're going to notice the sound your cane tip makes when you pass the kitchen," she explained, grabbing my cane about halfway down and tapping it against the tile floor. A distinct clicking echoed around me with the three quick raps. "Hear that? That echo lets you know the kitchen is on your left. If you walk a few feet further, there'll be a metal doorframe into the meeting room. Everything in there is carpeted, so there will be virtually no sound clues from your cane tip," she said, already walking into the next room.

Interesting, I thought with a bit of bewilderment, I've been blind for a year and never really thought of how to use the echo from the cane's tip. It took only that short walk to learn Trina was a master instructor. I couldn't believe someone sighted was so proficient in cane travel. *If the other teachers are this good,* I thought happily, *I'm going to learn more quickly than I imagined!*

Trina and I entered the meeting room and she showed me to a chair. "Just come in here sometime and get a feel of the area," she said, pulling up a chair, "That will help you more than any explanations I could give." As she sat down, Diane entered and spoke to the group of students.

"We've just received our newest student, Marcus Engel, from Missouri," she said with all the gusto of a M.C. I felt my face grow red with embarrassment. "Marc, Monday, Wednesday and Friday, we conduct 'Business Class.' This isn't about sales and marketing, but rather the business of being blind. We discuss all issues of blindness, everything from Braille and mobility to dating and friendships. This is an open forum. We want each student to realize that blindness can be thought of as a characteristic instead of a disability, much as some people have red hair and some people have fair skin."

That's stupid. One of the most dehabilitating handicaps is NOT the same as having red hair! I bit my tongue. No reason to get up in arms on the first day. Yet, I couldn't help wondering the obvious; if blindness was simply a characteristic, why wasn't the government providing social security for redheads? Still, I kept silent and waited through the rest of the discussion.

We exited the room and I followed the other students down the hallway, out the front doors and down three blocks to the bus stop, all the while knowing and fearing the truth; I was following the lead of other blind people. Without a sighted person amongst us, I was completely relying on the skills of the person at the front of the pack. *Someone has to be in the lead,* I thought, *and that person is going to be me just as soon as I learn how!*

As the bus pulled up, I followed the other students up the stairs, paid my fare and attempted to find a seat. After only a step or two, a husky voice on my right said, "Hey, Marcus, I'm Gabriel. I've got room next to me if you want it." I sat down and thanked him while shaking his hand. Soon, we were deep in conversation. I learned that Gabe had formerly been sighted, but due to a degenerative eye disease, his vision was rapidly fading. Like myself, his time at the school was a means to an end, nothing more. As we shared our initial impressions of the program and the other students, I realized Gabe's attitude mirrored mine.

"Man, it seems like some of the other people are here to learn how to learn about life. Me? I'm just here to learn the things I'll need to know when my sight finally goes for good. I'm not concerned with joining any organization or lobbying the government or any of that crap." I gave a silent smile, pleased to know there was someone else here who knew exactly what he wanted. "Yeah, I just need to learn how to use this cane, to cook and use computers. When I do, I'm outta here!" Gabe added as we stepped off the bus. He lit a cigarette and patiently waited for me to explore the area around the bus stop. "Man, I've gotta tell you, I'm kind of envious of you," Gabe said, turning to walk toward the front doors.

"Me? Why?"

"Because your roommate, Robert, is the coolest guy here. I know you haven't met him yet, but he's a great person, not like that dork I'm stuck with!"

Arriving at my new home, I unlocked the door just as the phone began to ring. "Hi there! How was your first day?" asked the cheery voice of my mother.

"It was okay, I guess," I said, not sure whether to boast of the things I'd learned from Trina, or to complain about the absurdity of Business Class.

"Well, we've decided to leave for home tonight," Mom said reluctantly, almost as if she were waiting for me to protest.

"Tonight? You mean now?" I asked with more than a little apprehension.

"Yeah, like now. We'll be by in a few minutes to say good-bye," she said before hanging up.

I knew they decided to leave immediately because, if they stayed, they might have second thoughts about leaving without me. It wasn't just the unfamiliar city and the trauma of the previous year that made the separation difficult. It was clear their presence was not welcome as a part of my rehab process.

Like it or not, this rehabilitation was necessary and it was time to get on with it. I hugged my mom and shook hands with my father, realizing I was about to sink or swim. To leave one's child in such a way had to feel like throwing me to the wolves, but my parents fought through their emotions to do what would ultimately benefit me. As tough as it was, they quietly said goodbye and walked out the door.

Not knowing what else to do, I sat down at the kitchen table with a slate and stylus and practiced writing Braille. Later, the phone rang and Doug, the junior Orientation and Mobility instructor, recited my assignment for the next day. "Meet me at the corner of Evans and Oneida at 7:20 tomorrow morning. We'll catch the bus to the center and I'll teach you some things along the way."

"No problem," I replied, knowing it was only a walk of about 100 feet. I'd be walking solo, but I figured I couldn't go wrong. My second logical assumption was that Doug and I would then cross the four lanes of Evans Avenue together. I'd never crossed a street by myself and damn sure didn't plan to do it my first day of training.

Confident that I understood my instructions, I arrived at the corner at precisely the assigned time. Five minutes passed with no sign of Doug. Then 10 minutes clicked by and I began to get worried. *Am I at the right place?* I asked silently. After another few minutes, I heard the scraping of a cane's metal tip coming down the sidewalk.

"Hi Doug!" I called out.

"Nope, came an unfamiliar voice, "I'm Jesse."

"Sorry about that," I said sheepishly. "Do you know where Doug is? He said to meet him at the corner, but I think he forgot," I said.

"He meant the other corner, where the bus stop is. We meet at that corner every morning." Jesse replied, completely unbothered by the fact I might have stood there all day.

I followed Jesse across the street, silently cursing Doug. In addition to being rude, it was dangerous. I didn't like putting myself in harm's way due to someone else's lousy means of communication. When Jesse and I safely navigated the street and arrived at the bus stop, Doug met us with a warm welcome. "You made it, Marc, and just in time! The bus is coming down the street right now!" I grumbled a response and continued to internalize my anger. If my first lesson was typical of the Center's approach to acquiring skills, then this wasn't going to be any fun.

Later that afternoon, I finally met my roommate, Robert. As we shook hands, he politely said, "Hi, how's it going? Sorry I wasn't around to help you move in the other day. Did you have any trouble?" I smiled as all my preconceived notions of death metal, black leather and satanic rituals melted away. As we chatted, I found Robert to be one of the kindest individuals I'd met. Gabe was right! My new roomie really was a cool person!

We spent the rest of the day getting to know one another. Only five years separated the ages of Robert, Gabe and me. Not only our number of years on this planet, but similar experiences helped to draw us together. After only a few days, the three of us became inseparable friends.

Some of the other students proved less sociable, thereby lending credence to Gabe's original assessment. Many seemed to live in a remote world that revolved around their disability. Some even had no friends or acquaintances that were sighted! Even their pastimes consisted of activities that had been hand created for the blind and nothing more; no television, no professional sports, no movies. I couldn't ignore the obvious differences between our threesome and most other students. The ages, ethnicity and socio-economic status of the students were all fairly similar, so why did our trio seem so different? I posed this question to Robert and Gabe one evening while we sat around a small table at a local watering hole.

"You haven't figured it out yet?" Robert asked, smiling at my obliviousness. "Think about it, Marcus… you, me, Gabe… each of us was once sighted, right?"

"Sure." I said, "But what does that have to do with anything?"

"Well, think of the other people around us. Most don't understand why we'd ever spend time in a place like this, right?" Robert said, making a quick motion with his hand to audibly indicate our surroundings. "It wasn't all that long ago that society shoved blind people into institutions. Plus, if people were born blind, they may have never learned to fly with their own wings. If someone's life has been sheltered from day one, that's a lot to overcome, ya know?"

Robert made a valid point. Those of us who had seen before seemed to regard ourselves as inhabitants of a sighted world, though we just happened to be blind. Many of our fellow classmates seemed to live in a world centered around blindness.

As we sat in the dingy tavern, I asked Robert about his loss of sight.

"I'll tell you everything you want to know," he said, leaning back in his chair before beginning his tale. Robert had been an insulin dependent diabetic since infancy. He had fought a lifelong struggle to regulate his blood sugars until complications caused his blindness two years before. "My lifestyle has never exactly been a healthy one," he stated, flicking open his cigarette lighter for emphasis, "and that probably had something to do with the loss of my sight. I hate being blind and I hate having diabetes, but there's nothing I can do about it now."

Being nearly the same age and having recently lost our visual worlds gave Robert and I common ground from the first night we met. Yet, with all our similarities, our outlooks on life couldn't have been more different. While I had decided to rebuild my life and was always engaged in adjustment and adaptation, Robert's world was a constant struggle; a struggle I tried to combat with encouragement and praise.

"Dude, I'm not trying to give you a motivational speech or anything, but you've got a ton of stuff going for you. Why are you so freaking down on yourself all the time?" I asked, trying to pin him down on his latest episode of self-bashing. Our threesome sat in the living room, stretched out on the couches and the floor, listening to a Led Zeppelin CD. Robert took a deep breath and paused, the room filling with tension. I'd just hit a nerve. Finally, Robert spoke.

"Because it's not just my blindness. I've never told you guys this, but before I lost my sight, I was married. The day I started going blind, my wife walked out on me," Robert's chin fell to his chest as he relived the painful memories. My jaw dropped open and Gabe swore under his breath. The selfishness of some people had me not only baffled, but angry. How could anyone look at Robert and only see his blindness, not the genuinely wonderful human being he was?

"That's not all. About a month before I started going blind, my dad died. He was 45, had been a diabetic all his life, too, and he was my hero. When he died, things started to go downhill. Then, when my sight started going and wife left, it just turned into an avalanche. My friends couldn't deal with me being blind and they pretty much all ditched me. Other than my girlfriend and my grandmother, I've really got no one."

I didn't know what to say. Racing through mental images of all the people who supported and encouraged me, I felt so different from my friend.

"Robert," I said sincerely, "I don't know how comforting this is for you, but from here on out, you've got me as someone on your side."

"Goes double for me," Gabe said, pulling himself up from the floor and grasping Robert's shoulder with a tight grip. From that moment, I knew I had two brothers for life. Several nights later while our threesome was hanging out, there was a knock at the apartment's flimsy door. Robert felt his way around the coffee table, opened the door and a female voice said, "Hi there, you!" before taking him in an embrace.

"Dude, it's not every day that random girls just knock on the door, walk in and hug you! I'd milk that for all it's worth!" I said to Robert, standing to introduce myself to the girlfriend I'd heard so much about. Kira and Robert had been dating for nearly a year; a year that Robert had gone through some of the worst emotional times imaginable. Ever since meeting him, he'd told of how Kira had helped bring him up when he was at his lowest.

"She's great, man, and you're going to love her," he said, smiling with a teasing tone to his voice, "But keep your filthy hands off her! She's mine!"

From that point on, the four of us spent nearly every night together. Sometimes it was an evening out on the town, but more often, we simply lounged around the living room, engrossed in deep conversation. Each of us brought our own backgrounds and stories to the table, each of which was tragic and traumatic in its own way. Our discussions invariably revolved around why these unfortunate events had occurred in our lives. Our nightly discussions became more like group therapy with all of us seated and sharing our souls inside the cramped and smoke-filled apartment.

The three of us mainly dealt with our feelings of loss associated with blindness. Unintentionally each discussion would target whichever one of us needed support the most.

One evening, Gabe arrived in a virtual fury. "I'm crossing the street today, wearing that damned blindfold so I don't rely on that little bit of sight I have when this woman comes up and just grabs me! Here I am, doing just fine on my own, but this person thinks, 'He's blind, he needs help, I'll help him!' Well, she ended up getting me all turned around and I walked three or four blocks before I figured out where I was!" Gabe vented, pacing between the kitchen and the living room. "I know she was just trying to help, but God I wish people would just leave me the hell alone! If I need help, I'll freaking ask for it!"

Robert and I could only mumble agreements. We'd been there before, attempting to negotiate a crossing when a well meaning pedestrian "helps" by tugging at an arm, or worse yet, grabbing the cane. It was Gabe's turn in "the hot seat" and for the next hour, he talked over his frustration at his depleting sight. Through angry tears, he recounted the day when the ophthalmologist had diagnosed the same eye disease as had been suffered by his ancestors before.

After his explosion, Gabe collapsed into silence. Then, his voice at a whisper he said, "I hate even saying this stuff to you guys. After all, I still have quite a bit of my vision. Neither of you guys have any and that makes me feel like the most selfish person in the world." Nothing I could say would change his mind, but I refused to let Gabe think that either Robert or I begrudged him for having partial vision. The conversation wound down and, after we felt like we had solved all the problems we could for one night, Gabe hugged us all goodbye and returned to his apartment. It wouldn't be long until the next of us needed the chance to unload some feelings.

One afternoon, a deliveryman showed up holding a package with my name on it. Unsure of who would be sending me anything, I asked Kira to help me decipher the handwriting on the return address. While she informed me of the sender, I smiled. My benefactor was a young lady I knew had a slight crush on me. As Kira searched the box, she exclaimed, "There's an envelope in here, Marc. Do you want me to open it?"

"Well, I sure can't read it on my own! Have at it!" I was giddy with excitement.

Kira flipped through the pages and said quietly, "There's a letter, and then several poems here, too. Where do you want me to start?"

Poems? And a letter? I was taken aback. My crush had never told me she wrote poetry, but I was about to get a taste of her talent. By the time Kira finished reading I was practically in tears.

"That letter really makes me feel like there's nothing wrong with me," I whispered.

Kira and Robert both gasped, "What?" Robert stepped onto shaky ground and asked, "Why would you say that, Marc? There IS nothing wrong with you, man!"

"Well, I'm blind, my face looks like it was run over by a semi-truck, and those things just aren't at the top of any girl's wish list for a partner!"

My friends were astute and knew this was a glimpse into my true feelings, not just some off-hand comment made at a stressful time. Now, it was my turn in "the hot seat" and I wasn't looking forward to it, but I had no choice. I couldn't take back my comments and the group was ready to help me figure out my feelings, just as I'd done for them.

Those nights when we'd sit and talk for hours, the stereo always played a choice CD with a depressing theme. The music seemed to be an elixir that would lubricate the tears to come, giving the person in the hot seat an extra reason to let their feelings out. Counting Crows and Tori Amos were my choices when it was my turn to cry, but Robert quickly introduced me to Pink Floyd's *The Final Cut*. The CD focused on loss, war, depression and suicide; lyrics which echoed our concerns for the future and our frustration with the present and the past. *The Final Cut* soon became melded with my time in Colorado much as R.E.M.'s song had been cast in stone with the Barnes Hospital experience. By the end of the CD, or the end of a time in the hot seat, each of us learned one universal truth: life will go on.

Often, I'd arrive at school, tired and dragging from a late night discussion with my partners. No matter what, I could not let myself slack off, not even for a day. I focused on the class in which I most needed instruction: Orientation and Mobility. Doug, for whom I still harbored a grudge, taught concurrent classes of O & M with Trina. During the lessons, Trina would don a blindfold and teach cane travel from the perspective of one of her students. I was simply amazed by her abilities. Not only could she travel well while blindfolded, she could teach the sound clues around the intersection simply by focusing with her ears. Bewildered, I asked, "So, do I officially suck if I leave here not being able to travel as well as a part-time blind person?"

Trina laughed and said, "Yes! However, you've got great natural skills with your ears and a good sense of direction, you'll pick this up quickly."

I wasn't so sure, but trusted her opinion. After all, Trina was the guru O & M instructor. If I could graduate with even half of her proficiency, I'd do fine in the real world. Trina soon became more than my teacher, she became my confidant. As the months dragged on and I learned more and more, I felt sure my progress toward the goal of all goals was on track.

One day I shared my plan with Trina. She was the only instructor I trusted with the secret that I was not going to stay at the Colorado Center for 18 months, no way, no how.

"Marc, you're an adult. You choose your own time frame. You've done well at everything I've seen you try and I have no doubt you're going to be fine with what you've learned," she said quietly, glancing around to be sure our conversation was private. "Even if you graduate early, you still need to do the drop."

I swallowed hard. Even equipped with superb O & M skills, I still feared, "The Drop." Upon my arrival in October, I had been informed that there were two requirements for graduation: the preparation of a meal for the entire facility and "The Drop."

"The Drop" was an exercise to determine one's Orientation and Mobility proficiency, yet originally sounded more like a death sentence. I would be driven around for over an hour, a time during which the car would barely go in the same direction twice.

After 60 minutes, I'd be dropped off at an unknown location and forced to find my way back to the school. I'd know nothing of my location and the entire procedure was done on the honor system; no one would follow me, there was no safety net. Gabe, standing nearby, heard other students explaining "The Drop" and stopped the conversation in mid-sentence. "They're right, Marc, but what they're not telling you is that when you're dropped off, you're only permitted to ask a single pedestrian one question, no more." *One question? Yeah, right,* I thought cynically, *no one can do that!*

As the weeks slipped into months, I saw daily improvement in caning proficiency. My travel skills soon surpassed those of some other students and I knew 'The Drop' was possible.

While I pushed myself relentlessly during my classes, we always found time to enjoy ourselves on the weekends. On Friday and Saturday nights, Robert, Gabe, Kira and I would often frequent the clubs on Denver's 16th Street Mall, an outdoor arrangement of shops, restaurants and the best nightlife the Mile High City had to offer. Late one night, we sat in a coffee bar, sipping lattes and talking about our future plans. My plans were known from day one, but Robert and Gabe were unsure of what their next step would be. Sadness encompassed us, each knowing this may be one of our last nights to be together.

"Well, guys, I think we're all better people for having come into contact with one another. I'm going to miss you guys when I'm gone," I said, and we held up our latte cups for a toast. Soon, a waitress came by to tell us the café was closing. Ten minutes later, we left the warmth and smells of fresh-ground coffee when Kira spotted a taxi pulling up to the front door. "Our chariot awaits!" she said, grabbing her coat and keys. As we piled into the cab, Robert, Gabe and I struggled to tuck all three of our awkward canes along the cab's frame. As we situated the canes and slammed the doors, the young cabbie turned to Kira, smiled and asked, "What's up with this? Do you collect blind guys or something?"

Kira leaned forward with a seductive grin and said, "I sure do! Blind guys do it with *feeling!*" Everyone howled as the cabbie took off for home.

As the next week passed, I knew it was time for yours truly to think about hitting the road. Finally, according to my personal schedule, the time had come. Quite predictably, the Center's administration balked at my decision.

"You've only been here for five months," Diane said in a hastily called staff meeting with me in the hot seat, though this wasn't a group session where I'd end up feeling loved and supported.

"I know, but in the last five months, I've accomplished more than most students who've been here three times as long as I have. I'm 110% sure I can do a drop and cook the graduation meal, too. So, the long and short of it is that I'm leaving next week. It's up to the staff to determine whether I leave as a graduate or a quitter."

A discussion and debate quickly erupted. No one wanted to see me, a student who'd accomplished so much, leave with the label of "quitter," but yet I was proposing a precedent that could derail the future of the program. Finally it was decided that I was indeed ready to go.

"Okay, Marc," the administrator said, "I'm comfortable with you graduating, but you will still need to perform the requirements of graduation. So, you know what that means!" I certainly did and I was ready for it! The drop was scheduled for two days later, and it couldn't get here fast enough!

On the morning of the drop, I donned a pair of Levi's, my black Doc Marten boots and a heavy sweatshirt. I hoped it would be enough clothing to ward off the chilly March breeze in case I got lost and spent several hours wandering around. The center's sighted secretary drove me, another student and Doug to my drop location. The area had specifically been picked for me. If I was going to push the program, they were no doubt going to pose a challenge for me, too. After nearly an hour of sporadic driving, the car finally pulled over to the curb and stopped. Opening the door into the brisk March breeze, I tried to appear confident. I knew I could do this, but when the moment of truth arrived, so did the butterflies.

"Remember, Marc…. you can only ask ONE question!" Doug said cheerfully before rolling up his window.

"Screw you," I muttered under my breath, half hoping he'd heard. I had no plan to ask even ONE question, much less cheat and ask more. If I'd come this far, there was no way I would cut corners in this, the last step of the Colorado leg of the journey. "I'll freeze to death before I ask a single question," I muttered under my breath, turning to follow traffic along the sidewalk. The Center was about to receive some instruction in the merits of an individualized learning program!

I began walking and found a sidewalk by dragging the tip of my cane in wide arcs. Turning down the sidewalk, I crossed several small streets with relatively no traffic. After what seemed like miles, but in reality was probably less than five blocks, I came upon a busy street. Cars whizzed past as I turned right and continued down the block. I had no idea which direction I was going, but it really didn't matter. After much thought about the drop, I realized the issue was conceptual. Soon, a plan fell into place. Using the skills Trina had imparted, I would walk in any direction until I happened upon a heavily traveled street. At that point, I would choose a direction and continue on until I reached another large street. With Denver having one of the premier bus lines in the nation, I would surely find a bus stop at the intersection of two busy streets. Soon, I heard the familiar echo from a shelter and several voices standing around it. I waited without speaking, eavesdropping on the conversations. Several minutes later, a bus roared to a stop and the driver, as is required by Denver law, called out the bus route number.

I boarded and took a seat just behind the driver. After a few minutes, he announced another intersection and I nearly laughed! Our location, plus approximately a mile of walking to locate the bus stop added up to nearly 25 miles! "Well," I said to myself, "you did say you wanted to be challenged, Engel!"

An hour and a half later, I walked back into the front doors of the center to a round of applause and cheering from my classmates. I shook hands with my closest friends and hugged Trina. "As a reward for completing your drop successfully, you get to go skiing tomorrow!" Trina said excitedly. Both times I'd tried skiing, it was painful to my leg and an annoyance to my pride. The last time, my guide had been an elderly volunteer who made me feel like I was sticking out like a sore thumb. "Here you go, put this on," the guide had said, handing me a plastic vest that strapped over and around my ski parka. "It's day-glo orange and identifies you as a blind skier," she said, having no idea that being labeled as such may have been a safety precaution, but made me feel like a freak. Once we had slid off the lift, she positioned herself in front of me, actually skiing backwards down the mountain while holding the tips of my skis with her hands. *She's gotta be bent over, going down the mountain butt first!* I thought warily. What a sight to be riding up the lift, look down and see a day-glo blind guy being led down the mountain by an old woman's ass! It wasn't an experience I necessarily wanted to have again.

"I think I'll pass on the skiing tomorrow," I said to Trina, "I've got some good-byes to say and I need to pack to go home!"

Home! It almost hadn't seemed real until that moment, but in just a few days, I'd be out of Denver, out of the Colorado Center and back on my journey once again!

That night, our foursome sat in the living room for what would probably be our last time together. Even though I'd gained so many new skills, the most profound benefit of my time in Denver was the bond I'd formed with Robert, Gabe, Kira and Trina. I owed each of them a debt of gratitude for believing in me, supporting my decisions and just for being there and making me feel like a normal person again. While the stereo cranked out Roger Water's voice and guitar, I almost felt as if I were at a funeral. I'd accomplished what I came here to do. It was time to move on.

Three days later, my sister and her fiancé arrived at my apartment, ready to help me move home.

After the last box had been packed into the trunk, Robert, Gabe and Kira met me at the front door. I shuffled my feet and said, "I guess this is good-bye, huh?" Before the tears could come, I hugged them tight and said, "Thank you guys so, so much! I can't even tell you how much you've helped me!" Without drawing out the parting, I turned and walked to the elevator, my canes tip echoing off of the courtyard. It was the last time I'd ever hear that sound and, strangely enough, I knew I'd miss it.

As we pulled away from the apartment complex and headed back to I-70, I couldn't help but think over my time spent in Colorado. In spite of all of my head bumping with the administration, I will always be the first to admit how much the Center helped me. I thought back to my first day of school and the first ever "business of being blind" class. I couldn't help but remember the director and her statement, "Blindness should be regarded as simply a trait like having red hair." At the time, I thought how absurd that idea was. Now, I wasn't so sure. After all, blindness still controlled my life, but the Center, my friends and my education had helped to create a person, me, who no longer thought of his blindness as such a limitation.

After several dull hours in the car, Cathy read a road sign that exclaimed, "Welcome to Kansas!" To me, it was a farewell, not a greeting. I wiped away a single tear, thinking over the friends I'd left behind. As I thought about the geographical and practical moves I was now making, the tears I held back were more from joy than sadness. Putting Colorado behind me meant I was one step closer to reaching my goal.

Soon, very soon, the dream of returning to college would become a reality.

Chapter 16

"The thin horizon of a plan is almost clear.
My friends and I have had a hard time
Bruising our brains hard up against change..." [23]

~ Indigo Girls

"Flight 722 with service to Newark is now boarding," came the scratchy voice over the P.A. system.

I stood and gave the attendant my ticket. Navigating my way down the ramp, I felt excitement beginning to grow. When the plane landed, I'd be in New Jersey and one step closer to achieving my goal. Tomorrow, I thought happily, I'll be getting a Seeing Eye dog! I was as ecstatic as a kid receiving a puppy for Christmas, but this was no ordinary puppy!

The Seeing Eye, Inc. in Morristown, NJ is the original guide dog training facility in the country. Only dogs that are raised and trained at this school may properly bear the name, Seeing Eye dog, rather than the general term, "guide dog." The rich history of the facility dates back to the early part of the 20th century when an increasing number of American soldiers returned from World War 1 after being blinded on the battlefield. The school soon blossomed into the flagship guide dog training facility in the country and gained global respect.

Unsure of what to expect during the month of training, I spent the flight thinking over the various possibilities. My choices for a breed were limited to Labrador Retrievers, German Shepherds and Golden Retriever; dogs that have the size, intelligence and temperament necessary for their work. I also wondered about what the training would be like.

An assistant from the Seeing Eye met me at the airport gate, helped collect my luggage and escorted me to the waiting car. An hour later the limo service pulled into the grounds of the Seeing Eye. As I stepped out of the car I received an enthusiastic greeting.

"Welcome to the Seeing Eye, Marcus! I'm Lori, I'll be your trainer while you're here." She gathered my suitcases and showed me to my home for the next month; a typical dorm room with a private bath.

"I'll need to collect the payment for your dog and then I'll give you a run down of what you'll be doing here," Lori said.

Reaching into my wallet, I pulled out three $50 bills, an embarrassingly small fee considering the estimated $25, 000 cost of training a Seeing Eye dog. Very few people could afford the training cost without the corporate and private financial donations to the not-for-profit institution.

"So, you're going to be a college student?" Lori asked, looking over the extensive paperwork I'd sent in.

"Yep! Once I'm done here, I'll be back in college," I said, hardly believing that my goal was on the horizon, almost within my grasp.

"So, what kind of dog will work best for you Marcus?"

"Uhhh, the only dog I've ever had was an obese beagle when I was a kid."

Lori laughed. "We'll make sure you get a dog that fits a college environment. One who will sit through classes and be quiet when necessary, but will also enjoy your social outings. Do you go to a lot of parties and sporting events?"

"Definitely!!" I answered; glad they didn't expect me to sit home all the time.

"Anything else you're looking for?"

I flashed a shy smile and asked, "Can you make sure the dog has a really cool name?" A two year old, fully trained dog's name was not going to be changed just to accommodate my ridiculous request.

Lori laughed and said sarcastically, "Oh, you're not picky at all, are you?" She gathered the paperwork, and said, "I'll be back in just a second."

Lori returned, handed me a leash, and said, "Give this a tug… as hard as you can!"

"You sure you want me to do that?" I asked, knowing from the height of her voice that she was a petite person.

"Yeah, go ahead. I won't break, " she promised, bracing herself. I pulled back on the leash, popping it hard.

Lori stepped forward with the momentum of the pull. Her muffled laugh told me that she was well aware my demonstration of strength was more powerful than necessary. "You could put a choke chain on a horse with a tug like that, Marcus," she laughed.

She scribbled down a few more notes on her clipboard and opened the door. "Okay, onto test number two," she said, stepping into the carpeted hallway. "Here, place your hand like this," she said, showing me where to grip the leather clad harness handle.

"Like this?" I asked, gesturing with my free hand.

"Yep, exactly! Now, keep your right arm straight, your palm flat and raise your arm like you're pointing straight ahead. As you raise your arm, you're going to use your dog's name and then say, 'Forward!'"

I felt a little foolish giving Lori commands like a dog, but did as I was told. She shot ahead as soon as "Forward!" was out of my mouth. I recoiled from the abrupt start, but quickly regained my footing and we were off! We walked for about 100 feet; long enough to get a good feel of speed and pull.

"Too fast or too slow?" came Lori's question as I trotted behind her.

"Let's kick it up a notch and see what happens!"

She quickened her pace until I was nearly being dragged behind her.

"How's this?" she asked, hearing my heavy breathing.

"Are you thinking of giving me a Seeing Eye cheetah?"

Lori smiled. "You'd be surprised at how fast some of these dogs walk, so make sure you're comfortable when we're testing this out." Finally, I decided on a pace that felt good and it was on to test number three.

"We need to see what sort of pull you want. Some dogs walk at a quick pace, but with very little tug on the harness. Some pull like they're hauling a dog sled, so find what's comfortable for you." We continued down the hall for a few minutes, testing every aspect of a dog's movements. By the time we were done, I was confused. I wasn't sure whether I'd passed the test or not, or if there even was a failing grade.

Once back inside, we joined the other students in the lounge. There were 25 students in this April session, but only four of us were first time dog users. As we introduced ourselves, I was surprised to meet people from so many other states; even a few from Canada.

Soon after our initial introductions, we met Pete Jackson, a lead coordinator of trainers and someone who would be personally overseeing my group. "We don't have a curfew around here, but be sure you're getting plenty of sleep. You might be walking 10 or 20 miles per day, so be ready." Pete explained in his distinct Jersey accent. Concluding his welcoming statements, he left us to get to know one another.

I turned and introduced myself to Jim, a sculptor from Pennsylvania who would be receiving his second dog. Within a few minutes, we were telling off-color stories and laughing like old friends.

"Have you been blind all your life?" I asked, hoping my prying was not offensive.

"Yeah, basically. I had partial vision up until I was 20 or so, enough that I could make out the centerfold in a Playboy magazine if I held it about three inches from my nose!" Jim was my kind of guy!

Just a few seats away, I heard a young sounding man with a thick Texas accent conversing with a woman from Long Island. His southern drawl stuck out around so many east coast voices. I stood up, changed seats and introduced myself to the Texan, a first timer to the Seeing Eye named Ron Graham.

"Pleasure to meet you," I said, shaking his hand.

"This will be your first dog, too?" he asked.

"Yep! I've been waiting for this day for the last year and a half, ever since I lost my sight."

"How'd you lose your sight?" Ron asked, not tiptoeing around the issue.

"Car crash," I said, "I lost my sight, broke every bone in my face, lots of bad stuff like that."

Ron paused, "Wow, I lost my sight in a car crash, too."

Really? I'd met scores of other blind people, but only one who had lost his sight in a car wreck. "How long ago?" I asked, feeling strangely apprehensive.

"About 18 months, give or take."

18 months? I felt an icy finger raise the hair on the back of my neck. "When exactly?" My voice quivered.

Ron paused for what seemed an eternity. "October 9th of '93."

My heart stopped. I took a deep breath, then another.

"No shit, dude?" I blurted out, my blood now pumping. "Ron, I don't know if you're going to believe this, but that's the night I lost my sight, too."

Ron was only able to choke out a one-word question, "Really?"

I grunted a reply and sat motionless, trying to believe what was happening. For the next hour, we compared notes about the horrific experiences we'd endured that fateful autumn night.

"Yeah, my wreck wasn't pretty, either," Ron said. "A buddy and I were driving back from Lubbock and we flipped a Dodge Intrepid into a cotton field at 110 miles per hour. I was thrown from the car and woke up face down in the dirt. I was in a coma for the next couple of months. I don't remember anything from that time." My heart thudded in my chest.

Ron and I talked late into the night, each of us hanging on the other's every word. I felt so shell shocked that I wanted to sit there speechless, but the "coincidences" that had led us to the same place at the same time were so unbelievable that I just had to learn more, to get the information in my brain as quickly as possible, almost as if it would slip away as soon as Ron and I parted company.

In the 18 months since losing my sight, I'd found no one who could really relate to what I'd been through. Suddenly, a thousand miles from either of our homes, I was sitting three feet away from someone who had been through a nearly identical experience.

As I retired to my room, my head was flooded with this astronomical improbability. Bewildered and exhausted, I could only believe something more powerful than us had arranged our meeting.

Early the next morning, I was awakened out of a sound sleep by the raucous barking of dogs outside my window. Far away, a voice could be heard calling commands, as the barking grew louder. "Any of you guys want to be paired with me?" I asked the glorious bedlam, grinning with the knowledge that, in just a few short hours, I'd have my very own Seeing Eye dog. After showering and dressing, I went to the dining room for breakfast where I sat with Ron. I was anxious to get to know him as a person, not just as a guy with whom I shared a not-so-happy anniversary.

Lori sat down with us and asked, "So, Ron, how's the knee doing?"

"It's doing a lot better. I still need to do exercises and wear the brace, but it shouldn't hold me up at all," Ron reported cheerfully.

"Did you hurt your knee in the crash?" I asked.

"No, actually I started this program back in January. I slipped on a patch of ice and tore some ligaments. I hobbled around on it for a few days until I just couldn't stand it any more. I went back home to Texas, had surgery and lots of physical therapy." I listened, not believing what I was hearing.

Ron continued. "Yeah, I started on January 5th, then slipped on the ice on January 11th. The Seeing Eye was kind enough to keep Quarry, my dog, in training and I'm anxious to get reacquainted with him."

January 11th? I felt that same icy finger slip up the back of my neck.

"Ron," I said calmly, "January 11th is the day the Seeing Eye called to tell me I'd been accepted for the April session."

I wasn't excited, wasn't bouncing off the walls with another "coincidence." In fact, I was a little afraid; afraid of just how obvious it was for us to now be together, almost like a master plan. We sat in stunned silence for a few moments, trying to let everything sink in. I was now convinced, beyond a doubt, our meeting had been arranged.

Finally Ron said, "I don't care what brought us to this place at this time, but I'm damned glad to know you, Marcus." I echoed Ron's sentiments.

Later in the afternoon, I was introduced to the four-legged reason I'd come to New Jersey. The Seeing Eye dogs, soon to be separated from their trainers, were now prepared to meet their new masters. Over lunch, Lori and the other trainers briefed us on what to expect.

"Keep in mind, these puppies have been trained here by us for the last five months. Some will take to their new master immediately, but not always. I've seen a few cases where the dogs cowered and hid from the students. If that happens, do not take it personally! They'll come around soon! The more love and attention you give your dog, the more quickly they will bond with you!"

I hoped and prayed my dog would like me. Could there be anything worse than being dissed by man's best friend?

An hour later, there was a knock at my door. "Ready to go meet your new pal?" Lori asked happily.

"Yep! Let's do it!" I said, trying to sound more confident than I felt.

Lori led me to the lounge and ushered me to a seat near the door. As I sat down, I could hear heavy panting coming from my one o'clock angle. The April afternoon was warm, but certainly not hot enough to warrant the heavy breathing that animal was putting out! "This panting guy in the corner is your dog, Marcus. His name is Dasher and he's a black Lab. I'm going to take him off his leash and you can call him to come to you," Lori said.

We'd been instructed that the dogs were probably just as nervous as we were, though I found this hard to believe. My hands trembled like the aftershocks from an earthquake. I held my breath while she unleashed the dog that would be my constant companion and guide.

I bent slightly at the waist to pat my leg and called, "Come here, Dasher!" It was the moment of truth and, for a microsecond, I wasn't sure if Dasher would obey. Then, from across the room, there came a thundering roar. Visions of stampeding cattle rushed through my mind. The next thing I knew, his paws were on my knees and there was a giant Labrador head bumping my chin. In a split second, Dasher flopped onto his back, all four feet in the air and begged for a belly rub. Reaching down to touch the soft fur of my new friend, I repeated his name.

"Hi Dasher!" I said warmly as I fulfilled his needs for some well deserved affection. "How ya' doing, boy?" I asked. His answer came in the form of his heavy tail thudding against the carpeting. He squirmed and batted my wrists with his paws, virtually saying, "Pet me! Don't stop!"

I sat on the floor for a few minutes, stroking his sides and head, overwhelmed by the fact I was actually touching the third portion of the journey back to college… and what a beautiful and energetic part of the goal he was!

"You guys think you'll get along?" Lori asked, smiling and giving Dasher an occasional pat on his thick snout. Dasher answered for me, hopping up in a flash, then giving a monstrous shake while his tail beat back and forth.

Once back in our room, I sat cross legged on the floor with my new friend. I slowly trailed my hand from his nose to the tip of his tail, getting to know every curve of his body. I just couldn't believe how beautiful he was! His fur was as soft as mink, ears like silk and a nose like a cold, wet thumb. He never tired of playing and I was more than happy to oblige.

After what seemed like hours, he laid down on the floor,

practically curling his body around my legs. He laid his head in my lap and let out a great, satisfied sigh. My fingers massaged his neck and silky ears, all the while his tail thumping the floor.

"Think you can handle college with me, big guy? It should be lots of fun for both of us! We'll be going to classes and parties, playing on campus, all sorts of good stuff!" His tail never stopped wagging, almost as if he could comprehend what I was saying. "I tell ya, Dasher, if you act this sweet to other people, there should be lots of belly rubs from cute girls, too!" Admittedly, this held more benefit for me, but I doubted Dasher would turn down attention from anyone!

That afternoon began a process of emotional rebuilding I didn't even know I needed. With the introduction of Dasher, my existence became a degree brighter. Seated on a tile floor in New Jersey with a black Labrador in my lap, I could only imagine what benefits my new friend would bring.

For the next four weeks, Dasher and I learned the ropes together. Our training quickly progressed from quiet neighborhood streets to large, difficult and crowded intersections. At every street crossing, Dasher would maneuver through the crowd of pedestrians and plant us on the wheelchair ramp that emptied into the street. As soon as I heard the parallel traffic begin to move, I'd command Dasher with the proper hand signal and by saying, "Forward!"

As we trained, I grew more confident with Dasher's ability to steer me around obstacles, as well as becoming more comfortable with putting my life in his paws. As we walked down South Street in Morristown, Dasher weaved in and out of tables, potted plants and racks of merchandise from shops. During the lunch hour, Dasher was especially tempted by the morsels of meals that had been eaten at the outdoor cafes. If he became distracted by food, other dogs or gutsy urban pigeons, a simple punitive word would set him back on the straight and narrow in a flash.

One afternoon as Dasher and I reached a corner, safe and sound, I bent down to give him some pats and praise as we waited for the light to change. When it was safe we stepped into the intersection. Dasher pulled forward with the gusto of a dog in control when, in a flash, he stopped, dipped his head and took three quick steps back. Just then, a truck shot in front of us, missing me by inches. The vehicle was so close I could feel the rush of the passing breeze and hear the song on the stereo.

I stood motionless, wondering what I should do when a quiet voice behind me said, "Marcus, give him his forward command." It was Lori, trailing me down the block incognito, observing my skill and Dasher's behavior along the way. When we reached the safety of the other corner, Lori stepped up and gave an enthusiastic, "Excellent job, you guys! Lots of praise for Dasher here, too! Do you know what happened there, Marc?"

"Um, yeah. Dasher and I almost got squashed by a car!" I replied, bending down to praise my friend.

"No, not at all. True, there was a car that swept around the corner. That is called a traffic check. Did you feel Dasher stop and take a step or two back?"

"Sure," I said, scratching Dasher under his chin.

"Good! The dogs are taught intelligent disobedience and that was a great example of it. If Dasher recognizes a dangerous situation, he will disobey commands in order to keep you safe. In this case, he saw a car coming, stopped dead in his tracks, then stepped back to move you out of the way," Lori explained.

I was amazed, but also a little shaken. What kind of disaster would there have been if Dasher hadn't been with me? I shuddered at the thought. Confidence in my four-legged friend jumped up a few more notches.

During the last week of training, only the four first time dog users remained. Ron and I had more time to train together and examine our other similarities in life. As we chatted one day with our instructors about the peculiarities of all our "coincidences," Lori looked down and exclaimed, "Oh my God! You guys are wearing the same shoes!" Ron and I just laughed at yet another mirror image of our personalities.

At breakfast the next morning, Pete Jackson said, "You guys ready to head into the Big Apple today?" Ron and I were both ready for the challenge, but not without some trepidation. We knew a trip into the city wasn't required, but we'd decided to do everything together our last days in New Jersey.

"I don't know about you, Ron, but this is a little scary for a small town boy like me!" I said, laughing.

Thirty minutes later, we met the trainers at the front doors, crowded into the Seeing Eye van and set out for New York. With all the stories I'd heard about the subway system, I was pretty apprehensive. Dasher didn't seem to be the least bit intimidated.

We traveled all over Manhattan by subway, by bus and by walking. Our training took us to the Empire State Building, the Port Authority, through Macy's Department store, and down the crowded fish and produce vendor lined streets of Chinatown. We finished our training with a celebratory meal at a great Italian restaurant in Little Italy. With every step I took down the streets of New York, my confidence in my own abilities, as well as Dasher's ability, grew to unimaginable proportions. On the van ride home, I leaned down and patted Dasher with compliments galore. "Dasher dog, if you can handle New York, the campus of SMSU is going to be a breeze."

Finally, the month in New Jersey drew to a close. I walked out the doors of the Seeing Eye feeling as though I'd just experienced one of the best times of my life. Ron and I hopped into the van, melancholy since our last outing would lead to our parting at the airport. I wasn't sure what to say on the ride and stayed silent most of the way. Leaving Ron was going to be nearly as hard as leaving Robert, Gabe and Kira in Colorado, but once again, it was time to move on.

After being dropped at the front doors of Newark Airport, we checked our bags and I fought back tears. Ron and I exchanged bear hugs as our paths were about to be diverted. We had grown so close in our month together that I felt like I was embracing my own brother. There was no way this friendship would be temporary or easily interrupted by distance.

As I sat down on the plane headed back to St. Louis I whispered to Dasher, "Hey, buddy, we're going to have an awesome life together." Dasher sighed happily. I wish it had been as easy to convince myself of the bright prospect for the future. With the words of promise I'd just made still ringing in my ears, I repeated my mantra. "No looking back, Engel," I whispered to myself, "Most definitely, no looking back!"

Chapter 17

"When the Bible is a bottle, and a hardwood floor is home,
When morning comes twice a day or not at all,
If I break in two, will you put me back together?
When this puzzle is figured out, will you still be around?" [24]

~ Uncle Tupelo

"**M**arcus! It's so good to meet you at last!" A young sound-ing man said as he approached. "I'm the residence hall director and everything is set for you to move in. All I need is a sig-nature on this form and you're ready to go!" As I signed the forms, my hands shook with anticipation. The entire three hour ride to Springfield had been spent fretting over anything and everything that could go wrong. The last two years had been like walking through a minefield of unexpected snags. Surely, now that I was again standing inside the dorm that was a virtual Mecca, nothing else could go wrong... could it?

"Here's your room key, security card and a welcome packet, too," he said, handing me a bag filled with ink pens and refrigera-tor magnets advertising a slew of pizza delivery places.

I thanked him and walked toward the hallway of the first floor. As I stepped out of the lobby, I felt like I was in a time warp. "God, this place even smells the same," I mumbled, turning to my right and facing the lounge. I could almost see the carpeted floors and seating area around the grand piano.

"This is surreal," I whispered as I slid the key into the lock of my new home.

We spent the rest of the afternoon arranging my belongings and setting up the brand new computer with adaptive software. *I was home again!*

The tension of the day, as well as carrying boxes by the score had caught up with me. Exhausted and aching, I crawled into bed and slept as if I'd downed a gallon of NyQuil.

The next morning, I walked around campus with my sister. As we strolled through the dorms and classroom buildings, memories of my days as a sighted student came flooding back. "Okay, Marc, the Student Union is on your right. Do you remember what's on your left?"

"Yeah, first is Wells House, then comes Siceluff Hall, right?" Being back on campus sparked all sorts of logistical memories. "As we make a left in front of Siceluff, we're on the quad, right?"

Cathy was amazed at the precision of my visual memory and, frankly, so was I! I had no idea how much those six short weeks of sight would help when traveling around campus.

I only registered for one class that summer, thinking it would be wise to ease back into the world of academia. The sociology class was scheduled for 7:30 a.m., Monday through Thursday. Two years ago the early morning class would have set off major complaints. Somehow, it no longer seemed much of an inconvenience.

The first morning of summer school, I woke at 5:30 a.m. to take Dasher out and get myself ready. I stood at the closet for what seemed like an eternity just figuring out what to wear. After all, this was my first day back to the dream that had sustained me for nearly two years. I was as close to Cinderella going to the ball as I was ever going to get! Finally I decided on a pair of shorts and a golf shirt. As I dressed and gathered my backpack up, I played out the potential scenarios. I'd done this no less than a thousand times the previous week, trying to think over every possible pitfall. Worries, doubts and fears still haunted me, but at least I was now about to find out if they had any validity. I shoved my laptop into my backpack, stepped into the hallway and locked the door. Pausing for a moment, I took a deep breath and composed myself. The last thing I needed was to get lost on the way to my first day of class.

"Okay, Dasher, here we go!" I said nervously. He took off like a shot as soon as "forward!" was out of my mouth. Soon, we were out of the dorm and headed down the sidewalk. As we walked along Harrison Street I thought, "So far, so good."

Dasher weaved around pedestrians and led me straight to the door of the correct building. As soon as my hand touched the familiar door handle, I bent down to hug Dasher for helping to make our first solo trip a success! Rubbing his neck and praising him, I whispered in his ear, "Now, lets go and see if we can find the right room!" Dasher's tail wagged furiously as we stepped into the building and down the short hallway. Hanging a quick right we stepped directly into the correct classroom.

"Good job, buddy! You rock, Dashman!" His tail swatted back and forth and he raised his chin high in the air, almost as if to say, "Yeah, you're right! I'm the bomb!"

I sat down and patiently waited while the rest of the sleepy students trickled in. A few minutes later, the professor entered and greeted us with warm sincerity.

"I'm Dr. Michael Carlie and this is Sociology 150," he said, smiling. Even as he took attendance it was obvious Dr. Carlie was a dynamic teacher and thoroughly enjoyed his job. I definitely wouldn't be slipping into any early morning naps during these lectures!

After the class had ended, he approached and asked if we could talk about how I would handle the assignments. "Sure," I said, thankful he recognized the fact there would be some differences between me and the other students.

"How do you prefer to handle the weekly quizzes, Marcus?" he asked, waiting for the final student to leave before posing the question.

"I guess I'll get an assistant from the disability support services office to read the test," I said, but Dr. Carlie was already shaking his head.

"Completely unnecessary. Each quiz is only 10 questions long. I don't want to have a reader get here at 7:30 in the morning for a five minute quiz. Would it be okay if you and I just stepped out into the hall and I read the quiz to you?"

Dr. Carlie had just empowered someone who was quite possibly the most helpless person in the class. How? Just by posing the simple question and allowing me to fill the role of decision maker. It was only the beginning of my introduction to just how incredible Dr. Carlie would be as the professor who aided my reentry to college.

Later in the week, the early morning class commenced by Dr. Carlie rolling in a video player and television. "Today, we're going to be watching a film on the interaction of rival street gangs in L.A.," he began. "I want you to see the different symbols each gang uses to identify one another, their common lingo and the division of power within the gang. Take notes, the video's information might be on the next quiz." As the other students grabbed notebooks and pencils, Dr. Carlie pulled up a seat next to me and whispered, "I'll give you a description of what's going on." Instead of announcing his plan to the class, he allowed me to retain a degree of anonymity.

I was pleased to find my classmates didn't seem especially interested in the fact I was a blind student. They were, however, quite intrigued by Dasher. During our breaks, I'd take off his harness and he'd flop on his back begging for belly rubs. Even the most disinterested students had to smile when Dasher would nuzzle up to their legs.

During our daily break, a small group of girls gathered to pet Dasher, showering him with the usual, "Oh, you're so cute!" comments. One of Dasher's fan club asked, "How old is he?"

"He just turned two a couple of months ago," I said.

This sparked another question from a different girl. The next thing I knew, we'd spent the entire break talking about Dasher, how he worked and what his jobs were. As Dr. Carlie began the second half of class, I patted Dasher on the head. "Good job helping me meet chicks there, buddy!" I whispered. Dasher just licked my hand and seemed to say, "No problem, Boss!"

My fantasies about returning to college and immediately throwing myself back into fun, friends, social life and flirtation with girls were soon deflated. I didn't see my friends nearly as often as I would have liked. Their lives had also changed during my absence, a fact I had a hard time swallowing that first summer back. Often my only social contacts in a full day were in Dr. Carlie's class; and it ended by 9:30 in the morning. I'd spend endless hours in my dorm room, wishing I could have a life like the one I remembered. After all, I was back in college, right? Tons of people my age, fun and parties all the time, right? Sadly enough, that was the furthest thing from what my life was like. My disappointment and loneliness grew with each passing day.

"Engel," I told myself, "You've got to get out of this rut. You need to go out and do some things on your own. Take walks, go grab a cup of coffee in the cafeteria, just do something, already!" But, I just couldn't. I was too self-conscious, too shy and too afraid that, if I did walk across campus, I might get lost and look foolish wandering around aimlessly. Insecurity and pride being the determining factors, I locked myself away from everyone and everything. I'd worked for two years to return to college, only to discover that "the goal of all goals" marked the end of a physical journey, nothing more. Now, a new goal emerged, one that seemed even more insurmountable than the first; to adapt to blindness and find happiness and contentment.

One Friday evening I was shocked when the phone rang.

"Marc? Hey, it's Jill. How's it going?" a smiling voice asked. Jill was a friend from high school, as well as a fellow SMSU student.

"Fine… what's going on with you?" I asked, hoping I'd not be spending another weekend night alone in my dorm room.

"The girls and I are hosting a little shin-dig tonight. You wanna come over?"

"Sure… sounds good," I said, trying to control the excitement in my voice. It was Friday night in a college town and I was heading for a party. Maybe things were looking up! Two hours later, I walked into Jill's apartment with Dasher in the lead.

"Hi there, sweetie! Oh, you're so cute!" said a female voice, already bending down to love on Dasher.

"Thanks, darling, you're not too bad yourself!" I said, pretending to think the compliments were for me. The girl, one of Jill's three roommates, laughed and introduced herself, disregarding my blindness and treating me like any other guest. Within an hour, the apartment was filled with college students, a blasting stereo and a cloud of blue smoke hanging over everyone's head. I was having a great time, learning to interact and make small talk for the first time in a couple of years. Jill didn't hover around to make sure I was okay, but instead just left me to learn to interact again on my own. It was the best thing she could have done and soon, I was even approaching unfamiliar voices and introducing myself.

As the night roared on, Jill slipped up beside me, reached into my arm and whispered, "My roommate thinks you're hot!" My heart did a little flip flop. *Really?* The possibility a female thought

I was attractive was an awesome ego boost, though I wasn't sure I believed it.

Later in the evening, I stood in the kitchen which grew smaller and smaller with every additional partygoer who entered. I stood talking with Jill's roommate when a flood of new people walked into the apartment. A cheer went up with the newcomers and the crowd grew even larger. The roommate and I were squeezed together as more people crowded into the kitchen. Soon, her body was pressed up against mine. Suddenly, she reached up behind my neck and pulled my head toward hers, placing her mouth on mine. For the first time in over two years, I was once again kissing a woman. Stunned, I wasn't quite sure what to do. I'd wondered if I'd ever again kiss a girl and, if I did get so lucky, what would it be like? Nerve damage in my face, limited jaw movement and all the dental work that had been done over the last two years all added up to the mechanics of kissing being in question. However, as I stood there in liplock with this virtual stranger, I was finding that all those things didn't really matter. Once I was certain I wasn't drooling down her chin, I settled in to enjoy it. After the party broke up, we kissed once more before I headed home. I was walking on air and felt, for the first time in two years, a little like the person I wanted to be.

As the summer continued, my old friend, Travis, helped me to map out the campus. One day, as we walked and talked, Travis asked, "You want to grab some dinner at happy hour? There's a great Tex-Mex place I want to show you." After a few more spins around the quad, we headed for some much needed refreshment.

While we ate and drank, Travis interrupted the crunch of nachos and said, "Well, man, I think I'm going to do it."

"Do what?" I asked, scooping up a tortilla full of sour cream.

"I'm going to pledge a fraternity this fall," he said, gauging my reaction.

My heart sank. "That's cool, I guess," I said, trying to sound pleased for him, but failing miserably. Secretly, I was worried. Pledgeship was a major time commitment. I had not moved heaven and earth to get back to college only to hear my friend say, "Sorry dude, I don't have time for you anymore." I was certain this was about to happen with Travis. I left dinner still hurt and feeling sure our time together would soon come to a screeching halt.

Plus, I was just plain jealous. I'd always wanted to pledge a fraternity. It sounded like such an incredible experience. Parties, girls, fun, secrets, tight brotherhood – all part of living the college life. However, when I should have been pledging, I was undergoing a 20-hour facial reconstruction and being fed through a tube. I considered the possibility of pledging with Travis, but quickly dismissed it. Would any fraternity want a blind guy with facial trauma and all the extra time Dasher and I required? I thought not.

As I laid in bed that night and thought about the upcoming fall semester, apprehension continued to form a tight fist in the pit of my stomach. What other crappy things were waiting around the next corner? What hadn't I even thought to worry about yet? Was I going to have any friends left? I fell asleep feeling the downward spiral was only beginning.

Soon after fall classes began, I received a call from my sister. "Marc, my friend Hilary has the same English class as you!"

"Is she hot?" I asked, completely serious.

Cathy sighed, "Yeah, she's cute, but she has a boyfriend." *Oh well, easy come easy go.* "Hilary said if you need any help with your English class to call her. She lives upstairs from you in New Hall, so she said it's no big deal to run down and read the stuff."

"She's not stupid, is she?" I asked, images flashing into my mind of a blubbering idiot with a book on her lap trying to sound out words.

"Hardly! She's pre-med, they don't have too many stupid people who are going to be doctors!" I fought off the urge to argue that I had, in fact, had quite a few doctors who were imbeciles.

The next day after English class, a quiet voice approached and said, "Hi Marc. I'm Hilary, Cathy's friend. She said you might need help with the readings?"

"Yeah, the books are being recorded now, but the tapes haven't come in yet."

"Well, just give me a call when you're ready," she said after we'd exchanged numbers. "I'm free all weekend, so whenever is best for you."

I hated to ask for help and loathed the possibility Hilary might think I was helpless and backwards, but I really had no choice. Until the books arrived on tape, I was stuck having to swallow my pride.

The following Sunday, I dialed Hilary's number, but hung up before it rang. God, I hated asking for help. With a shaking hand, I pressed re-dial and forced myself to let the call go through.

"Hilary? Hi, this is Marc Engel from English class. I was just wondering if you still planned on reading that assignment," I asked, fingers crossed.

"Yeah, I guess so. I've looked over it a little bit already. If you want me to come down and read it, I'm free this afternoon." I accepted and, an hour later, there was a knock at the door. "Hi there, it's Hilary," the same shy voice from English class said, "how's it going?"

"Fine, thanks for helping out with this. I really appreciate it."

"It's no problem. I've got to read it anyway, so I might as well read it out loud," she said, already making me feel like less of a charity case. "I'm warning you ahead of time, I'm probably not the best reader in the world. After today, you may never want to study with me again!" I chuckled.

The assignment was to read an article by a political scientist concerning the entrepreneurial spirit in America, a topic which interested both of us about as much as the early Romanian history of hammock weaving.

After an hour, in the middle of an especially dull sentence, Hilary burst out, "This is the most God-awful boring thing I've ever read! I'm really sorry I can't make this sound more exciting, but this assignment just sucks!" I laughed, realizing I was seeing a new side of Hilary. The ice was broken and we took a break from reading. The recess turned into an afternoon of just hanging out and getting to know one another.

"So, what do you think of that English teacher?" I asked, hoping Hilary's opinion was the same as mine.

"Oh, god, Marc!" she exclaimed, "This woman is the biggest flake! She's nice and all, but she's just one of those people you can look at and say, 'Yep, definitely a flake!'" I fell over laughing as Hilary's quietness faded and she went into a hilarious description of just how badly the professor dressed. That led into both of us laughing at how odd the other students in our class were.

"That girl you sat by the other day, remember her? This morning, I saw her doing a handstand on a park bench by the library... and she was wearing a skirt!" I was laughing so hard I almost peed my pants!

After another hour of chatting, Hilary said, "Well, I'd better get outta here. See you in class tomorrow!"

As the semester progressed, so did our friendship. Our social times became nearly as frequent as our study sessions and were much more enjoyable. Her shyness melted away around me and I no longer thought of her as a quiet person. I realized I was growing too. Just realizing I could still make friends with new people was like conquering the summit of a mountain.

At one of our weekly study sessions, I had some good news for Hilary. "I spoke to my rehab counselor today and he said the state actually gives out money to pay readers like you!" No college student in her right mind would turn down cash – or so I thought.

"I don't want it," Hilary said, throwing her backpack onto my bed, "You think I'm only helping you out? This is helping me, too. It forces me to actually read the assignment. Besides, I've made a new friend! That's worth more than five bucks per hour from the state," she said, and the matter was closed.

At the end of our study session, I said, "Okay, if you won't take the money, can I at least buy you dinner? I'm starving!"

"Yes," Hilary said, "I want pizza. And get sausage on it, Mister!" she teased as I dialed one of the dozens of delivery chains.

One afternoon I was approached by a student who pushed several small pieces of paper into my hand. "Here ya go! These are tickets to the SMSU Drama Team's production of 'Hair.'" I shoved the tickets in my pocket, having no real desire to go to a play.

Later that afternoon, Hilary called and whined, "There were people giving away tickets to *Hair* today, but I didn't get any! I want to see it, but I'm not going to pay for it!"

"Cheapskate," I teased, "Do you want to go? I was one of the lucky ones who got tickets!"

"Yeah, definitely! You know, Marcus P., you feed me all the time, and now you're giving me tickets, too! You rock!"

I laughed and asked, "I've only got two tickets. Can I go with, or do you want to take your boyfriend?"

"I don't think he really wants to go. Besides, this is the real version of *Hair*, like, they've got full nudity and everything, and I know how much you love naked people!" she said making a seductive growl intended to sound like a drunken tiger.

The next evening, we walked to the theater and chose seats away from the rest of the crowd. Hilary promised to describe the set and the visual aspects of the show that I would obviously be missing. Every few minutes, she'd lean over, give me the rundown on the costumes or the set changes and tell me any other tidbits I might need to know.

Halfway through the second act, in the middle of a screaming guitar solo, Hilary grabbed my arm and said, "We've got naked people! And oh my God, Marc, you're not missing anything! One of the girls is the biggest cow I've ever seen!" I nearly busted a gut laughing through the rest of the show.

The more time Hilary and I spent together, the more I let my guard down. No one beside Kista and my friends in Colorado really knew what went on inside my head during those early months and years of adaptation. Even though I didn't share many of my feelings with Hilary, she intuitively knew I was hurting.

Late one night, Hilary called to see what I was up to. "Hi, it's me!" she said. "I'm bored with studying and I'm taking a break. What are you doing tonight?"

"Nothing," I answered, but my slurred speech told her exactly what I'd been doing.

"Who are you hanging out with?" Hilary asked, concern creeping into her voice. She knew something was wrong.

"Um, Dasher," I croaked out through a stuffy nose.

"Want some company?"

"Um, you don't wanna be around me right now. I'm kinda a mess." I downed another swallow of the reason I was blind in the first place and winced.

"You're always a mess," she joked, "And I'm coming down anyway." She hung up and, within moments, was knocking at the door. Dasher ran to greet her.

"Hi, Dasher Man! Dasher, Dasher, Dasher… what are we going to do with your old man?"

I answered quietly, "Shoot him…"

Hilary took the nearly empty bottle from my hand, sat it on the nightstand and wrapped her arms around me. Feeling completely unworthy, I lost what little composure I had left.

"My life sucks! I hate this!" Through my sobs, Hilary remained strong and steady, never breathing an accusatory word. She let me rant and rave, cry and curse. I jabbered on for what must have felt like hours until, like waiting for the poison to pass, I was empty. When I was finished, Hilary spoke.

"Marc, sometimes I wish I knew what went on inside your head. Other times I'm glad I don't. Whenever I get a little taste of what you must be going through, I feel so helpless. I wish I could do something to help, but I just don't know what." I was about to protest, to tell her that her friendship did more than anything else in my life, but I just couldn't say the words.

She continued, "There's no way I can know everything you've gone through, Marc, and God knows I don't want to even imagine it. But I just wish you knew what an awesome person you are and how much I care about you." I was far too numb to fully appreciate what her respect meant. I took a deep breath and tried to control myself so I didn't miss the rest of her words. "Just being around you has helped me so much. You are my biggest source of inspiration," she said, her head resting on my shoulder. I didn't feel very inspirational as I pushed empty bottles out of the way.

"I wish I had half the confidence in myself that you seem to have in me," I said quietly, "God knows I don't deserve it."

"Yes, you do, Marc. Someday, you'll see why," she whispered. I could only hope she was right.

The next day, my head was filled with both pain and our conversation. In a daze, I walked across campus in my own little world. Suddenly, someone grabbed the leather loop on my backpack and I heard a familiar voice say, "Hey Marc, it's Kit." I turned around and shook his hand. "You want to get a workout in tonight?"

Two years before, Kit and I had formed a friendship while pushing up hundreds of pounds of iron. I showed up that evening, prepared to work out like we'd done in the old days.

"What do you want to do first?" Kit asked.

"I think I'll do cardio tonight and slowly work into weights," I said, already heading for the treadmill.

"Great! You do that, I'll watch out for Dasher," he said, and grasped my shoulder. Leaning in close he whispered, "Dude, this dog is going to bring all the babes to us!"

No longer able to exchange those sly glances about a good looking co-ed, Kit and I quickly devised codes to let me know the difference between "hottie" and "heinous."

As I walked on the treadmill, Kit threw Dasher's toy up and down the same long hallway I'd seen in my hallucination of running to the light. Dasher would sprint after his toy, loving to play his favorite game of retrieval.

Dasher adapted well to the social environment of college. His easygoing personality allowed me to take him to crowded parties and sports events. He simply scoped out the situation and, after taking off his harness, proceeded to get attention from anyone present.

This was never more apparent than at our evening playtime in the large grassy field behind my dorm. I would sit and throw his toy while he fetched and played tug-of-war until his tongue seemed like it would fall off from happy panting. The grassy lawn was a perfect area for play... not to mention my ulterior motive. The field was within full view of at least three sorority houses. I strategically planned Dasher's playtime during the dinner hour. It was fool proof! Girls always stopped to play with "the adorable dog."

As our nightly ritual continued, I met Laura and Heidi, two sophomores who lived in a neighboring dorm. "Hey Marc," Laura said one evening as they exited the cafeteria and found Dasher and I playing, or more appropriately "fishing for women."

"Want to go see a band with us tonight? Come over to our room around nine, we'll pre-party and then go hit the club!" I agreed and went inside to start getting ready.

An hour later, I knocked on their door, walked in and was immediately handed a cold bottle.

"Hey Marc! We're not quite ready yet, but it doesn't really matter, right? I mean, this is so cool! We can change and get ready with you sitting right here!" I laughed, knowing this was a common thought among my female friends. As we chatted, I heard one of them walk across the room to the closet. Saying nothing, she slid her shirt off and reached into the closet for a different outfit.

"Nice bra!" I said, my face focused on the topless girl just across the tiny dorm room. After a moment of shocked silence, they exploded with laughter. I'd made my point!

The school year stretched out into the early days of spring. One April afternoon during our routine workout, Kit posed a question. "Marc, do you think you'd be interested in working at Camp Mo-Val with me this summer?" The question caught me off guard and I didn't answer right away. I'd spent considerable time at Mo-Val during my high school years as both a camper and a counselor. In fact, on the patio outside the main lodge was where I'd first been introduced to Tom, long before the night of October 9th had forever changed my life. Memories of camping, canoeing, archery and nature hikes flooded my mind, and with them came a pang of sadness.

"Kit, I'd love to, but there's no way I can do the job. Singing and arts and crafts wouldn't be a problem, but dude, I can't lead campfire building and canoeing and the like," I said, crestfallen.

"Whatever, dude! About the only thing you wouldn't be able to do would be lifeguard and drive the tractor. I'm not even sure you couldn't drive the tractor better than half of the staff!" Kit said, sliding another weight onto our bench press. Seeing the self-doubt in my face, Kit changed his tactics. "Seriously, Marc. The campers could learn so much from you and Dasher."

"Yeah, but…" I began to protest. Kit cut me off.

"Promise me this, Marc." Kit said seriously. "Promise me that you'll at least think about it. I know we can find ways for you to do everything that everyone else does, okay? I'm telling you, we can make this work!"

A week later after much soul searching, I called Kit and asked, "You really think I should apply?"

Kit's tone was sure and confident, "I absolutely think you should, Marc."

"Then I'll do it," I said hoping that I sounded as confident as Kit. I applied for the position, went through the usual interviews and spent weeks nervously waiting for the outcome. Finally, Kit's boss, the camp director, called and offered me the job. I suppressed a shout of excitement until after I hung up the phone. I had received a lifetime of support from the friends I made at Camp Mo-Val. Now would be my opportunity to give something back.

Chapter 18

**"I can't remember all the times I tried to tell myself
to hold on to these moments as they pass"** [25]

~ Counting Crows

The Pontiac's headlights pierced through the snow that had just begun falling on the remote, two lane highway. I squinted, trying to see out the windshield that was, once again, fogging up. Pearl Jam blasted through the speakers as I turned south on a narrow blacktop road.

I glanced at the illuminated dashboard to make sure I wasn't in danger of running out of fuel. The last gas station was five miles behind me and, with so little traffic I could be sitting for a long time before anyone found the absent-minded teenager who hadn't filled up when he had the chance. I uttered a quick prayer of thanks as I saw the tank was half full; more than enough to make it to the camp.

As I continued winding through the steep hills, I thought back on the three previous winter retreats. The days between Christmas and New Year's Eve of my freshman year in high school introduced me to lots of fun and friends. That time was so enjoyable that I'd continued the tradition through my sophomore and junior years and always enjoyed every moment. Now, a senior, I was looking forward to my last official year as a participant.

A few moments later I reached the welcoming sign that announced Camp Mo-Val, quickly parked and jumped out into the frigid December air.

I stepped into the warmth of the registration room, complete with a roaring fire in the stone hearth. Looking around for my friends, I was pleasantly surprised to see some new and cute female faces. Almost instantly I spotted Tom across the room.

"I was wondering when you were going to get here, " he said smiling, "I didn't know if that piece of crap you drive would make it in the snow!" He knew I loved my "piece of crap" car and poked fun at it whenever he had the chance. Tom's girlfriend, Cherie, ran up from behind, wrapped her arms around my waist and playfully pretended to perform the Heimlich maneuver.

"Hey, Marcus!" she said brightly, spinning me around and playing with the weightlifting medals on my letterman's jacket. "What's with all these medals? Are you trying to show everyone you're a stud or something?" she teased.

Truth be known, yes, that is exactly what I was doing! The two football letters, two music letters and a variety of medals, patches and pins made for awkward wearing, but showed off my accomplishments nicely. What I was even more proud of than the awards was the big "93" attached to my right sleeve. "Yes! In just five months I'll be graduating! Then, this jacket probably won't mean so much, but for now, it is my pride and joy!"

I pulled up a chair and sat down next to Tom, made eye contact with a cute brunette sitting at the other end of the table and smiled in her direction. "What are you doing for New Year's Eve?" Tom asked, distracting my gaze from the girl.

"Nothing special. Why? Something going on?" I asked.

"How do hockey tickets and passes to the Arena Club sound?

"Excellent! That sounds awesome!" I exclaimed.

"Snowball fight by the lake in five minutes!" someone called over the crowd. Everyone rushed outside pulling on gloves and scarves. I trudged through the freshly fallen snow down a rocky path to the edge of the frozen water. Across the lake, a flock of Canadian geese circled an isolated cove where the ice dipped behind a small hill. The gray clouds overhead darkened the skies and the white snow fell with an even darker backdrop of evergreens.

"I wish I could stay here forever," I said quietly as Cherie silently walked up behind me to enjoy the scene, too.

"It's beautiful, isn't it?" she asked, turning and looking up at me, snow settling in her hair.

"It sure is. I'm going to miss not being able to come out here next year when I'm in college," I said, pulling my baseball cap down to shield my eyes from the flakes. "So, I'm just going to enjoy this now while I have the chance." At no time in recent memory had I felt more at peace.

Half an hour later, the snow battle ended and the warriors returned to the lodge for hot cocoa and freshly baked brownies. We feasted on the snacks around the fire and enjoyed the view of the lake through the south picture window. It was the most perfect place on earth.

Now, three and a half years later, I thought of those images as I arrived back at the very parking lot where I'd left my Pontiac as a 17 year old. This time, though, I'd traded the driver's seat for riding shotgun with a large black lab stretched out across the back seat. Things were definitely going to be different now. Nonetheless, I was excited that it was my job as a summer staffer to create memories for young campers.

After packing my camping gear into the cabin, Dasher and I returned to the lodge to meet the rest of the staffers. "Okay, we're going to take some time to get to know one another," Kit explained to the group. A dozen college aged students sat around picnic tables in the early June sun.

I was pleasantly surprised to find I knew almost all of the staff already from winter retreats. At least I'd not be starting with a bunch of strangers.

"We're going to take a tour of camp now," Kit said, gathering up his backpack, "Please pay attention. I'll be pointing out some of the dangers to avoid, areas that are off-limits to campers and storage places where you can get supplies. If you're lucky, I might even point out the plants NOT to use as toilet paper!"

Kit laid a hand on my shoulder and quietly said, "We're going to be walking through a lot of underbrush on the trails, man. If you want to let Dasher chill here in the air conditioning and use my shoulder, you're welcome to that." The last thing I wanted was Dasher to have a coat full of ticks and fleas, or worse, to have a run-in with a copperhead snake.

I grabbed Kit's shoulder and we set out to get an extensive look at camp.

Following the tour, we gathered on the patio overlooking the lake for some discussion time. After covering the usual safety precautions for campers, our evening drew to an end.

"Does anyone have anything they'd like to talk about before we close?" Kit asked.

"I do," I said quietly. "I'm really excited to be here, but I'm a little nervous. Does anyone have concerns or questions about working with me?" I paused and waited for someone to say something, anything.

"Marc, I'm just wondering how you're going to lead archery," Kevin, a new friend finally asked.

"Yeah, I'm kind of wondering that myself," I joked. "Seriously though, the kids have to stay behind a certain line when firing at the target, right? If I'm leading with someone else, I'll be in charge of crowd control. I'll make sure the rest of the campers are seated and not running in front of the target, remind the shooters to point the arrows at the ground when they're loading, that sort of stuff."

"What about canoeing?" asked Leah, a young lady I'd met briefly during the winter retreat my senior year.

"Well, I don't mind going out on the lake in a canoe with campers, which would be good if we have odd numbers or any kids who are feeling left out. Once I'm on the lake, I can hear if they are splashing with paddles or ramming the canoes into each other. I've got a pretty loud mouth and it shouldn't be hard to get them to stop," I replied. I hadn't thought of these things before, but the answers falling out of my mouth seemed right on.

"How about cookouts?" inquired Mike, the youngest staffer of the group.

"If the campers can bring me the sticks and wood from the forest, I'm perfectly capable of lighting the fire."

Kit piped up and said," Yeah, I hate to admit this, but I've had to take a lot of lessons in campfire building from campers. Last summer, I was having trouble getting a campfire started and this third grader, some superstar Boy Scout, had to show me why it wasn't working! I felt like an idiot taking instructions from a kid on how to do my job!" We all chuckled, knowing full well that none of us were professional campers, but college kids who were usually only in the woods during the summers.

Before we retired for the night, I said, "I feel like there is some reason I'm here this summer, a reason that I don't really know yet. I want to show everyone who comes to Mo-Val the abilities of someone with a disability, and I hope you guys will challenge me to do my best."

A week later staff training came to an end. Had it really only been a few days since I'd settled into my cabin and started getting to know the other staffers? I shouldn't have been surprised. "Mo-Val Magic" happened every minute of the summer; total strangers becoming as close as family in less time than it took to roast a marshmallow.

The summer's first camp was split between two very different groups; DDA camp for developmentally disabled adults, and a concurrent work camp for senior high students. I volunteered to help with the work camp, thinking I'd challenge myself with manual labor.

My fellow staffer, Mike, and I worked diligently alongside our crew building footbridges and digging drainage ditches. Not wanting to appear to be helpless I consistently worked on the heaviest jobs.

"Hand me that chain saw," I said to Mike as we came to an overgrown section of a trail.

"You're kidding, right?" Mike asked nervously.

"No, dude, hand me the chainsaw. I'm going to clear this tree off the path," I said, extending my hand.

"I take no responsibility for this," Mike said, chuckling, but handing over the saw. I spent a few moments feeling the sides of the log, an oak with a girth of about three feet. The tree had fallen, struck by lightening and was now blocking the trail. Mike gave a quick lesson in how to work the saw before asking, "You're really going to do this?" I didn't answer, just pulled the starter cord and the saw roared to life. Ten minutes later, we had firewood and the trail was cleared.

As I turned off the chain saw, I said in a monotone, "Oops. I forgot to wear safety goggles."

Halfway through the week, the director of the DDA camp invited me to give a presentation on being blind and having a guide dog. I accepted the offer, but was unsure how to go about the lesson. Explaining all my adaptive techniques was one thing, but teaching these concepts to individuals with cognitive disabilities was a new challenge.

When it was time for my presentation, I carefully chose basic terms to explain how I used each of my "blind toys." Then I engaged the students in a discussion.

"How many of you like to read? Say 'me!'" I'd told them right up front that raising one's hand at a blind person wouldn't exactly get their attention.

"Me!" the audience shouted back. They'd caught on nicely!

"Can blind people read books?" I asked the group.

"No!" came their enthusiastic answer.

"Sure blind people can read! I read all the time. Except that now I read my books on tape! The books are recorded by someone who can see, then I play the tape and the words come into my ears!" I said, hoping my explanations were elementary enough. "Would you guys like to read like blind people?"

"Yes!" came back their excited response.

"Okay, close your eyes and I'll press the play button. Then you can read like blind people!" I paused a moment while they closed their eyes, then started the tape. The voice of a male reader came through the speaker and sounds of wonder came from the audience. After the "Ooh" and "Ah" responses quieted down, I was able to make out the words of the narrator; and I was horrified! The book launched into graphic tales of a grisly murder scene; walls smeared with blood, bodies strewn about and the smell of death in the air. "Oh, crap!" I thought, remembering that I'd been reading "Helter Skelter," an account of the Charles Manson murder spree. Staff training had been so packed with activities that I hadn't read in over a week and had, in fact, forgotten what book was in the player. My fingers quickly fumbled for the off switch.

"Great! Now all of you know how blind people read!" I concluded brightly, hoping I hadn't traumatized them for life! A lesson learned: Always check the cassette tape before show and tell!

After the presentation, Kit said, "Man, that was great! I didn't know any of that stuff about blindness… or Charles Manson, for that matter! Do you think you could do something like this for other camps?"

"Sure, why not?" I responded, embracing the challenge.

With the exception of the DDA group, campers were ages seven to seventeen, each group spending one week participating in the usual summer camp activities. Kit titled my small group learning sessions, "The Marc and Dasher Show."

"Yeah, dude, we can even make up some theme music for you guys," Kit teased, humming a tune that sounded like a Saturday morning cartoon. We laughed.

The next week my first group of third and fourth graders gathered around Dasher and I, ready to learn about blindness and Seeing Eye dogs.

"Hi guys! You guys know me, and I'm sure you know Dasher, too. I'll tell you more about him in a few minutes, but first, I want to ask some questions. What kinds of things do you like to do that you couldn't do if you were blind?"

"Well, blind people can't play sports!" a talkative boy answered.

"Well, you're right. There are some sports blind people can't play, but there are lots that they can play. For example, there are blind people who swim races at swim meets and some who ride and race tandem bikes. I know a blind guy who used to wrestle in high school, too. Plus, there are special volleyballs and softballs with beepers inside so blind people can hear them and play like everyone else," I explained.

"Yeah, but blind people can't play video games, can they?" a little girl asked.

"There are all kinds of computer games that are specially made for blind people. In fact, I have several on my laptop. Wanna see?" They gathered around my computer and were shocked at how cool the games were.

As their questions continued, I'd answer each and explain the adaptations a blind person would have to make. My mission was accomplished when, in every group, the question was unconsciously rephrased from "Blind people can't..." to, "So how do blind people...?" That simple change in phrasing signaled a different perspective and new set of expectations.

After the first few camps ended and kids went home having witnessed "The Marc and Dasher Show," letters began flooding into the camp office from parents excited that their children had learned so much from Dasher and me.

One afternoon, I walked into the staff lounge to a chorus of laughter. "What's so funny?" I asked innocently.

One of my fellow staffers spoke up and said, "Um, Marc, the 'Marc and Dasher Show' has been renamed by the volunteer director," he said before bursting into more laughs.

"Oh, God," I said, bracing for the title that had my friends doubling over.

Kit, laughing, choked out, "He's calling it 'Sightless Wonders!'" He and the rest of the staff were nearly incapacitated, actually struggling to catch their breath between howls. By now, they'd all become accustomed to my slightly self-deprecating humor. They knew I wouldn't be insulted, just bewildered at such a stupid title.

"Sightless Wonders? Dude, people are going to think I'm Stevie's brother!"

While I thought of myself as just another staffer, I have to admit there were a couple of times I surprised myself. One afternoon, I was sitting on the edge of the pool while the primary aged campers jumped and splashed around. With nearly 100 bodies of pure energy packed into the swimming pool, it was necessary for all staff to be present to control the melee. As my legs dangled in the water, I would call, "Walk, please!" to the campers I heard running on the slippery deck.

Suddenly a small voice just a few feet in front of me whispered, "Help!" It was the quietest "Help!" I'd ever heard.

I bent down toward the little girl and asked, "Are you okay?" She was barely out of arm's reach, struggling in the five-foot deep water.

"Help me!" she choked out again. Stretching out into the water, I pulled her toward me. Hooking my hands under her arms, I lifted her out of the pool and stood her upright on the concrete deck. She snapped her swimming suit back into place and yelled, "Thank you!" as she ran for the diving board.

"Walk, please!" I called after her. I sat with my feet in the water for a few seconds listening for other running campers when I felt a hand on my back.

Kit knelt down and said quietly, "Do you realize you just made the first save of the year?"

"No kidding? It only took a second and really was not a big deal. The little girl was in water over her head and I just gave her a hand."

"Whatever, dude!" Kit said excitedly, "I've got all those official Red Cross certifications to be a lifeguard, but it wasn't me who pulled that kid out! See, this just goes to prove that you might actually be better with your ears than those of us who can see."

As a lookout, my primary duties were to keep rowdiness to a minimum, provide crowd control, and now, save occasional little girls from drowning. I'd been certified in CPR and first aid, but technically, being a lifeguard required sight. Now that I'd made a save, the only difference between the true lifeguards and myself was the fact they were acknowledged by the Red Cross and had one piece of service equipment that I did not: a whistle.

"Man, we need to get you a whistle since apparently you can save kids better than the rest of us," Kit said as the last campers pulled themselves out of the pool.

Lifeguarding was practically the only task I couldn't officially do, so of course, that became what I wanted most. There was no way I could be certified, but I figured Kit was right; I deserved a whistle. The quest for the shiny little object soon became a focus of my personal mission. One of these noisemakers only cost $3.00 and would symbolize my equality in the eyes of the other staffers. I could have easily bought my own at the local discount store, but I wanted one to be issued to me, just like the others. The next day during a staff meeting, Kit's boss closed by asking, "Does anyone have anything else to discuss?"

I piped up, "Yes, I'd like a whistle." With a sigh, the director patiently recited the Red Cross rules, which required that each lifeguard be able to visually spot a troubled swimmer in the water. "When the Red Cross certifies you, then you'll get a whistle," I was informed.

"I'm not asking to be a lifeguard, I just want a whistle," I said, matter-of-factly. There was nothing stating a lookout couldn't be issued a whistle, but the answer was still no. I didn't care if I only received a token whistle; I wanted one! The denial of my request was more than a little annoying!

On his day off, a fellow staffer purchased a huge, red and incredibly obnoxious plastic whistle at an amusement park. Phil slipped it around my neck like an absurd Olympic gold medal. It was the size of a softball and included a cartoon depiction of the Tasmanian devil.

"Here ya' go, Marc! Your official whistle!" Phil said, smiling. It had to be the biggest, ugliest whistle Phil could find… and I loved it! I couldn't hide my enormous appreciation for his thoughtfulness.

"Don't sweat it, Marc!" he said, pleased his gift was appreciated. "I know you want a real lifeguard whistle. You earned it."

As the summer progressed, I was given new and different tasks, jobs that were probably not considered within my ability the first day of camp. After campfires and pool saves, archery and canoeing, no one had reservations about handing me tasks when our shorthanded staff suffered lack of manpower. One of these jobs was to deliver and serve food to a satellite camp nearby which lacked kitchen facilities. Along with Kevin and Leah, the chore wouldn't take long. Plus, any time the three of us were together, something usually happened that ended up with all of us rolling on the ground laughing like hyenas.

After dinner and clean up, we loaded the coolers and serving trays in the back of the van and were ready for the one-mile drive back to Mo-Val. As Leah loaded the last of the gear into the van, I snuck up to the driver's door, opened it and climbed in. Fingers fumbling for the keys, I cranked up the radio and yelled for Kevin and Leah to hop in. Without considering that what we were doing was illegal, they just did it. I shifted the van into gear and listened carefully while Kevin instructed me down the driveway back to the road that would take us to Mo-Val.

"Little to the left… keep it straight, now just a hair to the right…straighten it out, Engel," he coached. Being on the campgrounds was one thing, but when we arrived at the gates onto the main road, Kevin said, "Now, cut it hard to the right!" It wouldn't be a drive of more than three minutes, even at the snail's pace we were traveling, but there was no way I wanted to be on a public road, even one void of other cars and drivers.

"No way, dude!" I said loudly as I threw the van into park. "The last thing I need is a ticket!" I jumped out of the van and felt my way around the hood to the front passenger's seat. That short trip and experience being back in the driver's seat felt foreign, but somehow, it didn't seem to matter.

The summer had shown me in hundreds of ways who I am, what I am capable of doing and that, even without sight, the world can still be a wonderful and productive place. To those who passed through Camp Mo-Val that summer, I hope I touched your life… thank you for changing mine.

Chapter 19

"Tomorrow's right around the corner
I'll get there somehow
But I'm stuck in the meantime, and I love the now" [26]

~ Jimmy Buffett

"Dude, this stuff reeks!" I said, tossing a handful of damp clothes into a laundry bag.

"Is that mildew I smell?" Kit asked, shocked, but smiling. A week ago, I'd have picked up one of the shirts, thrown it on and headed out the screen door of Red Cedar Cabin. Now, back in the dorm with bone dry air set at a comfortable 65 degrees, the clothes seemed so filthy I debated whether to throw them in the laundry… or the dumpster.

"That's the difference between here and camp," I said, motioning around the dorm room, "When you're at camp, you realize it's not someone's image, but what's inside them that counts."

"Yeah, you're right," Kit said, giving me a hand with a box of souvenirs from the summer. I unpacked my pocketknife, bandanas and canteen; items that symbolized a 180 degree turnaround from the Marc of the spring semester. Insecurity and inebriation were now replaced with confidence and energy – something that seemed impossible just a few months earlier.

Three months of being challenged in a leadership position helped re-claim a good portion of the Marcus from before. After all, I'd never stopped being that guy – I'd just lost track of him for a while. When I returned for the fall semester, it was with a gigantic boost in confidence, a new goatee and a killer tan.

"Okay, last box!" Kit said, ripping off the tape.

Just then the phone rang. Kit knew I'd be preoccupied and excused himself. "I'll call you later!" I waved as he exited into the crowded hallway.

"Hello?" I said into the receiver.

"Good! You're home! I'm coming down!" said a peppy voice that could belong to no one but Hilary. Before I had a chance to respond, the line went dead. Half a minute later, she burst in through the door and screamed, "Marcus P.! Dasher D.!" before practically jumping into my arms. In a heartbeat, she was on the floor rubbing Dasher's belly and whispering, "Dasher boy, tell Marc to let you go for a jog with me!" Normally, I didn't like others walking Dasher, but he needed the exercise after a three hour car ride, and I was beat.

I handed the leather leash to Dasher's new jogging partner. An hour later, dog and girl returned, rousing me from a sound sleep.

"Did you two have fun?" I asked, still groggy.

Hilary jumped on the side of the bed. "Yep! We ran all over campus and around the track a few times, then one of us drank a bowl of water and peed on the soccer field."

"You can get arrested for peeing in public, Hil," I said, trying to sound serious while we both rubbed Dasher furiously. He, too, was glad to be back at school and hanging out with his other best friend.

For the next two hours, Hilary and I caught up on all the happenings since we'd parted ways. Halfway through a story of my weekend trip to Memphis, Hilary cut me off.

"What happened to you this summer?"

"What do you mean? I've been telling you for the last half hour!"

"No, I mean, what happened to YOU? What happened to the down-in-the-dumps Marc from last year? You've changed, buddy… I mean, a lot!"

"Yeah, I guess I learned some pretty important stuff out there. Camp was the best thing that has ever happened to me, present company excluded, obviously," I teased and playfully punched her in the arm.

"Well, Marcus P., there's one change I don't like! For the love of God, what is that furry thing growing around your mouth?" she laughed, poking me in the ribs.

I traced two fingers over my goatee in feigned horror. "Oh my God! One of camp's timid little woodland creatures has attached itself to my face!" As we laughed, I thought, *It's good to be back…it's really good to be back!*

The next day began the fall semester, and I was soon reminded that college was a not-so-nurturing environment. Dasher and I walked to my English class feeling more confident and happy than a year ago when I thought I had just accomplished the ultimate goal. I arrived at Pummill Hall, found the classroom and waded through uncomfortable wooden desks to the front row. No matter the class, I always tried to sit in the first row. That way, Dasher had plenty of room to stretch out. No more than 15 students occupied the tiny area.

A few moments later the professor came in, walked to the teacher's desk just in front of me and laid her briefcase down, all the while chattering with the students. She walked to the board, picked up a piece of chalk and scrawled something. As she finished, she tapped the chalk against the board and said, "That's me!"

"What's you?" I thought, confused.

Generally, if I sat in the front row, it served as a quiet reminder to the professor that at least one student needed written notes to be spoken.

"Can anyone pronounce my name?" she asked, almost offering a dare. A young man from the rear of the classroom spouted off a word that contained more than an adequate number of vowels. The teacher exaggerated applause.

"Very good! How did you know that?"

"I had your husband last semester," the student said, bored with the conversation.

"Good!" she said, popping open her briefcase and pulling out a stack of papers, "I don't expect you to pronounce it right, but I DO expect it to be spelled correctly. This is English 220. We've got a small class and we're going to get to know each other well. First, I want to tell you about me." I settled back and reached down to scratch Dasher.

I always liked it when professors gave some of their background, provided they weren't academic snobs bent on bragging about their every award, degree and published article. In addition to showing the professor's humanity, it gave an idea of their personality. I took those nuggets of information, filed them away and tried to regurgitate them when writing a paper.

"I'm originally from Manhattan which is why I don't have a southern accent," she said, the second part of her statement taking on a playful cynicism. "I went to a private college in New York for both my undergrad and my grad degrees. I've now been at SMSU for four years. My husband is also a professor on campus." She walked within an arm's reach of me and sat down on her desk.

"Enough about me, let's look over the syllabus," she said, surveying the class. "Rule number one. No cheating, copying, plagiarizing, etc. Don't even let me think you're trying to be dishonest. Because of this, no baseball caps, visors, sunglasses or hats of any type are to be worn in here." She paused, looked up and waited for something to happen.

"The rule says, 'no sunglasses.' You... please take them off... now," she said evenly.

I sat quietly and waited for the student who was wearing sunglasses to remove them. Many professors have such a rule because one can hide their eyes with such headgear. It is an understandable guideline, one most students have no problem abiding by.

"Excuse me! You need to take off your glasses!" she repeated, more sternly this time.

A tense silence fell over the room. Suddenly, I realized she was speaking to me!

"Me?" I blubbered, shocked.

"Uh, yeah, you." the instructor replied with more than a touch of condescension. She must be kidding, I thought, still completely stunned. I'd been wearing Oakley sunglasses since I was released from the hospital and I never left home without them. I was just more comfortable covering up the uneven bridge of my nose and the drooped left eyelid. Surely, common sense exempted me from the anti-sunglasses rule!

"Why?" I shot back, clearly conveying we were at an ugly stand off. My face burned crimson with humiliation.

"Because I want to see my students' eyes when they are in class," she retorted in an imperious tone.

"Tough shit! Like I'm going to cheat off of the person next to me or something!" I knew I was pushing my luck by using profanity, but I was well past the point of caring. If she wanted to lock horns, she'd better be ready to do battle... and that was a fight she wasn't going to win! One more word about this and I would

walk out of class and go straight to the head of the department…
or possibly the president's office, depending how much she pissed
me off! I took a quick breath and tried to calm down.

"Look, I'm going to tell you this one time and one time only,"
I said, barely controlling my rage. "I'm blind and I don't even take
my shades off around my family. I'm damned sure not going to
take them off for you!" In the moment of complete silence that
followed, the class held it's collective breath.

"I'm sorry," the instructor said at last, backing down. "Okay,
never mind then…" It was obvious to everyone, especially the
new teacher, that she was not off to a rousing start.

I sat in furious silence until a possibility hit me. *Maybe she
didn't realize I was blind!* It only took a moment to quickly dismiss
that idea. Dasher was less than two feet from her. If she couldn't
see him, then *she* was the one who needed a Seeing Eye dog!
Firmly convinced that she was just as obnoxious and stupid as she
sounded, I left the class feeling I should have been more rude and
profane. On the walk home, the late August sun burned down, but
it couldn't even compare to the heat of my temper.

As the semester progressed, I reluctantly admitted that I enjoyed the class and, other than the attacks of the first day, I also
enjoyed the professor. Spicy debates were encouraged which
not only got our minds working, but helped us get to know one
another.

The three students who sat behind me were fraternity brothers who seemed to especially enjoy challenging the professor's
ultra liberal viewpoints. "Yeah, but how can you say that when
American society would falter?" one asked after the teacher had
proclaimed that the American legal system was outdated and the
Constitution should be scrapped. The rest of the class nodded in
agreement as another student piped up with his two cents worth.

I snickered under my breath when I realized he was taunting the professor into rationally explaining her argument, something she wasn't able to do. The debater, a political science major, had her up against the ropes. She chose the path of least resistance and called the conversation to a halt. I couldn't help laughing at the fact that, no matter what, the student had won.

I turned around and whispered, "Good job, man!"

"Hey Marcus, see you next time," said Ben, one of the other fraternity brothers as students exited after class.

"Later, dudes," I echoed, still smiling at the humility they had inflicted upon the instructor.

I couldn't help but like these three guys and always enjoyed eavesdropping about the latest party or drunken incident at the house. Originally, I'd looked upon members of the Greek system as arrogant and snobby, yet these guys were nothing but friendly. My previous attitude toward Greeks was unfounded, especially since I never picked up a bit of condescension from Travis or his Kappa Sigma brothers. Travis' pledgeship was long since over and had never caused him to focus on his house and forget about me, as I had feared. I felt a twinge of shame for all the trash I'd talked about the Greek system, comments that were made out of insecurity rather than substantive experience.

I walked back to the dorm, ready to get the weekend started off right. After taking off Dasher's harness, I hit 'play' on the answering machine.

"Marc, it's Travis," came the scratchy voice, "There's going to be a party at the house tonight, if you're interested. Ought to be lots of girls, should be a good time. Call me." As soon as the recording ended, I dialed his number and we set the plans in motion. After a healthy, pre-weekend nap, I met Travis at the dorm's front door and we drove the few blocks to the fraternity house.

"Are you sure it's cool for me to be here? I thought these sorts of parties are restricted to members," I asked, not wanting to step on anyone's toes.

"No, it's cool, don't worry about it. If anyone asks who you are, just say you're my friend," Travis said, pulling into the lot of the fraternity house. Girls by the score started showing up just minutes after we arrived, everyone ready to party and dance. I was having a great time, getting to know the members, but spending a fair amount of time talking to the girls, too. Travis tapped me on the shoulder, slipped Dasher's leash from my hand and said, "Go shake your ass!" He grabbed a girl I was speaking with and pushed us toward the dance floor. Soon, we were buried amongst a group of hot, sweaty bodies all doing 70's disco dances, as the party had been themed.

"I've gotta go find my hound," I said to the girl at the end of the song. She took my hand, placed it on her shoulder and we crowded out of the packed room.

"I saw Travis take him outside," she said, patting my hand and cutting through the crowd. We pressed on and reached the outside stairs to find Travis, Dasher and three or four other fraternity members waiting.

"Thanks for the dance!" she said, hugging me before heading back in. I sat down next to Travis, scratching Dasher behind the ears for behaving without me.

"Engel, this is Adam, this is Tucker and this is Nathan," Travis said, introducing me to his brothers. I shook each of their hands and thanked them for allowing me to party with them.

"No problem, man," one said, pulling up a chair beside me, "I told Travis he could bring you back any time you wanted to come." *Really?* I hadn't considered that these guys would accept me as willingly as any other person, but apparently Travis wasn't the only guy in the house who saw some potential in me. "Yeah, in fact, I was telling Travis that we should give you a bid to join Kappa Sig. Have you ever thought about rushing a fraternity?"

"Yeah, I've thought about it, but I didn't know if it was the right thing for me," I lied, figuring this was not the time to explain my freshman year of insecurity.

"Well, how about Travis and I take you to lunch tomorrow and we can see what sorts of questions you have." I agreed and we made plans to meet the next afternoon. Over burgers and fries, I peppered them with questions about pledgeship, costs, duties, etc. For more than an hour, each brother answered the questions they knew the most about.

"Marc, you don't have to make a decision until the beginning of next semester. Just take time to think about it. If you decide to do it, we'd love to have you as a brother," Travis said. I agreed, but already knew in which direction I was leaning.

On the last day of the semester, my fellow students and I walked into English class, anxious to fill out the class evaluations and evacuate. It was university policy that the instructor excused him or herself while students completed the forms and expressed their opinions. When everyone was done, they turned their papers over and chatted with their neighbors; all but one person, that is. Evidently, Ben, one of the three fraternity brothers, still had a few things to say. Long after everyone else was finished, he sat hunched over writing furiously.

"Hey, Ben... you writing a love letter to the prof or something?" one of his friends asked, chuckling.

"Nope," he said quietly, turning to face me just a few feet away. "Marcus, I'm telling her what I think about how she treated you on the first day of class." I hadn't forgotten the confrontation, but had long since filed it in the category of more water under the bridge. "The way she acted made me sick, Marcus. I almost got up, walked out and went straight to the department head's office," he continued, still angry about the events of that day.

I was surprised this episode had made such an impression on him. All I could muster was, "Thanks, dude."

A chorus of, "Oh yeah, I had forgotten about that..." comments came from the other students as they turned over their evals and proceeded to shred the professor's behavior.

Immediately, I halted my internal debate about whether or not to join a fraternity. This guy wasn't even in Travis' house or a friend of mine. He was just a decent guy who hated to see people walked on. If those are the sorts of people the Greek system attracts, I wanted to be part of it. I made a mental note to phone Travis as soon as I got back to my room. I sat in humble silence for the rest of the class, thankful to Ben and his friends for showing me in actions the kind of integrity and composure bred by fraternities.

"Hey, Trav," I said into the receiver as soon as I got back to my dorm room. "Want to grab dinner? I need to talk to you." An hour later, we were seated at the same Tex-Mex restaurant we'd dined at when I'd returned to SMSU a year and a half earlier.

"Well, I think I'm going to do it," I said to Travis as soon as the waitress had taken our order.

"Do what?" Travis asked, genuinely baffled.

"I'm going to pledge Kappa Sig in the spring," I said, feeling déjà vu from a year before when we'd had the exact same conversation with the two of us playing different roles.

"Marc, that's great! Make sure you are doing this for you. I don't want you to join just because I want you to, or you think it's expected," he said cautiously.

"Not at all. It's something I've always wanted to do, and now is the time. I'm ready!"

Travis smiled. "It's going to be great having you as a brother!" he said, toasting his glass against mine.

The fall semester came to a close, finals flew by and soon it was Christmas break. Anticipating my involvement with the fraternity, vacation raced past and I was, once again, living back in New Hall dormitory, looking forward to the spring semester. On an Arctic night in early February, I met five other young men who would also be pledging Kappa Sigma. We met near the dorm, each anxious about what pledgeship would be like... or more specifically if the horror stories about hazing were true. We walked to the house in silence and were met outside by the chapter's president.

"Gentlemen, you need to wait in the garage while the brotherhood prepares your pinning ceremony," he said, pointing to a darkened building detached from the house. We cautiously walked in, pulled up cold metal chairs around a single candle and waited for further instructions. While the wind whipped outside, the candlelight illuminated the dreary cinder-blocked walls and added to the foreboding mood.

After an hour of nervous anticipation, a fraternity member stepped into the center of our candlelit circle and made a quiet warning.

"Gentlemen, you are about to enter the initial realms of the brotherhood of this order. Tonight you will receive a pledge pin and take the obligation of a pledge. I must warn you, nothing done in ritualistic fashion with this fraternity is to be spoken of unless it is to another member. Do I make myself clear?" he asked ominously. We all nodded in agreement and he instructed us to stand, follow him into the house and receive the first of many rituals.

Kappa Sigma soon filled a void I hadn't even realized existed. The other five pledges soon elected me their president. This only meant that I was the one who had to explain to the members why my pledge brothers had failed their tests or skipped a house clean-up; an honor I got to do about every other day. Their immature antics and laziness were to be expected from freshman, something I had trouble relating to since I was three years older. One day, I'd had it. I walked into a pledge meeting, ready to kill.

"I studied my butt off for that test and every one of you failed. Hell, I even got the extra credit questions right! Since none of you could even get a passing grade, we all have to clean the house at dawn tomorrow! Thanks a lot, you freaking bunch of slackers!"

"Engel, chill out, dude," one said as he kicked his feet onto the coffee table and lit a cigarette, "It's not the end of the world." I was so livid I couldn't speak. Turning my back on them, I walked out. Halfway down the hall, I had an epiphany.

"Engel," I said to myself, "You're three years older than those guys, you've got so much more life experience and you've been dreaming of pledging for years. They're acting like kids because, well, they ARE kids." A pang of guilt struck me for lashing out at them and I turned around and went back to the meeting. I rapped a couple of soft knocks on the door and walked in with my head down.

"Guys, I'm sorry. I'm really stressed out. I've got mid-terms next week and I'm behind in my classes because I'm always doing fraternity stuff. I'm just tired of having no time to myself," I said humbly. Our session concluded and I walked home, feeling good about the forgiving nature of my pledge brothers.

As soon as I walked in the door, the phone rang. A low voice I didn't recognize growled, "Have your pledge brothers at the house at midnight. Everyone needs to be there, no excuses." Then, the line went dead. I called my pledge brothers and relayed our directions. Because of our performance on tests and clean-ups, the midnight session probably wasn't going to be pretty.

At five minutes before twelve, we met outside the high wooden fence that surrounded the fraternity house. Inside, music of crashing drums and heavy bass guitar rattled the windows.

"What do you think they're going to do to us?" one of my cohorts asked, his voice shivering, though it wasn't due to the March breeze.

"I don't know, but there's no way I'm screwing any goats!" another joked. No one laughed.

At exactly midnight, we opened the gate and entered the grounds.

"Pledges, to the garage," the fraternity president said as soon as the gate was closed. We obediently walked to our familiar waiting place and sat silently, worrying about what was to come. Somewhere outside, there was a succession of breaking bottles. The candle had again been put in the midst of our circle, the light only adding to the fear of the unknown. In the dark, a door squeaked open.

"Engel, come with me," a deep voice said. I rose, handed Dasher's leash to one of my pledge brothers and took the shoulder of my unknown guide, trusting only the fact the fraternity would not harm me. As we walked the narrow sidewalk toward the house, the music grew louder. Somewhere inside, a bottle crashed against something metal and howls of evil laughter floated up. My guide knocked with a succession of raps that sounded like Morse code and, on the final rap, the house fell silent as death. I stepped into the doorway, prepared to brave whatever was to come.

Fifteen minutes later, I emerged out that same door, smiling and feeling on top of the world, my fears washed away. What a great snow job the brothers had just pulled! The shoulder my hand rested upon belonged to Travis who, after the ceremony, could now officially be called my big brother.

"So, were you scared?" he asked as we stepped back into the yard.

"Dude! Look at my pants!" I said gesturing like I'd just pissed myself. "Y'all are breaking bottles and screaming and stuff, then I walk in and it's like a surprise party! Now that I've got a big brother, I'm just excited to be one step closer to membership!" I said, my heart still fluttering a little.

"I was with you every step of the way, but I didn't want you to know I was your guide," Travis said. "Plus, I was just having fun watching your face go pale! You looked like you'd just been sent to the principal's office!" There's no other way to put it; I was glowing!

"I've got one more gift for you," Travis said, lightly socking me in the stomach with a brown paper bag filled with the traditional libation of our "family tree." I smiled, clutched the gift I'd just been given and could only say, "Thank you."

Chapter 20

"Now this whole damned mess is becoming quite clear" [27]

~ Uncle Tupelo

"**W**ell, Marcus," the woman seated across the desk said, "I guess the question is, 'What do you want to be when you grow up?'"

This seemed a simplistic way to plan the rest of my college career, not to mention my future, but she was exactly right. If I knew what I wanted to do with my life, declaring a major would be the first step.

"Ma'am, I have no idea," I said, giving a serious answer to her playful question.

"Well, so far you've taken four courses in sociology and two in criminal justice. It looks like you're interested in human interaction, is that right?"

"Yeah, I guess."

"Well, why not continue that line of study? You always have the option to change your major later."

Easier said than done, I thought.

With no other major standing out, I nodded and said, "Okay, let's do it then!"

She smiled, scribbled something down on my transcript and said, "Congratulations, Marcus! You are now majoring in sociology!"

While I wasn't sure where the degree would take me, I was, at least, enjoying college and college life. My social world expanded and grew almost every day, thanks to my recent initiation into Kappa Sigma. Late night fraternity parties were starting to be a way of life. Though sometimes I didn't arrive back to the dorm until 3 a.m., I almost always managed to drag myself out of bed for class. Since I was a junior, I figured I should put forth effort to take my education seriously. Following class, I'd head back home, fall into bed and nap half of the afternoon. Ah, the life of a college student!

One day during a marathon napping session, I was awakened by the phone. I fumbled for the receiver and groggily asked, "Hello?"

"Marc? It's Sarah," the young girl at the other end answered. A jolt of fear shot through me. Sarah and her family were longtime friends as well as members of my church in High Hill. My first thought was that her parents or one of her four siblings had been hurt and she was calling to deliver the news.

"We just had a senior class officer's meeting about graduation. We are looking for a commencement speaker and someone suggested you. Would you be interested in giving the speech?" she asked hopefully.

A speech? My mind replayed my own high school graduation just five years before when I sat in those uncomfortable chairs wearing a royal blue mortarboard. At least 2000 people had been packed into the gym.

"Um, I don't know. You guys really want me to speak?" I asked, left in a rare state of stunned silence. Usually commencement speakers were accomplished at something – business leaders, educational administrators. Not 23-year-old college students that partied all night and napped all day. I'd spoken in public about the crash and recovery, but never like this. Twenty minutes in front of a couple thousand people was daunting.

While I made a mental list of why I couldn't do it, I suddenly remembered what a friend, Pat, had said while I was still laying in Barnes Hospital, questioning if I could pick up the fragments of my former life and return to college. "Come on, Marc! After this, everything else in your life will be a breeze!" And, she was right! After this, what could ever compare to the trials I'd endured? After this, what could ever be as bad as the pain from a 20-hour surgery? After this, nothing could be as traumatic as learning I would never see again. I'd been through horrors no human should endure and, having "been there, done that" I knew I could do anything!

With that thought in mind, I took a deep breath and said, "Sarah, I'll do it."

Before the speech even had a shape, I knew that I had to include the Bob Dylan quote that had changed my life, "negativity don't pull ya through." I mulled over how I could craft the 20 minutes into a performance that would show everyone that our choices, not our circumstances, are what bring us ultimate happiness and fulfillment.

The next several months were spent in preparation for the speech – at least when I could work it in between naps. When the semester ended, I returned to my parents home for a two-week holiday before heading to Mo-Val for my third and final summer. During my vacation, I'd give the graduation speech and then be able to relax for a few days before taking off for the welcome session at camp. Since I was back in High Hill, I phoned Kista to try to set up a time to get together and catch up.

"Hey kiddo! Whatcha doing?"

"Hey Marc!" she responded, "I was just going to call you! I heard you are giving the commencement talk for graduation. Need a lift?"

"Only if you let me drive!" I said, deadpan.

"After the ceremony. I'm not going to be responsible for us showing up late because you decided to play *Dukes of Hazzard* on the back roads!"

Two days later, I once again found myself flying down the highway in Kista's VW convertible. Had it really been four years since she had rescued me from the doldrums of my parents' living room and revived me with a cruise for sodas? Had even more time than that passed since I was incapacitated with laughter as she played Adam Sandler in my hospital room?

As we drove to the high school, the wind whipping through our hair, we chatted about the kids we'd been during those horrid times. Heavy silence encompassed us when the conversation rolled around to her father's passing.

"That was such an awful time, Marc, and it was so good to have you there with me. You were a constant then, and you still are now. I can't tell you how thankful I am for that," she said, pulling off the highway.

"If I hadn't been in that wreck and you hadn't lost your dad, do you think we ever would have stayed friends after high school?"

"I don't know," she said, turning to face me while we waited for a stoplight, "and I really don't care. You're one of the most important people in my life and no matter how long or hard that road was, I'm just glad I had someone to walk it with me."

"Who'd have thought we'd ever get to this point? I guess time heals old wounds, but between the two of us, those were some pretty deep cuts; both physical and emotional," I said.

"And look at you now!" she said enthusiastically, "You're getting ready to stand up and talk in front of the whole town. That takes more guts than anything!" This brought a few butterflies to my stomach, but I dismissed them remembering Pat's words from years before, "Marc, after this…nothing else in your life can ever be as tough as what you've already been through…"

Kista and I entered the high school, walked to the very stage where we'd acted in the school play five years prior and laughed and joked over memories of all our wild times as a cast. I took my seat with the school board and administrators as the crowd finished filing in.

When it came my turn, I was ready. I strode to the podium, welcomed the audience, congratulated the graduates and launched into the speech I'd been preparing for months. After a few seconds of nervousness, everything began to come together and, before I knew it, I was actually enjoying the delivery. I didn't feel like I was even giving a speech, but rather, just talking with friends.

I expected nothing more than a polite round of applause at the end of the 20 minutes, figuring everyone would want out of that stifling auditorium. I couldn't have been more wrong.

As I finished, I turned away from the podium; but not before the crowd erupted with a deafening cheer. My former principal turned and called over the noise, "The audience is standing for you, Marc!"

The graduates soon completed the ceremonial hat toss and filed out of the gymnasium. I took the cue with the administration and exited the stage into the crowded hallways. Once I stepped past a row of lockers, I was swarmed by dozens of people.

A man approached after the crowd had scattered and shook my hand. He choked back tears and said, "You're the most amazing person I've ever met." Speechless and slightly embarrassed, I simply shook his hand and thanked him. I didn't feel very amazing and was uncomfortable being viewed that way. Glad to have the speech over and relieved I had not embarrassed myself, I went home to relax.

By the next morning, I had already mentally shifted gears. I was in my bedroom packing for camp when the phone rang.

"Phone call, Marc," my mother called as I threw my camping tools into a duffle bag and picked up the line.

An unfamiliar voice belonging to an elderly woman politely asked, "Are you Marcus Engel, the young man who gave the speech yesterday?"

"That's me!" I responded.

"I was at my granddaughter's graduation yesterday and heard you speak. I just wanted to tell you how proud I am of you. Your speech really changed my life."

Unsure of what to say, I simply said "thank you," expecting that would end the conversation.

She continued, sounding as if she were fighting tears. "My son died from cancer several years ago. It was the worst thing that could happen to a parent. I don't know how your parents ever could have gotten over seeing how badly you were hurt, Marcus. Up until yesterday, I felt like my son had been robbed from me. When I left graduation, I realized it was okay for me to be happy and not be disloyal to his memory."

I didn't feel I said anything all that inspiring and was humbled by her compliments. After all, I had only talked about my life and how I had chosen to live. After a few minutes she brought the conversation to a close. Before I fell asleep that night, the phone would ring no less than a half dozen times with similar calls, some from acquaintances, some from total strangers.

As I lay in bed, I thought of the intensity and sheer volume of responses I'd received from the speech. Was it possible that what I had to say was relevant to so many people? Would it have the same effect outside of my hometown? I began considering if I could give speeches on a professional basis. Trying to fall asleep, I couldn't stop thinking about the possibilities.

The next morning, I felt incredibly peaceful and clear minded as I discussed my thoughts with my parents.

"Even the classes I've taken seem to have led to this." I said.

"Who do you want to speak to, Brother?" Dad asked.

"I think I'd like to go into high schools and colleges and give assemblies."

"So, are you going to speak about drunk driving?" Mom asked.

"That'll be a part of it, just by the nature of my story. However, I think the majority should be showing people they can go through the worst hell imaginable and can come out smiling if they take on the right attitude."

"You're not going to drop out of college to do this, are you?" my father asked, a touch of concern in his voice.

"Are you kidding? Of course not!" I answered emphatically, "I worked my tail off for two years to get to college! I've got to finish what I started!" I paused and smirked, "Besides, I'm moving into the fraternity house this fall and I'm not giving up that experience for anything!"

The next morning, I went to a local printer and had business cards created. When the prints came back, bam! I was a speaker!

After three months at camp, I returned to college still excited about my new career, but even more excited about my new living situation in the Kappa Sigma house. I planned to savor my last semesters with every last mindless party that went on in the old dwelling. *Ah! Home!* I thought happily as the stench of smoke, mold and mildew hit me when I carried my first box of belongings into my new room.

Dewain, my roommate, was more enthusiastic about having Dasher as a roommate than me! Dasher's reputation as a secret weapon for attracting co-eds who want to "pet the adorable dog" preceded him. "Engel! This dog is going to get all the honeys up here! When they come up those stairs and start petting my buddy, Dasher, that is right about the time you need to go and hide in your room!" he teased.

Parties raged all weekend inside the house. One typical Saturday night, the house was filled with hot, sweaty bodies moving to the dance music that poured out of the sound system. Figuring it was getting a bit crowded for Dasher, we headed outside for a little relief from the heat. Just as we rounded the corner, I was grabbed by the arm and chest. "Oh my God! What a beautiful dog! Why did you bring your dog here?" a girl slurred. In typical fraternity house fashion, she was helping to reinforce the reputation of college students. She was at just the right level of intoxication for me to have a little fun with her.

"Hey chicky pooh! This is my Seeing Eye dog, Dasher. He goes everywhere with me," I said in my best "ladies man" voice.

"Seeing Eye dog? So, you're blind?" she asked, confused.

"Um, yeah, those are usually the kinds of people who have Seeing Eye dogs," I said. If anyone had been standing nearby, they would have laughed at my playful condescension.

"Okay, since you're blind… here! Feel my face!" she said excitedly, grabbing both of my hands and lightly pressing them to her sweat-soaked cheeks. "I'm really pretty, aren't I?!"

"Yeah, pretty arrogant!" I muttered under my breath. Then, a brainstorm! With my palms still on both of her flushed cheeks, I pressed the tip of her nose upward with my thumb, giving her the image of Porky Pig. "Oink, oink!" I said loudly before pulling away and hustling for cover! "That's all folks!"

While parties and exchanges with sororities were fun, I forced myself to set aside time for some serious research. Now that I had a career, it seemed wise to find an internship that would help create a strong foundation for the business. If I planned to motivate my young audiences to make responsible decisions, I'd need to immerse myself in the subject as I had with my other adaptation skills.

I first called the Mothers Against Drunk Driving office in Jefferson City. MADD had advocated for my family during the legal phase that followed the crash and I felt they might be a good place to start. Bud, the Victim's Advocate, had been extremely helpful to my parents during some hard times dealing with defense attorneys. I called him and reintroduced myself.

"I've just started a career in professional speaking and I'd like to work with young people. I'm looking for as many opportunities to speak as possible," I explained.

"Marcus, call the Missouri Division of Highway Safety. They're a State organization and may have more opportunities for you," Bud said, becoming more enthused about his suggestion. I took down the phone number and thanked him. "Ask for Joyce, the executive director, and tell her I told you to call. By the way, I think you know her." he added.

"I know her?"

"Joyce's daughter, Melanie, used to live across the hall from you in the dorm. Joyce was the director of MADD at the time of your wreck and told me she'd met you when she was helping Melanie move in."

"What a small world!" I said, smiling.

Three years later, that brief introduction would turn into the entrée for an internship. The "coincidences" felt like they were mounting.

As more and more things fell into place with perfect precision, the idea that nothing is a coincidence was reinforced all the more. The answer to my request for some meaning in the loss of my sight had finally, finally been granted. After all this time, everything was becoming clear, piece by piece.

Chapter 21

"Lifetimes are catching up with me..." [28]

~ Pearl Jam

"Hi, Marcus! Welcome to the Division of Highway Safety!" a bubbly woman said, grasping my hand. "It's so good to finally meet you, I'm Tempe! I'll show you to your office and then introduce you to everyone." She turned and headed into the rows of cubicles, Dasher following close at her heels. Joyce, the executive director and mother of my college dorm friend, had excitedly accepted my proposal for an internship, but had the foresight to ask Tempe, the Youth Safety Specialist, to be my supervisor.

After seven semesters of college courses, I needed a break. A nine-month sabbatical would be both a perfect vacation and learning opportunity.

After leaving me a few moments to get to know my new office space, Tempe returned to the cubicle and asked, "Are you ready to go meet your co-workers?"

"Sure! Let's do it!" We walked through the hallways meeting those who filled the various roles: public relations, law enforcement liaisons, alcohol awareness specialists, child safety experts and the secretarial staff. While there were only a couple of dozen employees, it still added up to a lot of new voices to learn and personalities to figure out. I was definitely up for the challenge!

Over lunch, Tempe briefed me on the various programs she directed and how I'd be involved with each. Every conference sounded better than the next. It didn't take long to realize that this internship was not only going to be productive, but a heck of a lot of fun, too!

In no time, I was comfortable in the office and growing to love my co-workers, especially Tempe, who became my traveling partner when I was booked to speak around the state.

One day, we piled into the van for a two hour road trip. As soon as the doors were closed, Dasher eased his way in between the front seats and laid his big head in Tempe's lap.

"No, Dasher," I said, grabbing his collar.

"It's okay," Tempe said, stroking his soft Labrador ears, "He's not bothering me. If he gets in the way of my driving, I'll let you know." With that, we set out for yet another program where I'd share my story with high schoolers.

On the weekends, I'd return to my parents' home just to escape the boredom of my tiny, barren apartment. It was during this time that I began to speak to my father about a love of his; the Masonic Lodge. I'd been 14 at my grandfather's funeral when I first had an inkling of the family tradition the Engel men had as Masons. Even at that young age, I knew that someday I would also take that sacred obligation. At 23, I was of legal age to take on the degrees and join the fraternal brotherhood.

"Marc, you'll be the third Engel in a direct lineage to do this, and that's not so common in Lodge any more," my Dad said as we filled out my petition for membership. "You're joining an organization that dates back hundreds of years and includes people like George Washington, Benjamin Franklin and Harry Truman. It's a pretty neat thing to be able to say you're a member of such an ancient order, especially one which has developed so many great leaders."

Two weeks later, my father and I drove to my first ever Masonic Lodge meeting. "I think when you arrive tonight your jaw is just going to drop open," Dad said, smiling and acting like he had a secret.

An hour later, I was seated in the Lodge's waiting room as the members filed in for their regular communication. I reached down to scratch Dasher's ears when someone gave my shoulder a friendly squeeze.

"Hey Marc, how's it going man?" asked a voice so familiar that I could remember it before the effects of puberty.

"R-Rodney? What are you doing here?" I asked, my mouth agape. I'd not seen Rodney in years, but I could never forget the sacrifice he, David and Jeff made the first night of my hospitalization. Driving the 150 miles just to be with my parents still ranks as one of the kindest things anyone has ever done for me.

"I came for your initiation, just like everyone here!" Rod exclaimed, playfully punching me in the shoulder.

"But, you've got to be a Mason to be in there," I said, never considering one of my best friends may have already walked this path.

"You're right... and I'm still here! I went through my degree work late last year," he said matter-of-factly. "I saw your Dad at a Lodge meeting a few months ago and he said you were going to be joining. This is something I couldn't miss!"

As if the family tradition and qualities taught by Masonry weren't enough, I would now be able to sit next to one of my biggest supporters in an organization that bonded us as more than friends.

"Gotta run, man," Rodney said as the Master called for Lodge to come to order. "See you when I can call you something other than 'Marc!'"

What did he mean, "something other than, Marc?"

An hour and a half later, the ritual was complete. I was returned to the waiting room and, after just a few minutes, Masons by the dozen came flooding in, my father leading the pack with Rodney close at his heels. "Congratulations, Brother!" he said, shaking my hand. I'd never before seen such pride emitting from the man. "I wanted to be the first to call you, "Brother'," he said, resting his hand on my shoulder.

Brother. My dad's childhood nickname had now taken on a new and unfathomable dimension. I truly was a brother, and now I could call one of my best friends the same!

The summer came and went and, before I knew it, the internship was over, I'd met hundreds and hundreds of wonderful people and I was ready to return to SMSU for my final year. The experience and speaking skills I gained in a short time would have been impossible without the Missouri Division of Highway Safety.

My sense of the correct pieces falling into place continued to click in my mind as I again moved back into the Kappa Sigma house. The internship had been a nice break, but now I was ready for one last year of irresponsibility and fun!

"God! This place still stinks!" I said to my roommate as I moved back in my old room. "Haven't you guys cleaned since I left?"

"I didn't smell anything until you walked in, Engel," a brother teased as several guys helped with the unpacking. It was good to be back! A big, stinky house, drafty windows and all night parties were fine by me!

Spring came, the days grew warm and, suddenly, graduation was only a few days away. The eminence of a diploma in my hand caused lots of reflection about the last seven years.

The "Goal of All Goals" had been to take back control of my future. Graduation proved that I had accomplished just that.

The night before commencement, I walked down the creaking front staircase of the Kappa Sig house and sat down on the concrete front steps. It was well after midnight, and finals week was officially over. The campus was virtually dead, except for the occasional car that drove past on Elm Street. Final exams were over, senior seminar reports had been turned in and all that was left was the official ceremony. "This time tomorrow, Engel," I thought, "College will be over."

That possibility seemed forever away when sitting in solitude under the gigantic front porch. The night was warm and quiet. I could not stop the thoughts that filled my head. Had I really come to the end? It was something I couldn't and almost didn't want to accept. The memories I would treasure. The friends I made were too priceless to be allowed to slip away.

Here, within a one-mile radius of where I now sat, I had regained my sense of self as a young, happy and in control person. The direction in which my life moved hadn't always been straight ahead, but regardless of the detours, I always learned valuable lessons. I never wanted to lose touch with how that felt. I never wanted to forget the fear of leaving my dorm room and the fear of failing. I never wanted to forget what loneliness and solitude felt like. I never wanted to forget what it felt like to hate myself, hate my appearance and take that hatred out on those around me. Although these were not my favorite memories from my early college years, they were priceless. As I thought back, those painful feelings stabbed at my heart. I wasn't ashamed of the person I had been, but I never wanted to revisit him.

And why should I? Feeling that loneliness and frustration in the pit of my stomach did nothing but remind me just how far I'd come. It had been a long road, but through the good and bad, I was always learning, always adapting, always growing and, most importantly, always figuring out my place in this world.

How was it possible then or now to adequately define all of the life lessons I've learned since October 9th, 1993? I'm still discovering new things every day. Redefining happiness was and will remain one of my most important lessons. Happiness is a choice, not an outcome.

True, I could not control a drunk driver's irresponsible choice to drag race on the night of October 9th. In fact, due to that, there were a multitude of aspects resulting from his decision that I cannot control. However, the one single thing I have that no one can take away is my attitude. Whether it is in relation to that horrid event, or dealing with whatever difficulties arise in daily life, I am in charge of my perception. To not have taken charge of how I viewed my life was to relinquish that power to the drunk driver himself. My overriding thought? He took enough from me then, he can't have my attitude now!

I'm happy to be alive and my life is great! In fact, my life is better than great! I'm sure some will read the words of this book and feel the hurt and frustration I felt lying in that hospital bed. Some may also wonder how anyone could live through that shit and now say their life is better than great. Again, my life will be as great or as horrible as I decide it will be; and I frankly see no reason to have anything but a happy life.

Does that mean I don't get down? Of course not. I am human, after all. However, there is only one direction in which I know how to move. That direction is straight ahead with no turning back. If I were to spend time lingering in the misery of the past, how will that, in any way, help me move ahead? It won't, so I don't.

Soon after my own graduation, I was invited to speak to a small, informal group at St. Louis University. Hoping for a chance to catch up with Dennis Fuller after my presentation, I invited him to attend. It came as no surprise when he quickly accepted and boomed, "You bet, dude! I'll be there!"

The next Sunday night, a group of about 50 students filled the dormitory's lobby for my program.

Afterwards I opened the floor for questions to give the students a much more personal glimpse into the life of a survivor and a blind person. After we'd expended the inquiries about the drunk driver's sentence, how I pick out my clothes and how Dasher worked, a student posed a question I wasn't expecting.

"How did this experience affect your family?"

I thought for a moment and then answered truthfully, "I don't really know. Everyone was so focused on helping that they protected me from their own emotional trauma. However, there is someone here who can probably answer that better than I. You want to field this one, Dennis?" I directed my question to the back of the room where I heard his deep laugh at an earlier funny moment.

"Do you want me to?" Dennis asked quietly. His voice wasn't the echoing baritone, but now seemed thin, almost fragile.

"If you would, yes. You know more than I do..."

There was a pause and I waited to hear details that were still withheld by my family. The pause became longer and I couldn't figure out why this usually boisterous person wasn't jumping right in with all the flare of an M.C. Then, as he spoke, his voice cracked. Had I overstepped my boundaries? When he treated me in the hospital, I thought of Dennis as a rock. And now, my simple question had him fighting back tears? Dennis was the first person who made me laugh when I thought nothing could ever be funny again. Not until that moment did I realize he had not been laughing on the inside.

"Every time I went into Marcus' room, I didn't see Marcus lying in that hospital bed. I saw my own son. The worst thing I can imagine is to have something happen to one of my kids... and there were Marcus' parents living out every parent's worst nightmare." He paused a moment and swallowed. "At the time, Marcus had so many injuries that no one could stop long enough to worry about his mental state. Let me tell you… it isn't easy to treat someone when you're imagining that the kid on the operating table could be your own. Every time I'd work with Marcus, I'd just think how senseless it all was."

I slowly began to understand the special connection that had existed between my favorite rehab team members and me. They had looked at me and seen their own loved ones; their children, their siblings, their friends. For so long, I'd imagined that to everyone except Barb, Dennis and Rick, I was just another patient; just another body in just another hospital bed. Dennis' words showed me that this was just not true. My providers had given me more than their best possible care; they had given me a piece of themselves. It was the only thing they had to try and compensate for all that could not be healed. Family, friends, doctors, nurses, therapists and a multitude of others; There had been more than just one victim.

As I lay in a hospital bed, stripped of all but the most fundamental of human emotions, I learned the most basic human need… the need for love. In my most desperate personal state, all I longed for was someone to be there and tell me they loved me. That raw emotion is the basic need around which revolves every human action. Clinging to life, reaching for whatever I could grasp, what I needed most was love. Whether it came from a family member, a friend or a medical specialist, I simply wanted to know I was not alone in this world of darkness.

The only way I know how to repay the kindness of the people who took care of me and gave me part of themselves is to live well, practice these truths and make my life a positive force for change. I have found love, acceptance and meaning for my life. I hope this book will, in some way, help you to find those truths, too.

Epilogue

How do you finish an on-going story? You don't. You take a writing break and a good, long look at the present.

Three summers ago, the original self-published edition of this autobiography was released. Thank you to the thousands who read, loved and provided feedback on the original manuscript. Since then, I've sweated over every word of this book. Finally, this is my story; the way I want to tell it.

While the last stages of *After This...* were being completed, I continued to travel the country giving speeches. One morning in an anonymous hotel room, Dasher woke me with his usual morning greeting; a cold nose in my face. As I reached out to give him a good morning scratch, my fingers slipped over a hard nodule on his neck. *A lump? Another one?* Every time I noticed a new blemish on this nine-year-old dog, my heart skipped a beat. *What if this wasn't just one of those fatty lumps that old dogs get? What if this was cancer?*

A trip to the vet proved that the lump was not, in fact, the big C. However, these constant fears about Dasher's health, combined with little slippages in his working behavior, all pointed to the dreaded "R" word: retirement. This decision wrenched my guts for weeks on end while I slaved over an equally difficult task: finding someone I trusted who was willing to adopt my best friend. After all, it takes an incredibly special soul to take a dog in his twilight years.

To this end, I could not have been more blessed. Tempe, my co-worker from the days of my college internship, said she and her family would love to adopt Dasher. As I handed over his leash on a hot August afternoon, I felt as though a part of me was being amputated. Tempe hugged me as the tears fell and said, "I'll take care of him like he's one of my own." No words could have been a greater comfort.

Two months later, a 19-month-old black lab came charging into my life. Still chock-full of youthful exuberance, Carson's Seeing Eye dog duties quickly overtook his puppy behaviors. In no time, he fell into line with my lifestyle and has readily accepted the challenge to travel the country, sharing the platform and breaking down the barrier between the audience and me.

Life is great and, even more importantly, improving all the time. Professionally, I am blessed beyond measure to have a career I dearly love; not to mention one that affects so many people. Personally, the friends I retain are priceless; the new people who enter my life on an almost daily basis are welcomed in with open arms, just like we've known each other for years. Writing has become a daily joy and has reinforced many of the life lessons I sometimes forget. If this book has helped you learn some of those lessons I learned the hard way, please, share it with a friend.

Thank You

"There are nights I don't remember and pain that's been forgotten,
and a lot of things I choose not to recall
There are faces that come to me in my darkest, secret memories,
faces that I wish would not come back at all.
But in this dream parade of lovers from the other times and places,
There's not one that matters now no matter who,
I'm just thankful for the journey and that I survived the battle
And that my spoils of victory is you." [29]

~ Johnny Cash, "Soldier Getting Over the War"

As a reader, I get pretty darned annoyed when I am forced to wade through the names of every person the author has ever met. Come on, Mr. or Ms. Author, no one really cares to read a bunch of names known only to you. What's even worse is that crap is always right up front before the book ever starts. It's sorta like whacking through the jungle underbrush to get to the oasis that is the book I wanted to read in the first freaking place.

Writing a book is a gigantic pain in the butt. Seriously, try it sometime and you'll see. So, now I empathize more with authors' feelings of gratitude. After working on this manuscript off and on for the last few years, I have to, I mean seriously have to, give props to all who've helped this journey. Besides, many of these names should be familiar to you; after all, they're part of the story you just read. So, my apologies if you're one of those folks who has to read every single word of a book or else you feel cheated.

Hey, at least I saved these for the end, right? If nothing else, I hope this will amuse you… and, if you're one of the people on this list (or not on this list, for that matter) please know my gratitude towards you is immeasurable…

Thanks to…

My Family:

My father, Phillip Engel, for teaching me to find humor in a world that isn't perfect

My mother, Nancy Engel, for being my mother in every way imaginable

My sister, Cathy Dickey, for becoming only mildly frustrated at my mountain of requests when I returned to college

My grandmothers, Bernice Schroer and Virginia Engel, for cookies, chicken salad sandwiches and lima beans

My aunt and uncle, Elaine and Steve Slater, for teaching me things I could have never learned in High Hill. You have given me more guidance and positive advice than you may ever know

My late uncle, Doug Engel, for showing me life goes on when parts of the body fail

Doug's woman, Sharon Wattonville, for a million funny stories about the nut house, and for trusting me with Doug's most priceless tangible possessions

Carl, Susan, Carla and Scott Schroer for playing taxi for the hundreds of hospital visitors who, in turn, helped me get out of that place

The Jenkins/Judd family for helping me tell time when I couldn't see the clock on the wall

The Ken Schroer family for great meals while I was in Denver and for legal guidance when I had bigger things to worry about

High school friends:

Jeff Deering, Rodney Devlin and David Payne for Sweet Natalie in our younger years and for continued friendship now. You guys did a hell of a lot for me back then; well above the call of duty. I will always, always be in your debt

John Woods for getting me my first and only "real" job at Texaco.

Ted Fischer for continued friendship since Mrs. Cutright's 4th grade class

Kista River – shit, where can I even start? Words can't tell you what you mean to me and how grateful I am for you being in my life. You helped me more than you'll ever know...I love you...

Amy Clendennen for one of my longest standing friendships, for a million concerts, for REK road trips and for never letting our friendship slip by the wayside

Ben Leech for a talking goat, being my roomie in New Hall and Charlie in Vegas

Tim Hubbard for being the only person who could drop a few hundred bucks at Crazy Horse

Dennis Klein for teaching me to rub some dirt on it and get back in the game

Larry Luetjen for empowering me as a 16 year old to change the things within my control

Those who had anything to do with my recovery:

Dr. Tim Jones for doing the impossible; putting me back together again

Dr. Don Gay for putting up with my bullshit. You are nothing short of a master craftsman

Dr. Sam Marwit for doing your best to understand your atypical patient

Dr. Gayle Neely for helping me to retain my main sense

Special thanks to Dr. Dennis Fuller for teaching me to laugh when nothing was funny. You were nothing short of a miracle. Thanks for marrying my first editor, too

Barb Dewalle for compassion and kindness that I'll never be able to repay. Your presence is proof that angels walk among us

Rick Ochs for treating me like a guy, not a patient

Colorado, New Jersey and College Friends:

Robert Dyson for making me hold up a mirror to my own words

Gabriel Stokes for never doubting my goals

Trina Boyd for being an island of normalcy in an ocean of insanity

John Vollertsen for giving me the most memorable Thanksgiving ever

Judy and Rick Burch for showing me everyone doesn't believe certain blind philosophies

Ron Graham for slipping on the ice and making it possible for us to meet. Never lose touch with me, my brother!

The staff of the Seeing Eye, Inc. for Dasher and Carson who have, in turn, changed my life

Dr. Hilary Warren for writing my college papers and for being one of the best friends I'll ever have…I love you, Hil!

Laura Gawlack for introducing me to Big Smith, Don and Norman and for showing me lingerie!

Kristen Alexander for taking care of my fish while I was trying to get back to college

Dr. Michael Carlie for teaching me to love sociology and for treating me like an individual

Dr. Marvin Prosono for helping me understand the medical nightmare I went through

Jana Long for not requiring me to fit into a "blind mold"

Julia Poling for squirrels and showing me I can still be friends with my past girlfriends

Kacee Austin…You're funny, Kong A!

Brothers of Kappa Sigma:

Travis Franke for being my big brother and for Glinmorange

D.J. "House" Grimwood for pissing me off as a pledge and becoming a confidant when we both grew up. You're one of my best friends and I don't want that to ever change

Justin "Kong E" Kennedy for being "the wind beneath my wings"

Brian "The Babe" Hills for fancy dinners at Red Lobster (har har)

Dewain "Devain" Riddle for Dr. Katz and for never doing the dishes

Andy "Art Boy" Netterville for sharing a common goal of keeping people safe and for good times in Vegas. Know where I can get some waffles?

Also thanks to Fannin, C.P., Boulay, Tommy, and the rest of you punks…AEKDB

Various other folks:

Chris and Carrie Serra for PJ's and to Carrie for being my best girlfriend

Steve Serra for staying in touch while living in two different cities

Kit Norton for being a fellow conservative and for ticks in unmentionable places

Jake Engelman for being a Dylan fan, TNDC and a million burned CDs

Keith Dooley for funny hat poker nights

Kevin Dooley for unlimited rides to and from Springfield

Jeff Williams for Tuesday Nights and Treasures

Leah Atkinson for countless hours of advice on women and gas

Melissa Dooley for allowing me to guess things I touch

Mike Podorski for selling me my first guitar

Tracie Podorski for support in the fall of 98

Brian Skelly for putting a golf club in my hand for the first time

Phil Barbeir for my Taz whistle

Cherie Stolze for putting your fist in your mouth

Kathy Oberle for always being my friend and for White Castle burgers

Tom Cannady for friendship through the toughest times we'll ever know (hopefully…)

Vicki Jochimsen for E-mail, coffee, literature and smiles

Colleen Schott for ranch dressing, bumming me treats and gag bars

Pat Vollertsen and family for always having a place for me to crash

Kevin Zimmer for treats, introducing me to The Urge and convincing me to work at camp

Tom and Betty Taggart for dinners out and financial advice

Larry Dooley for great services for the first 18 months of my business

To everyone with whom I came into contact with during my internship at the Missouri Division of Highway Safety, but especially to Tempe Humphrey and family for adopting Dasher and for giving him the best retirement any dog could have.

The National Speakers Association-St. Louis chapter. You have helped me, challenged me and befriended me. Thanks to all, especially Shep Hyken for being my mentor.

And finally, thanks to you. Yes, you. For whatever reason, you've read this book and taken an active interest in the events of my life. Thank you for showing me that there really WAS some purpose for all this.

Endnotes

[1] Emily Saliers, "Wood Song" from the compact disc "Swamp Ophelia", performed by Indigo Girls, Sony Music Entertainment, Inc., 1994.

[2] Phil Collins, "In The Air Tonight" from the album "Face Value", performed by Phil Collins, Atlantic Recording Corporation, 1981.

[3] Kiedis, Balzary, Smith, and Frusciante, "Under the Bridge" from the album "Blood Sugar Sex Magik", performed by Red Hot Chili Peppers, Warner Brothers, Inc., 1991.

[4] U2, "Sunday Bloody Sunday" from the album "War", performed by U2, Blue Mountain Music Ltd., 1983.

[5] Dickens, Charles, <u>A Tale of Two Cities</u>. Signet Classics; Reissue edition, 1997.

[6] Bob Dylan, "Sign Language" from the album "No Reason To Cry", performed by Eric Clapton and Bob Dylan, Polydor Records, 1976.

[7] Eric Bogle, "The Band Played Waltzing Matilda", from the album "Rum, Sodomy and The Lash", performed by The Pogues, Island Music Ltd., 1985.

[8] James Keelaghan, "Cold Missouri Waters" from the album "Cry, Cry, Cry", performed by Richard Schindel & Dar Williams, Razor and Tie Records, 1998.

[9] Bob Dylan, "Stuck Inside of Mobile With The Memphis Blues Again" from the album "Blonde on Blonde", performed by Bob Dylan, Columbia Records, 1966.

[10] Elton John and Bernie Taupin, "Levon" from the album "Madman Across The Water", performed by Elton John, Universal Records, 1971.

[11] Gram Parsons and Chris Hillman, "Juanita" from the album "Return Of The Grievous Angel: Tribute To Gram Parsons", performed by Sheryl Crow and Emmylou Harris, Alamo Sounds, 1999.

[12] Bob Dylan, "Shelter from the Storm" from the album "Blood on the Tracks", performed by Bob Dylan, Columbia Records, 1975.

[13] Emily Saliers, "Closer to Fine" from the compact disc "Indigo Girls", performed by Indigo Girls, Sony Music Entertainment, Inc., 1989.

[14] Jerry Garcia and Robert Hunter, "Casey Jones" from the album "Working Man's Dead", performed by Grateful Dead, Warner Brothers Records, Inc., 1970.

[15] Bruce Springsteen, "Tunnel of Love" from the album "Tunnel of Love", performed by Bruce Springsteen, Sony, 1987.

[16] Berry, Buck Mills and Stipe, "Nightswimming" from the album "Automatic For The People", performed by R.E.M., Warner Brothers Records, Inc., 1992.

[17] Neil Young, "Long May You Run" from the album "Long May You Run", performed by the Stills – Young Band, Reprise / Wea, 1976.

[18] Bob Dylan, "Just Like Tom Thumb's Blues," from "Highway 61 Revisited", performed by Bob Dylan, Columbia Records, Inc., 1975.

[19] Adam F. Duritz, Daniel J. Vickrey, Charles Gillingham & Counting Crows, "Daylight Fading" from the album "Recovering the Satellites", performed by Counting Crows, Geffen Records, 1996

[20] James Hetfield and Lars Ulrich, "One" from the album "...And Justice For All", performed by Metallica, Elektra Records, 1988.

[21] Bob Dylan, "Shelter from the Storm" from the album "Blood on the Tracks", performed by Bob Dylan, Columbia Records, 1975.

[22] Steve Earl, "Tom Ames Prayer" from the album "Train A Coming", performed by Steve Earl, Warner Brothers, 1985.

[23] Emily Saliers, "Wood Song" from the compact disc "Swamp Ophelia", performed by Indigo Girls, Sony Music Entertainment, Inc., 1994.

[24] Farrar-Tweedy-Heidorn, "Still Be Around" from the album "Still Feel Gone", performed by Uncle Tupelo, Rockville Records, 1991.

[25] Adam F. Duritz, "A Long December" from the album "Recovering the Satellites", performed by Counting Crows, Geffen Records, 1996.

[26] Jimmy Buffet, "I Love The Now" from the compact disc "Floridays", performed by Jimmy Buffet, MCA, 1986.

[27] Farrar-Tweedy-Heidorn, "Life Worth Living" from the album "No Depression", performed by Uncle Tupelo, Rockville Records, 1990.

[28] Pearl Jam, "Elderly Woman Behind The Counter In A Small Town" from the album "Vs.", performed by Pearl Jam, Sony, 1993.

[29] Johnny Cash, "Like a Soldier" from the compact disc "American Recordings", performed by Johnny Cash, Lost Highway Records, 1994.

**Visit Marcus on the web at
www.marcusengel.com**

**and check out his blog at
www.marcusengel.blogspot.com**

FIFTH EDITION

YOUR LIVING TRUST & ESTATE PLAN

HOW TO MAXIMIZE YOUR FAMILY'S ASSETS AND PROTECT YOUR LOVED ONES

HARVEY J. PLATT

ATTORNEY-AT-LAW

Allworth Press

Allworth Press books may be purchased in bulk at special discounts for sales promotion, corporate gifts, fund-raising, or educational purposes. Special editions can also be created to specifications. For details, contact the Special Sales Department, Allworth Press, 307 West 36th Street, 11th Floor, New York, NY 10018 or info@skyhorsepublishing.com.

15   14   13   12   11   5   4   3   2   1

Published by Allworth Press,
an imprint of Skyhorse Publishing, Inc.
307 West 36th Street, 11th Floor, New York, NY 10018.

Allworth Press® is a registered trademark of Skyhorse Publishing, Inc.®, a Delaware corporation.

www.allworth.com

Cover design by Mary Belibasakis

ISBN: 978-1-62153-262-0

Library of Congress Cataloging-in-Publication Data is available on file.

Printed in the United States of America